TEXT BOOK OF INDUSTRIAL PHARMACY - II

[According to latest syllabus of B. Pharm - VII semester of Pharmacy Council of India]

Dr. Anirbandeep Bose

Associate Professor

Department of Pharmaceutical Technology,

School of Medical Sciences,

Adamas University (West Bengal)

Dr. Ruchi Gaikwad

Associate Professor

Oriental College of Pharmacy,

Bhopal (Madhya Pradesh)

Mrs. Anju Baniwal

Associate Professor

Ganpati Institute of Pharmacy,

Bilaspur, Yamuna Nagar (Haryana)

Ms. Arti Solanki

Assistant Professor

Bansal College of Pharmacy,

Bhopal (M.P.)

Dr. Kamaldeep Singh

Associate Professor

Lala Lajpat Rai College of

Pharmacy,

Moga (Punjab)

First Edition 2024

Published by:

NOTION PRESS

Publisher and distributor

Head office: Notion press Media Pvt. Ltd.

7, Red cross Road,

Egmore, Chennai,Tamil Nadu 60008

E-mail publish@notionpress.com

Website: www.notionpress.com

The authors feel great pleasure in presenting the first edition of the book **"Text Book of Industrial Pharmacy - II"** for graduate and post graduate students. The present book on **Text Book of Industrial Pharmacy - II** has been written according to the syllabus of B. Pharm - VII semester of Pharmacy Council of India and covers full course of the subject.

THE SALIENT FEATURES OF THE BOOK ARE: -

- *Easy to understand style of writing* which makes the book a self-study material.
- *Each new concept has been introduced through day-today problem of interest* to the students which makes the subject matter interesting.
- *The language of the book, on the whole, is lucid and easy to understand.*
- Wherever needed *neatly labeled figures have been drawn.*

The authors hope that the students, teachers and other readers will find the book interesting and to the point covering the course. We hope that the students will receive the book warmly.

I express a sincere thank you to the Management of Department of Pharmaceutical Technology, School of Medical Sciences, Adamas University, Oriental College of Pharmacy, Ganpati Institute of Pharmacy, Bansal College of Pharmacy and Lala Lajpat Rai College of Pharmacy, for their support during the writing of this book.

Every effort is made to keep the book error free. The author will gratefully acknowledge the suggestions to improve the book to make it more useful.

Wishing our readers success in examination and life ahead. The authors feel that their efforts will be fully rewarded if the book serves the purpose for which it is written.

TEXT BOOK OF INDUSTRIAL PHARMACY - II
CONTENTS

    a. Central Drug Standard Control Organization (CDSCO) and State Licensing Authority:

- Organization
- Responsibilities
- Certificate of Pharmaceutical Product (COPP)
- Regulatory requirements
- Approval procedures for New Drugs

CHAPTER - 1

PILOT PLANT SCALE UP TECHNIQUES

INTRODUCTION:

Pilot plant scale-up is a critical phase in the development of new products and processes, bridging the gap between laboratory-scale experiments and full-scale industrial production. This process ensures that the results obtained on a small scale can be reliably and efficiently reproduced on a larger scale. It involves meticulous planning, design, and testing to mitigate risks and optimize performance before committing to full-scale production.

1. Definition and Purpose of Scale-Up:

Scale-up is the process of increasing the batch size or production capacity of a process from the laboratory scale to the pilot plant and eventually to full-scale production. The main purposes are:

   a. **Validation**: Confirm that the process works under scaled-up conditions.
   b. Optimization: Identify and refine critical parameters for efficiency and quality.
   c. **Economic Evaluation**: Assess the feasibility and cost-effectiveness of the process at a larger scale.
   d. **Regulatory Compliance**: Ensure the process meets necessary standards and regulations.

2. Key Considerations in Scale-Up:

a. **Geometric Similarity**: Ensure that the equipment and processes are geometrically similar to those used in the lab, maintaining the same ratios of dimensions.

b. **Dynamic Similarity**: Maintain consistent flow patterns and mixing times across scales.

c. **Kinematic Similarity**: Ensure similar velocities and accelerations of particles within the system.

d. **Chemical and Physical Properties**: Understand how changes in scale affect heat transfer, mass transfer, reaction kinetics, and material properties.

3. Steps in the Scale-Up Process:

a. Laboratory Development:

- Conduct small-scale experiments to develop the process.
- Establish baseline data for reaction kinetics, heat and mass transfer, and other critical parameters.

b. Pilot Plant Design:

- Design pilot plant equipment to mimic lab-scale conditions as closely as possible.
- Consider modular designs for flexibility in testing different configurations.

c. Pilot Plant Operation:

- Operate the pilot plant under controlled conditions.
- Collect data on process performance, including yield, purity, reaction rates, and energy consumption.

d. Data Analysis and Optimization:

- Analyze data to identify scaling issues and optimize process parameters.
- Use statistical and computational tools to model and predict full-scale performance.

e. Scale-Up to Full Production:

- Transition from pilot scale to full-scale production, incorporating lessons learned from pilot testing.
- Conduct validation and commissioning of full-scale equipment.

4. Challenges in Scale-Up:

a. **Heat and Mass Transfer**: Differences in surface area-to-volume ratios can affect the efficiency of heat and mass transfer.

b. **Mixing and Flow Dynamics**: Ensuring uniform mixing and avoiding issues like dead zones or channeling can be more challenging at larger scales.

c. **Material Handling**: Scaling up can introduce issues with the handling and transport of materials, especially with solids or viscous liquids.

d. **Equipment Design**: Customizing equipment to handle larger volumes while maintaining performance can be complex.

e. **Cost**: Pilot plants are expensive to build and operate, and scaling up involves significant financial risk.

5. Case Studies and Examples:

a. **Pharmaceutical Industry**: Scaling up the production of a new drug from lab to pilot plant involves ensuring consistent quality and efficacy, as well as meeting stringent regulatory requirements.

b. **Chemical Industry**: For processes like polymerization or catalysis, scale-up must account for changes in reaction dynamics and heat transfer.

c. **Food and Beverage Industry**: Ensuring that the taste, texture, and safety of products are maintained when scaling up from small test batches to full production runs.

6. Modern Tools and Techniques:

a. **Computational Fluid Dynamics (CFD)**: Used to model and simulate fluid flow and mixing in reactors and other equipment.

b. **Process Analytical Technology (PAT)**: Real-time monitoring and control of processes to ensure consistency and quality.

c. **Advanced Control Strategies**: Implementing advanced control systems to manage process variables and maintain optimal conditions.

d. **Modular Pilot Plants**: Using modular, flexible pilot plant designs to facilitate rapid testing and iteration.

GENERAL CONSIDERATIONS - INCLUDING SIGNIFICANCE OF PERSONNEL REQUIREMENTS, SPACE REQUIREMENTS, RAW MATERIALS

When scaling up from the laboratory to the pilot plant, several general considerations are crucial to ensure a successful transition. These include personnel requirements, space requirements, and raw materials management. Addressing these factors comprehensively helps mitigate risks, optimize operations, and ensure that the pilot plant can effectively bridge the gap to full-scale production.

1. Personnel Requirements

Scaling up production from a laboratory to a pilot plant involves a variety of challenges and considerations that are critical for successful operations. Among these, personnel requirements, space requirements, and raw materials play a significant role. Understanding and addressing these factors is essential for ensuring that the scale-up process is efficient, safe, and compliant with regulatory standards.

a. Importance of Skilled Personnel:

i. **Expertise**: Scaling up processes requires personnel with expertise in both the specific product and general process engineering. This includes knowledge of the equipment, materials, and methods used at both lab and pilot scales.

ii. **Training:** Staff must be thoroughly trained in standard operating procedures (SOPs), equipment handling, safety protocols, and quality control measures. Continuous training programs are necessary to keep up with technological advancements and regulatory changes.

iii. **Multidisciplinary Team**: A successful scale-up requires a multidisciplinary team, including process engineers, chemists, quality assurance (QA) specialists, and regulatory experts. Collaboration among these professionals ensures comprehensive oversight of the scale-up process.

b. Roles and Responsibilities:

i. **Process Engineers**: Design and optimize the scale-up process, ensuring it can be replicated on a larger scale without compromising product quality.

ii. **Production Technicians**: Operate the pilot plant equipment, monitor processes, and maintain records. They need to be adept at troubleshooting and making real-time adjustments.

iii. **Quality Assurance/Quality Control (QA/QC):** Ensure that the scale-up adheres to quality standards and regulatory requirements. QA/QC personnel conduct in-process checks, validate equipment, and oversee final product testing.

iv. **Regulatory Affairs Specialists**: Ensure compliance with all relevant regulatory guidelines and assist with documentation and submission to regulatory bodies.

c. Communication and Coordination:

i. **Regular Meetings**: Regular cross-functional team meetings help address issues promptly and ensure alignment on project goals.

ii. **Documentation:** Meticulous documentation and record-keeping facilitate communication and compliance with regulatory standards. This includes maintaining batch records, equipment logs, and validation reports.

2. Space Requirements

a. Facility Design:

i. **Layout**: The layout of the pilot plant should optimize workflow and safety. This includes designated areas for raw material storage, production, quality control, and packaging.

ii. **Flexibility:** Facilities should be designed with flexibility in mind to accommodate different processes and products. Modular setups can help achieve this flexibility.

iii. **Containment and Safety**: Proper containment measures are necessary to handle hazardous materials safely. This includes dedicated areas for handling and storing such materials, as well as appropriate ventilation systems.

b. Equipment Placement:

i. **Efficient Use of Space**: Equipment should be arranged to minimize the risk of cross-contamination and to facilitate easy movement of materials and personnel.

ii. **Scalability:** Space should be allocated with scalability in mind, allowing for the addition of new equipment or expansion of existing processes.

c. Environmental Controls:

i. **Temperature and Humidity**: Controlled environments may be necessary to maintain the stability of certain products or processes. This is particularly critical for biopharmaceuticals and other sensitive products.

ii. **Cleanrooms**: Depending on the product, cleanrooms or controlled environments may be required to meet GMP standards. These areas must be designed to prevent contamination and ensure product quality.

3. Raw Materials

a. Sourcing and Quality:

i. **Supplier Qualification**: Raw materials must be sourced from qualified suppliers who can provide consistent quality. Supplier audits and certifications are essential for ensuring reliability.

ii. **Material Specifications**: Detailed specifications for raw materials, including purity, potency, and stability, must be established and adhered to. This ensures that the materials will perform as expected during scale-up.

b. Inventory Management:

i. **Storage Conditions**: Proper storage conditions must be maintained to preserve the integrity of raw materials. This includes controlled temperature, humidity, and protection from light.

ii. **Inventory Control**: Effective inventory management practices, such as Just-In-Time (JIT) inventory, help minimize waste and ensure the availability of materials when needed.

c. Quality Control:

i. **Incoming Inspection**: Raw materials should be inspected upon receipt to verify they meet established specifications. This can include physical, chemical, and microbiological testing.

ii. **Traceability**: All raw materials should be traceable from receipt through to the final product. This is crucial for quality control and regulatory compliance.

Space Requirements

The design and layout of a pilot plant are critical for the efficient and safe scale-up of production processes. Adequate space planning ensures that the plant operates smoothly, with optimal workflow and compliance with regulatory standards. This section details the considerations for space requirements in pilot plant scale-up techniques, highlighting their significance alongside personnel and raw material requirements.

1. Significance of Space Requirements

Proper space allocation and design in a pilot plant are vital for several reasons:

i. **Operational Efficiency**: A well-designed layout facilitates smooth workflows, reduces bottlenecks, and enhances productivity.

ii. **Safety**: Adequate space ensures safe movement of personnel and materials, reducing the risk of accidents and contamination.

iii. **Compliance:** Regulatory standards often mandate specific space requirements, particularly for cleanrooms and hazardous material handling.

iv. **Scalability**: Sufficient space allows for future expansion and the addition of new processes or equipment without major disruptions.

2. Key Considerations for Space Requirements

a. Facility Design and Layout:

i. **Workflow Optimization**: The layout should be designed to optimize the sequence of operations, from raw material storage to processing, packaging, and quality control. This minimizes material handling and reduces transit times.

ii. **Segregation of Areas**: Different areas for raw material storage, processing, quality control, packaging, and waste handling should be clearly defined and separated to prevent cross-contamination and ensure compliance with good manufacturing practices (GMP).

b. Equipment Placement:

i. **Efficient Use of Space**: Equipment should be strategically placed to maximize space utilization while allowing easy access for operation and maintenance. Adequate clearance should be provided around equipment for safety and maintenance activities.

ii. **Flow of Materials and Personnel**: Paths for the flow of materials and personnel should be clearly marked and free of obstructions. This ensures safe and efficient movement throughout the facility.

c. Environmental Controls:

i. **Temperature and Humidity Control:** Certain processes and materials require specific environmental conditions. Dedicated HVAC systems may be needed to control temperature and humidity, particularly in areas such as cleanrooms.

ii. **Cleanroom Requirements**: Depending on the product, cleanrooms or controlled environments may be necessary. These areas must be designed to maintain strict environmental conditions, including air quality, pressure differentials, and contamination control.

d. Flexibility and Scalability:

i. **Modular Design**: A modular design allows for easy reconfiguration of the space to accommodate different processes or products. This flexibility is crucial for adapting to changing production needs or scaling up operations.

ii. **Future Expansion**: Sufficient space should be allocated for future expansion, including the addition of new equipment or production lines. This foresight can prevent costly renovations or relocations in the future.

e. Compliance and Safety:

i. **Regulatory Standards**: The design and layout must comply with regulatory standards, such as those set by the FDA, EMA, or other relevant authorities. This includes requirements for space allocation, cleanroom classifications, and safety protocols.

ii. **Safety Measures**: Adequate space for safety equipment, such as emergency showers, eye wash stations, and fire extinguishers, must be included. Additionally, clear evacuation routes should be planned.

3. Detailed Space Allocation

a. Raw Material Storage:

i. **Dedicated Storage Areas**: Separate storage areas for raw materials, intermediates, and finished products to prevent cross-contamination.

ii. **Controlled Environment**: Storage conditions should be controlled and monitored, especially for temperature-sensitive or hazardous materials.

iii. **Inventory Management**: Efficient layout for easy access and inventory management, including space for receiving and inspecting incoming materials.

b. Processing Areas:

i. **Processing Zones:** Designated zones for different stages of the manufacturing process, ensuring a logical flow from one stage to the next.

ii. **Containment**: Areas for handling hazardous materials should have appropriate containment measures, such as fume hoods or containment booths.

c. Quality Control and Testing:

i. **QC Laboratories**: Dedicated space for quality control laboratories, equipped with necessary instruments and safety measures.

ii. **Sample Handling**: Areas for receiving, preparing, and testing samples to ensure they are handled under appropriate conditions.

d. Packaging and Storage:

i. **Packaging Areas**: Space for packaging operations, designed to prevent contamination and ensure product integrity.

ii. **Finished Goods Storage**: Adequate space for storing finished products before distribution, with controlled environmental conditions if necessary.

e. Utilities and Support Services:

i. **Utility Rooms**: Space for housing utilities such as water purification systems, HVAC systems, and electrical panels.

ii. **Support Areas**: Break rooms, changing rooms, and administrative offices should be included to support personnel.

4. Example Layout

a. Example Layout Components:

i. **Raw Material Storage**: Near the entrance for easy delivery and inspection.

ii. **Processing Area**: Central location with clear separation between different stages (e.g., mixing, granulation, drying).

iii. **Quality Control Labs**: Adjacent to the processing area for quick access to samples.

iv. **Packaging Area**: Near the processing area but with a clear separation to prevent contamination.

v. **Finished Goods Storage**: At the far end, allowing for easy access to shipping docks.

b. Workflow Example:

  i.   **Receiving Dock**: Raw materials are delivered and moved to storage.

  ii. **Raw Material Storage**: Materials are stored under controlled conditions.

  iii. **Processing Area:** Materials are moved to processing zones as needed.

  iv. **Quality Control**: Samples are taken to QC labs during and after processing.

  v.   **Packaging:** Finished products are packaged in a dedicated area.

  vi. **Finished Goods Storage**: Packaged products are stored before distribution.

Raw Materials Management

Effective raw materials management is essential for the successful scale-up of manufacturing processes in a pilot plant. Proper handling, storage, and quality control of raw materials ensure consistent product quality, regulatory compliance, and operational efficiency. This section provides a detailed overview of raw materials management within the context of pilot plant scale-up techniques, emphasizing its significance along with personnel and space requirements.

1. Significance of Raw Materials Management

Proper raw materials management impacts several critical aspects of pilot plant operations:

  i.   **Quality Assurance**: Consistent quality of raw materials ensures the final product meets predefined specifications and regulatory standards.

  ii. **Cost Efficiency**: Efficient management minimizes waste and reduces the costs associated with material handling, storage, and inventory control.

  iii. **Process Optimization**: Reliable supply and availability of raw materials facilitate smooth production processes and help avoid delays.

iv. **Regulatory Compliance**: Adhering to regulatory guidelines for raw materials handling and storage ensures compliance with industry standards and reduces the risk of regulatory actions.

2. Key Components of Raw Materials Management

a. Sourcing and Supplier Qualification:

i. **Supplier Selection**: Choose suppliers based on their ability to provide consistent, high-quality materials. This involves assessing their manufacturing processes, quality control measures, and reliability.

ii. **Supplier Audits**: Conduct regular audits of suppliers to ensure they comply with Good Manufacturing Practices (GMP) and other relevant standards.

iii. **Material Specifications**: Define detailed specifications for each raw material, including physical, chemical, and microbiological properties. Suppliers must adhere to these specifications consistently.

b. Receiving and Inspection:

i. **Receiving Procedures**: Implement standardized procedures for receiving raw materials, including proper documentation and initial quality checks.

ii. **Inspection and Testing**: Perform incoming inspections and tests to verify that materials meet the specified quality standards. This can include physical inspections, chemical analysis, and microbiological testing as necessary.

iii. **Quarantine Area**: Use a designated quarantine area for materials awaiting inspection and testing. Only materials that pass these checks are moved to approved storage areas.

c. Storage and Inventory Management:

i. **Controlled Storage Conditions**: Maintain appropriate storage conditions for raw materials, such as temperature, humidity, and light control, to preserve their integrity. Different materials may require different storage environments.

ii. **Inventory Control Systems**: Implement robust inventory control systems to track the quantity and location of raw materials. This includes real-time monitoring and automated reordering systems to ensure a steady supply.

iii. **First-In-First-Out (FIFO)**: Adopt FIFO practices to ensure that older materials are used before newer ones, reducing the risk of material degradation and waste.

d. Handling and Usage:

i. **Handling Procedures**: Develop and implement standardized procedures for the safe handling of raw materials, including the use of appropriate personal protective equipment (PPE) and safe handling practices.

ii. **Material Dispensing**: Use precise and accurate dispensing methods to ensure that the correct quantities of materials are used in the manufacturing process. This can include automated dispensing systems to improve accuracy and reduce human error.

iii. **Batch Documentation**: Maintain detailed batch records for each production run, documenting the specific raw materials used, their quantities, and their sources. This enhances traceability and accountability.

e. Quality Control and Assurance:

i. **In-Process Quality Checks**: Conduct regular in-process quality checks to ensure that raw materials are performing as expected during production. This helps identify any issues early and prevents defects in the final product.

ii. **Stability Testing:** Perform stability testing on raw materials to determine their shelf life and ensure they remain within specifications throughout their storage period.

iii. **Change Control**: Implement a change control process to manage any changes in raw materials, such as sourcing from a new supplier or changes in material specifications. This process should include a thorough impact assessment and revalidation if necessary.

f. Documentation and Compliance:

i. **Material Safety Data Sheets (MSDS):** Ensure that MSDS are available and up-to-date for all raw materials. These documents provide critical information on the handling, storage, and disposal of materials.

ii. **Regulatory Documentation**: Maintain comprehensive records of all raw materials, including certificates of analysis (CoA), supplier audits, and inspection reports. These records are essential for demonstrating compliance during regulatory inspections.

iii. **Training**: Provide regular training for personnel on raw materials management practices, regulatory requirements, and safety protocols.

Example Workflow for Raw Materials Management

1. Sourcing and Supplier Qualification:

    a. Select qualified suppliers based on rigorous assessment criteria.

    b. Conduct initial and periodic audits to ensure compliance with standards.

2. Receiving and Inspection:

    a. Receive raw materials and move them to a quarantine area.

    b. Perform quality checks, including physical inspections and laboratory testing.

    c. Approve materials that meet specifications and move them to storage.

3. Storage and Inventory Management:

    a. Store materials under controlled conditions based on their specific requirements.

    b. Use inventory control systems to track quantities and locations.

    c. Implement FIFO practices to manage stock rotation.

4. Handling and Usage:

a. Follow standardized handling procedures to ensure safety and accuracy.

b. Dispense materials precisely as required for each production batch.

c. Document the use of materials in detailed batch records.

5. Quality Control and Assurance:

a. Conduct in-process quality checks during production.

b. Perform stability testing to ensure long-term quality.

c. Manage changes in materials through a robust change control process.

6. Documentation and Compliance:

a. Maintain up-to-date MSDS and regulatory documentation.

b. Ensure all records are complete and accessible for regulatory review.

c. Provide ongoing training for all personnel involved in raw materials management.

Process Scale-Up Specifics

Process scale-up is a critical aspect of transitioning from laboratory-scale development to pilot plant production. It involves adapting manufacturing processes to larger scales while maintaining product quality, efficiency, and regulatory compliance. This section explores the specific considerations for process scale-up within the context of pilot plant operations, emphasizing its significance alongside personnel, space, and raw materials requirements.

1. Significance of Process Scale-Up

Process scale-up plays a crucial role in the successful commercialization of pharmaceutical products for several reasons:

i. **Product Quality**: Ensuring that the manufacturing process can be replicated at larger scales while maintaining product quality and consistency.

ii. **Efficiency:** Optimizing processes for larger batch sizes to maximize production throughput and minimize costs.

iii. **Regulatory Compliance**: Demonstrating to regulatory authorities that the scaled-up process meets quality standards and complies with regulatory requirements.

iv. **Technology Transfer:** Facilitating the transfer of manufacturing processes from research and development (R&D) to full-scale production facilities.

2. Key Components of Process Scale-Up

a. Process Optimization:

i. **Identifying Critical Parameters**: Determining the critical process parameters (CPPs) that significantly impact product quality and ensuring they are controlled within acceptable limits.

ii. **Scale-Up Studies**: Conducting scale-up studies to optimize process parameters such as mixing times, temperatures, pressures, and reaction times for larger batch sizes.

iii. **Quality by Design (QbD)**: Applying QbD principles to design robust processes that consistently produce high-quality products across different scales.

b. Equipment Selection and Validation:

i. **Suitable Equipment**: Selecting equipment that is scalable, robust, and suitable for pilot plant operations. This includes reactors, mixers, dryers, and other process equipment.

ii. **Equipment Validation**: Validating equipment performance and ensuring that it meets regulatory requirements for accuracy, precision, and reliability.

c. Personnel Training and Expertise:

i. **Process Knowledge**: Providing personnel with a deep understanding of the manufacturing process, including its critical parameters, potential risks, and mitigation strategies.

ii. **Training Programs**: Implementing comprehensive training programs to ensure that personnel are proficient in operating equipment, following procedures, and maintaining quality standards.

iii. **Cross-Functional Collaboration**: Facilitating collaboration between process engineers, chemists, quality control specialists, and other stakeholders to optimize the scale-up process.

d. Space Requirements and Facility Design:

i. **Layout Optimization**: Designing the pilot plant layout to accommodate larger equipment and facilitate efficient material flow, process integration, and personnel movement.

ii. **Flexibility**: Incorporating modular designs and flexible layouts that allow for easy reconfiguration to accommodate different processes and batch sizes.

iii. **Cleanroom Considerations**: Ensuring that cleanroom requirements, if applicable, are met to maintain product quality and comply with regulatory standards.

e. Raw Materials Management:

i. **Material Compatibility**: Ensuring that raw materials are compatible with larger-scale processes and equipment to avoid issues such as agglomeration, degradation, or contamination.

ii. **Supply Chain Optimization**: Establishing robust supply chain management practices to ensure a reliable and consistent supply of raw materials at the pilot plant scale.

iii. **Quality Control**: Implementing rigorous quality control measures for raw materials, including incoming inspection, testing, and documentation.

3. Process Scale-Up Workflow

a. Process Evaluation:

i. Assess the feasibility of scaling up the process based on product characteristics, equipment capabilities, and regulatory requirements.

ii. Identify critical process parameters (CPPs) and establish target specifications for the scaled-up process.

b. Scale-Up Studies:

i. Conduct small-scale experiments to optimize process parameters and assess scalability.

ii. Perform risk assessments to identify potential challenges and develop mitigation strategies.

c. Equipment Selection and Validation:

i. Evaluate equipment options and select suitable equipment for the pilot plant scale.

ii. Validate equipment performance through qualification and testing protocols.

d. Personnel Training:

i. Provide comprehensive training to personnel on operating equipment, following procedures, and maintaining quality standards.

ii. Ensure that personnel are proficient in safety protocols and emergency procedures.

e. Facility Design and Layout:

i. Design the pilot plant layout to optimize space utilization, workflow efficiency, and regulatory compliance.

ii. Incorporate cleanroom requirements, if applicable, to maintain product integrity and compliance with GMP standards.

f. Raw Materials Management:

i. Establish protocols for sourcing, receiving, inspecting, and storing raw materials.

ii. Implement inventory control systems to ensure a steady supply of materials and prevent stockouts or overages.

PILOT PLANT SCALE UP CONSIDERATIONS FOR SOLIDS AND RELEVANT DOCUMENTATION

Scaling up processes involving solids presents unique challenges compared to liquids or gases. These challenges stem from the handling, mixing, and processing properties of solid materials. This section details the considerations for scaling up solid-based processes in a pilot plant and the relevant documentation required to ensure a successful and compliant scale-up.

Considerations for Solids in Pilot Plant Scale-Up

Scaling up solid dosage forms in a pilot plant presents unique challenges compared to liquid or semi-solid formulations. These challenges include powder flow properties, blending uniformity, compression characteristics, and content uniformity. This section explores the specific considerations for solids in pilot plant scale-up, along with relevant documentation practices.

1. Powder Flow Properties

    a. **Importance:** Powder flow properties significantly affect the manufacturing process, including blending, compression, and granulation.

    b. **Characterization**: Conduct flowability tests such as angle of repose, Carr's index, and Hausner ratio to assess powder flow properties.

    c. **Optimization**: Optimize particle size, shape, and surface properties to improve powder flow and minimize segregation during handling and processing.

2. Blending Uniformity

    a. **Critical Parameter**: Ensuring uniform distribution of active pharmaceutical ingredients (APIs) and excipients is crucial for product quality and efficacy.

    b. **Sampling Plan**: Develop a robust sampling plan to collect samples from multiple locations within the blender to assess blending uniformity.

    c. **Blend Time Optimization**: Determine the optimal blending time based on blend uniformity studies to achieve homogeneity without overmixing.

3. Compression Characteristics

a. **Tablet Compression**: Understand the compression behavior of the powder blend, including tablet hardness, friability, and disintegration properties.

b. **Tablet Press Settings**: Adjust compression force, dwell time, and turret speed to optimize tablet quality and production efficiency.

c. **Tablet Tooling**: Select appropriate tooling designs and materials to minimize wear and ensure consistent tablet dimensions and weight.

4. Content Uniformity

a. **Regulatory Requirement**: Content uniformity is a critical quality attribute mandated by regulatory authorities to ensure consistent dosage delivery.

b. **Sampling Strategy**: Develop a statistically sound sampling plan to test individual dosage units for API content uniformity.

c. **Analytical Method Validation**: Validate analytical methods for API quantification to ensure accuracy, precision, and robustness.

Relevant Documentation Practices

1. Process Development Report:

a. Document the results of powder characterization studies, including flow properties and particle size distribution.

b. Summarize blending studies, including blend uniformity testing and optimization of blending parameters.

2. Scale-Up Protocol:

a. Outline the scale-up strategy, including equipment selection, process parameters, and validation requirements.

b. Specify the target scale-up factor and expected outcomes based on laboratory-scale data.

3. Batch Records:

a. Record all manufacturing activities, including raw material usage, processing steps, and equipment settings.

b. Document in-process testing results, such as blend uniformity, tablet weight variation, and hardness testing.

4. **Validation Protocols:**
   a. Develop validation protocols for equipment qualification, process validation, and cleaning validation.
   b. Include acceptance criteria and test methods for demonstrating process robustness and product quality.

5. **Change Control Documentation:**
   a. Implement a change control system to manage modifications to equipment, processes, or formulations.
   b. Document the rationale for changes, risk assessments, and impact assessments on product quality and regulatory compliance.

Relevant Documentation for Pilot Plant Scale-Up

Documentation is crucial throughout the pilot plant scale-up process for solid dosage forms. It ensures that the process is well-documented, reproducible, and compliant with regulatory requirements. Here are some relevant documentation practices:

1. **Process Development Report:**
   a. Document the initial laboratory-scale experiments, including formulation development, powder characterization, and preliminary process optimization.
   b. Summarize the results of powder flow tests, particle size analysis, and blending studies.
   c. Provide details on any challenges encountered during process development and the strategies employed to overcome them.

2. **Scale-Up Protocol:**
   a. Outline the scale-up strategy, including the rationale for scale-up, target scale-up factor, and expected outcomes.

b. Specify the equipment to be used in the pilot plant, including any modifications or adaptations required for scale-up.

c. Detail the process parameters to be monitored and controlled during scale-up, such as blending time, compression force, and tablet weight variation.

d. Define the validation requirements for the scaled-up process, including equipment qualification, process validation, and cleaning validation.

3. **Batch Records:**

   a. Record all manufacturing activities during pilot plant-scale production runs, including:

      i. Raw material usage, including batch numbers, quantities, and suppliers.

      ii. Processing steps, including blending, compression, and packaging.

      iii. In-process testing results, such as blend uniformity, tablet weight variation, hardness, and disintegration testing.

      iv. Any deviations from the approved process, along with corrective actions taken.

   b. Document environmental conditions, equipment settings, and personnel involved in each production run.

4. **Validation Protocols:**

   a. Develop validation protocols for equipment qualification, process validation, and cleaning validation.

   b. Include acceptance criteria and test methods for demonstrating process robustness and product quality.

   c. Perform risk assessments to identify potential hazards and mitigation strategies for the scaled-up process.

5. **Change Control Documentation:**

a. Implement a change control system to manage modifications to equipment, processes, or formulations.

b. Document any changes made during the scale-up process, including the rationale, impact assessment, and approval process.

c. Ensure that all changes are communicated to relevant personnel and are properly documented for regulatory compliance.

6. Analytical Method Validation:

a. Validate analytical methods used for in-process and finished product testing, including assay, impurities, and dissolution testing.

b. Provide documentation on method development, validation protocols, and validation reports.

c. Ensure that analytical methods are suitable for use at the pilot plant scale and meet regulatory requirements for accuracy, precision, and specificity.

7. Regulatory Submission Documents:

a. Prepare documentation required for regulatory submissions, including Investigational New Drug (IND) applications or New Drug Applications (NDAs).

b. Include summaries of pilot plant-scale production data, process validation results, and quality control testing.

c. Provide comprehensive documentation to support product registration and approval by regulatory authorities.

PILOT PLANT SCALE UP CONSIDERATIONS FOR LIQUID ORALS AND RELEVANT DOCUMENTATION

Scaling up the production of liquid oral formulations involves unique challenges related to maintaining product quality, consistency, and regulatory compliance. This section covers the specific considerations for scaling up liquid oral formulations in a pilot plant and the relevant documentation required to ensure a successful transition from lab to full-scale production.

Considerations for Liquid Orals in Pilot Plant Scale-Up

Scaling up liquid oral formulations in a pilot plant involves several considerations to ensure product quality, process efficiency, and regulatory compliance. This section explores specific considerations for liquid orals in pilot plant scale-up, along with relevant documentation practices.

1. Formulation Optimization:

a. **Ingredient Compatibility**: Ensure compatibility of active pharmaceutical ingredients (APIs), excipients, and solvents in the formulation.

b. **Solubility Enhancement**: Optimize solubility through the selection of suitable solvents, co-solvents, surfactants, and pH modifiers.

c. **Stability Studies**: Conduct stability studies to assess the physical, chemical, and microbiological stability of the formulation under different storage conditions.

2. Equipment Selection and Compatibility:

a. **Mixing Equipment**: Select mixing equipment suitable for liquid blending, such as stainless steel tanks, high-shear mixers, or homogenizers.

b. **Filtration and Sterilization**: Ensure compatibility of filtration and sterilization equipment with liquid formulations to maintain product sterility.

c. **Packaging Compatibility**: Choose packaging materials and containers compatible with the liquid formulation to prevent interactions or leaching.

3. Process Parameters Optimization:

a. **Mixing Parameters**: Optimize mixing parameters, including mixing speed, duration, and order of addition, to achieve uniform dispersion of ingredients.

b. **Temperature Control: Maintain** temperature control during mixing and storage to prevent phase separation, crystallization, or degradation.

c. **pH Adjustment**: Control pH within the desired range using appropriate buffers or pH modifiers to enhance stability and palatability.

4. Quality Control Testing:

a. **In-Process Testing**: Implement in-process testing to monitor critical quality attributes (CQAs) such as pH, viscosity, density, and particle size distribution.

b. **Finished Product Testing**: Conduct comprehensive testing of finished products, including assay, content uniformity, microbial limits, and preservative efficacy.

c. **Validation of Analytical Methods**: Validate analytical methods for accuracy, precision, specificity, and robustness to ensure reliable quality control testing.

Relevant Documentation Practices:

1. **Formulation Development Report:**

   a. Document the formulation development process, including ingredient selection, compatibility studies, and stability testing results.

   b. Summarize formulation optimization efforts and rationale for final formulation selection.

2. **Scale-Up Protocol:**

   a. Outline the scale-up strategy, including equipment selection, process parameters, and validation requirements.

   b. Specify the target scale-up factor and expected outcomes based on laboratory-scale formulation data.

3. **Batch Records:**

   a. Record all manufacturing activities during pilot plant-scale production runs, including:

      i. Raw material usage, including batch numbers, quantities, and suppliers.

ii. Processing steps, including mixing, filtration, sterilization, and packaging.

iii. In-process testing results, such as pH, viscosity, and density measurements.

iv. Any deviations from the approved process, along with corrective actions taken.

4. **Validation Protocols:**

   a. Develop validation protocols for equipment qualification, process validation, and cleaning validation.

   b. Include acceptance criteria and test methods for demonstrating process robustness and product quality.

5. **Change Control Documentation:**

   a. Implement a change control system to manage modifications to equipment, processes, or formulations.

   b. Document any changes made during the scale-up process, including the rationale, impact assessment, and approval process.

6. **Regulatory Submission Documents:**

   a. Prepare documentation required for regulatory submissions, including Investigational New Drug (IND) applications or New Drug Applications (NDAs).

   b. Include summaries of pilot plant-scale production data, process validation results, and quality control testing.

   c. Provide comprehensive documentation to support product registration and approval by regulatory authorities.

Relevant Documentation for Pilot Plant Scale-Up

Documentation plays a critical role in pilot plant scale-up for liquid oral formulations, ensuring traceability, reproducibility, and compliance with regulatory requirements. Here are relevant documentation practices for pilot plant scale-up in the context of liquid orals:

1. **Formulation Development Report:**
   a. Document the formulation development process, including the selection of excipients, solvents, and APIs.
   b. Summarize compatibility studies, stability testing, and formulation optimization efforts.
   c. Provide rationale for final formulation selection based on stability, efficacy, and manufacturability.

2. **Scale-Up Protocol:**
   a. Outline the scale-up strategy, including equipment selection, process parameters, and validation requirements.
   b. Specify the target scale-up factor and expected outcomes based on laboratory-scale formulation data.
   c. Detail the process validation plan, including the number of batches to be produced and acceptance criteria for process performance.

3. **Batch Records:**
   a. Record all manufacturing activities during pilot plant-scale production runs, including:
      i. Raw material usage, including batch numbers, quantities, and suppliers.
      ii. Processing steps, including mixing, filtration, sterilization, and packaging.
      iii. In-process testing results, such as pH, viscosity, density, and particle size distribution.
      iv. Any deviations from the approved process, along with corrective actions taken.

4. **Validation Protocols:**
   a. Develop validation protocols for equipment qualification, process validation, and cleaning validation.

b. Include acceptance criteria and test methods for demonstrating process robustness and product quality.

c. Perform risk assessments to identify potential hazards and mitigation strategies for the scaled-up process.

5. Change Control Documentation:

a. Implement a change control system to manage modifications to equipment, processes, or formulations.

b. Document any changes made during the scale-up process, including the rationale, impact assessment, and approval process.

c. Ensure that all changes are communicated to relevant personnel and are properly documented for regulatory compliance.

6. Analytical Method Validation:

a. Validate analytical methods used for in-process and finished product testing, including assay, impurities, and dissolution testing.

b. Provide documentation on method development, validation protocols, and validation reports.

c. Ensure that analytical methods are suitable for use at the pilot plant scale and meet regulatory requirements for accuracy, precision, and specificity.

7. Regulatory Submission Documents:

a. Prepare documentation required for regulatory submissions, including Investigational New Drug (IND) applications or New Drug Applications (NDAs).

b. Include summaries of pilot plant-scale production data, process validation results, and quality control testing.

c. Provide comprehensive documentation to support product registration and approval by regulatory authorities.

PILOT PLANT SCALE UP CONSIDERATIONS FOR SEMI SOLIDS AND RELEVANT DOCUMENTATION

Scaling up semi-solid formulations, such as creams, gels, ointments, and pastes, involves unique challenges related to their viscosity, rheology, and stability. This section covers the specific considerations for scaling up semi-solid formulations in a pilot plant and the relevant documentation required to ensure a successful transition from lab to full-scale production.

Considerations for Semi-Solids in Pilot Plant Scale-Up

Scaling up semi-solid formulations in a pilot plant involves several considerations to ensure product quality, process efficiency, and regulatory compliance. This section explores specific considerations for semi-solids in pilot plant scale-up, along with relevant documentation practices.

1. Formulation Optimization:

    a. **Ingredient Compatibility**: Ensure compatibility of active pharmaceutical ingredients (APIs), excipients, and bases in the formulation.

    b. **Viscosity Control: Optimize** viscosity using suitable rheological modifiers to achieve desired texture and consistency.

    c. **Stability Studies**: Conduct stability studies to assess physical, chemical, and microbial stability under different storage conditions.

2. Equipment Selection and Compatibility:

    a. **Mixing and Homogenization Equipment**: Select mixing and homogenization equipment suitable for semi-solid formulations, such as planetary mixers, homogenizers, or emulsifiers.

    b. **Temperature Control**: Ensure compatibility of heating and cooling equipment with semi-solid formulations to maintain stability and homogeneity.

    c. **Packaging Compatibility**: Choose packaging materials and containers compatible with semi-solid formulations to prevent interactions, leaching, or contamination.

3. Process Parameters Optimization:

a. **Mixing Parameters**: Optimize mixing parameters, including mixing speed, duration, and order of addition, to achieve uniform dispersion of ingredients.

b. **Temperature Control**: Maintain temperature control during mixing, heating, and cooling processes to prevent phase separation, crystallization, or degradation.

c. **Homogenization**: Ensure thorough homogenization of the formulation to achieve uniform distribution of APIs and excipients.

4. **Quality Control Testing:**

a. **In-Process Testing**: Implement in-process testing to monitor critical quality attributes (CQAs) such as viscosity, pH, density, and microbial limits.

b. **Finished Product Testing**: Conduct comprehensive testing of finished products, including assay, content uniformity, microbial limits, and preservative efficacy.

c. **Validation of Analytical Methods**: Validate analytical methods for accuracy, precision, specificity, and robustness to ensure reliable quality control testing.

Relevant Documentation Practices:

1. **Formulation Development Report:**

a. Document the formulation development process, including the selection of bases, rheological modifiers, and preservatives.

b. Summarize compatibility studies, viscosity measurements, and stability testing results.

c. Provide rationale for final formulation selection based on stability, efficacy, and manufacturability.

2. **Scale-Up Protocol:**

a. Outline the scale-up strategy, including equipment selection, process parameters, and validation requirements.

b. Specify the target scale-up factor and expected outcomes based on laboratory-scale formulation data.

c. Detail the process validation plan, including the number of batches to be produced and acceptance criteria for process performance.

3. **Batch Records:**

   a. Record all manufacturing activities during pilot plant-scale production runs, including:

      i. Raw material usage, including batch numbers, quantities, and suppliers.

      ii. Processing steps, including mixing, heating, cooling, and packaging.

      iii. In-process testing results, such as viscosity, pH, and density measurements.

      iv. Any deviations from the approved process, along with corrective actions taken.

4. **Validation Protocols:**

   a. Develop validation protocols for equipment qualification, process validation, and cleaning validation.

   b. Include acceptance criteria and test methods for demonstrating process robustness and product quality.

   c. Perform risk assessments to identify potential hazards and mitigation strategies for the scaled-up process.

5. **Change Control Documentation:**

   a. Implement a change control system to manage modifications to equipment, processes, or formulations.

   b. Document any changes made during the scale-up process, including the rationale, impact assessment, and approval process.

   c. Ensure that all changes are communicated to relevant personnel and are properly documented for regulatory compliance.

6. **Analytical Method Validation:**

   a. Validate analytical methods used for in-process and finished product testing, including assay, impurities, and microbial limits.

   b. Provide documentation on method development, validation protocols, and validation reports.

   c. Ensure that analytical methods are suitable for use at the pilot plant scale and meet regulatory requirements for accuracy, precision, and specificity.

7. **Regulatory Submission Documents:**

   a. Prepare documentation required for regulatory submissions, including Investigational New Drug (IND) applications or New Drug Applications (NDAs).

   b. Include summaries of pilot plant-scale production data, process validation results, and quality control testing.

   c. Provide comprehensive documentation to support product registration and approval by regulatory authorities.

By maintaining detailed documentation throughout the pilot plant scale-up process for semi-solid formulations, companies can ensure compliance with regulatory requirements and facilitate successful commercialization of the product. These documents serve as a valuable resource for process optimization, troubleshooting, and future scale-up efforts.

Relevant Documentation for Pilot Plant Scale-Up

1. **Formulation Development Report:**

   a. **Purpose:** This document summarizes the formulation development process for semi-solid formulations, detailing the selection of excipients, APIs, and bases, along with any compatibility studies and stability assessments conducted.

   b. **Content:**

     i. Description of formulation components and their functions.

     ii. Results of compatibility studies, including physical, chemical, and microbial stability assessments.

     iii. Summary of formulation optimization efforts, including viscosity adjustments and texture enhancements.

  c. **Importance**: Provides a comprehensive understanding of the semi-solid formulation, its stability, and the rationale behind the chosen ingredients, guiding scale-up decisions.

2. **Scale-Up Protocol:**

  a. **Purpose**: This document outlines the strategy and procedures for scaling up the semi-solid formulation from laboratory-scale to pilot plant-scale production, ensuring consistency and reproducibility.

  b. **Content**:

     i. Overview of scale-up objectives, including target batch sizes and expected outcomes.

     ii. Equipment selection criteria and specifications for pilot plant-scale production.

     iii. Process parameters and control strategies, such as mixing speeds, temperatures, and homogenization methods.

     iv. Validation plan for equipment, processes, and analytical methods.

  c. **Importance:** Provides a roadmap for executing the scale-up process, ensuring that all aspects are carefully planned and documented for regulatory compliance.

3. **Batch Records:**

  a. **Purpose: Batch** records document all activities and data related to each production batch of the semi-solid formulation, ensuring traceability and compliance with Good Manufacturing Practices (GMP).

b. **Content:**

    i. Details of raw materials used, including batch numbers, quantities, and suppliers.

    ii. Step-by-step description of the manufacturing process, including mixing, heating, cooling, and packaging.

    iii. In-process testing results, such as viscosity measurements, pH values, and any deviations from target specifications.

    iv. Equipment calibration and maintenance records.

c. **Importance:** Provides a detailed record of all production activities, facilitating batch-to-batch consistency and enabling traceability in case of quality issues or regulatory audits.

4. **Validation Protocols:**

a. **Purpose**: Validation protocols outline the procedures and acceptance criteria for validating equipment, processes, and analytical methods used in pilot plant-scale production of semi-solid formulations.

b. **Content:**

    i. Validation plan for equipment qualification, including Installation Qualification (IQ), Operational Qualification (OQ), and Performance Qualification (PQ).

    ii. Process validation protocols, detailing the approach, test methods, acceptance criteria, and sampling plan for demonstrating process robustness and consistency.

    iii. Analytical method validation protocols, including validation parameters, test procedures, and acceptance criteria for assay, impurities, and content uniformity testing.

c. **Importance**: Ensures that all equipment, processes, and analytical methods are properly validated and meet regulatory requirements for product quality and consistency.

5. **Change Control Documentation:**

   a. **Purpose**: Change control documentation manages and documents any changes made to equipment, processes, or formulations during pilot plant-scale production of semi-solid formulations.

   b. **Content:**

      i. Description of the proposed change, including its rationale and potential impact on product quality and regulatory compliance.

      ii. Risk assessment to evaluate the potential risks associated with the proposed change and mitigation strategies.

      iii. Approval process, including authorization by relevant stakeholders and implementation plan.

   c. **Importance:** Ensures that any changes made during the scale-up process are thoroughly evaluated, documented, and implemented in a controlled manner to maintain product quality and compliance.

6. **Regulatory Submission Documents:**

   a. **Purpose:** Regulatory submission documents provide comprehensive data and documentation to regulatory authorities for product registration and approval.

   b. **Content:**

      i. Summary of pilot plant-scale production data, including batch records, validation reports, and stability studies.

      ii. Process validation results, demonstrating the consistency and reproducibility of the semi-solid formulation manufacturing process.

      iii. Quality control testing data, including assay, impurity profiles, and microbiological testing results.

   c. **Importance:** Supports the regulatory approval process by providing evidence of product quality, safety, and efficacy, based on data generated during pilot plant-scale production and validation studies.

By maintaining detailed documentation throughout the pilot plant scale-up process for semi-solid formulations, companies can ensure compliance with regulatory requirements, facilitate successful commercialization of the product, and mitigate risks associated with scale-up activities. These documents serve as essential records of the scale-up process, providing valuable insights for process optimization, troubleshooting, and future scale-up efforts.

SUPAC GUIDELINES

The Scale-Up and Post-Approval Changes (SUPAC) guidelines, issued by the U.S. Food and Drug Administration (FDA), provide a regulatory framework for the pharmaceutical industry to manage changes in the manufacturing process, equipment, and site for approved drug products. These guidelines help ensure that any changes made during the scale-up process do not adversely affect the quality, safety, or efficacy of the drug product. This section details the SUPAC guidelines relevant to pilot plant scale-up techniques.

1. Overview of SUPAC Guidelines

SUPAC guidelines are divided into different categories based on the type of drug dosage form, such as immediate-release (IR) solid oral dosage forms, modified-release (MR) oral dosage forms, and non-sterile semisolid dosage forms. Each guideline provides detailed recommendations on managing changes related to:

a. Components and Composition

b. Manufacturing Sites

c. Scale-Up/Scale-Down of Manufacturing Processes

d. Equipment Changes

e. Manufacturing Process and Controls

2. SUPAC Guidelines for Different Dosage Forms

a. SUPAC-IR (Immediate-Release Solid Oral Dosage Forms):

1. **Levels of Change**: Changes are categorized into Level 1 (minor changes), Level 2 (moderate changes), and Level 3 (major changes). Each level has specific requirements for documentation, testing, and regulatory filing.

   a. **Level 1:** Minor changes that require minimal documentation and testing (e.g., small changes in batch size).

   b. **Level 2:** Moderate changes that require additional in vitro dissolution testing and stability studies (e.g., changes in equipment of the same design and operating principles).

   c. **Level 3**: Major changes that necessitate extensive testing, including bioequivalence studies (e.g., significant changes in the manufacturing process).

b. SUPAC-MR (Modified-Release Solid Oral Dosage Forms):

1. **Categories of Change**: Similar to SUPAC-IR, changes are categorized by their impact on the product.

   a. **Level 1:** Minor changes with minimal regulatory impact.

   b. **Level 2**: Moderate changes requiring thorough documentation and specific testing.

   c. **Level 3**: Major changes with a significant impact on product performance, requiring comprehensive regulatory submissions.

c. SUPAC-SS (Non-Sterile Semisolid Dosage Forms):

1. **Types of Changes**: Changes are grouped into three levels based on their potential impact on product quality.

   a. **Level 1**: Minor changes, such as slight modifications in batch size.

   b. **Level 2**: Moderate changes, including changes in equipment that maintain the same operating principles.

   c. **Level 3:** Major changes, such as changes in the formulation or manufacturing process.

3. Specific Considerations in SUPAC for Scale-Up

a. Components and Composition:

1. **Minor Changes**: Adjustments in excipient quantities within approved ranges are considered minor. Documentation should include justification for the change and supportive stability data.

2. **Major Changes**: Substitution or significant alteration of excipients requires extensive stability data and potentially bioequivalence studies.

b. Manufacturing Sites:

Site Changes: Moving production to a different site involves Level 2 or Level 3 changes. Required documentation includes site qualification, validation data, and stability studies.

c. Scale-Up/Scale-Down of Manufacturing Processes:

1. **Batch Size Changes**: Minor changes in batch size within the approved range typically fall under Level 1. Larger changes may require additional validation and stability studies.

2. **Process Changes**: Adjustments in the manufacturing process must ensure that the critical quality attributes (CQAs) of the product remain consistent. This may include changes in mixing times, drying conditions, or coating processes.

d. Equipment Changes:

1. **Same Design and Operating Principles**: Equipment changes that do not alter the design or operating principles usually fall under Level 1 or Level 2, requiring documentation of the change and comparative data.

2. **Different Design or Operating Principles**: Significant changes in equipment design or operating principles require extensive validation and potential bioequivalence studies.

e. Manufacturing Process and Controls:

1. **Process Optimization**: Adjustments to optimize the manufacturing process, such as changes in temperature or pressure, must be validated to demonstrate no adverse impact on product quality.
2. **Control Strategies**: Changes in in-process controls or final product testing methods must be justified and validated to ensure consistent product quality.

4. Documentation Requirements

a. Regulatory Submissions:

1. **Annual Reports**: For minor changes, documentation may be included in the annual report to the FDA.
2. **Supplemental Applications**: Moderate and major changes require the submission of a Changes Being Effected (CBE) supplement or a Prior Approval Supplement (PAS), depending on the level of change.

b. Validation and Testing:

1. **Validation Protocols**: Detailed protocols for process validation, including rationale, acceptance criteria, and testing methodologies.
2. **Stability Studies**: Stability data to demonstrate that the product remains within its specified shelf-life parameters post-change.
3. **Comparative Studies**: Data comparing the pre-change and post-change product to ensure no significant differences in quality attributes.

c. Reporting and Record-Keeping:

1. **Change Control Documentation**: Comprehensive records of all changes made, including justifications, impact assessments, and approval from relevant authorities.
2. **Batch Records**: Detailed batch records showing adherence to the validated process post-change.
3. **Testing Data**: Complete data from in-process and final product testing, demonstrating compliance with quality specifications.

INTRODUCTION TO PLATFORM TECHNOLOGY

Platform technology in the context of pharmaceutical manufacturing refers to the use of standardized systems, processes, and technologies that can be applied across multiple products or projects. This approach can streamline the scale-up process, improve efficiency, reduce costs, and ensure consistent quality. This section provides a detailed introduction to platform technology and its application in pilot plant scale-up techniques.

1. Definition and Principles of Platform Technology

a. Standardization:

Platform technology involves standardizing equipment, processes, and protocols across multiple projects. This reduces variability and simplifies the scale-up process.

b. Modularity:

Using modular systems that can be easily adapted or expanded for different products or batch sizes. This flexibility allows for quick adjustments and scaling.

c. Integration:

Integrating data management and process control systems to ensure seamless communication and monitoring throughout the production process. This integration enhances traceability and control.

d. Reusability:

Developing processes and systems that can be reused for different products, reducing the time and cost associated with developing new manufacturing processes from scratch.

2. Benefits of Platform Technology in Pilot Plant Scale-Up

a. Efficiency:

1. **Reduced Development Time**: Standardized processes and equipment shorten the development time for new products.
2. **Simplified Training**: Staff can be trained on a standardized set of equipment and processes, reducing the learning curve.

b. Cost Savings:

1. **Economies of Scale**: Using the same technology across multiple products allows for bulk purchasing of equipment and materials, reducing costs.

2. **Reduced Validation Costs**: Standardized processes reduce the need for extensive validation for each new product.

c. Quality Consistency:

1. **Uniform Processes**: Standardized processes ensure consistent product quality and reduce batch-to-batch variability.

2. **Enhanced Monitoring**: Integrated data systems provide real-time monitoring and control, ensuring adherence to quality standards.

d. Flexibility and Scalability:

1. **Modular Systems:** Easily adapt to changes in production volume or product specifications.

2. **Quick Adjustments**: Rapidly adjust processes for different products without extensive revalidation.

3. Applications of Platform Technology in Pilot Plant Scale-Up

a. Biologics Manufacturing:

1. **Cell Culture Platforms**: Standardized bioreactor systems and protocols for cell culture processes.

2. **Purification Platforms**: Modular chromatography and filtration systems that can be adapted for different biologics.

b. Solid Dosage Forms:

1. **Granulation Platforms**: Fluid bed granulation systems that can be used for various formulations.

2. **Tableting Platforms**: Standardized tableting equipment with adjustable parameters for different tablet sizes and compositions.

c. Liquid and Semi-Solid Dosage Forms:

1. **Mixing and Homogenization**: Standardized mixers and homogenizers for consistent production of liquids and semi-solids.

2. **Filling and Packaging**: Automated filling and packaging systems adaptable to different container types and sizes.

4. Key Components of Platform Technology

a. Equipment Standardization:

1. **Modular Equipment**: Use of modular, scalable equipment that can be easily reconfigured for different products.

2. **Automated Systems**: Integration of automation to ensure precision and repeatability in manufacturing processes.

b. Process Standardization:

1. **Standard Operating Procedures (SOPs)**: Developing SOPs that can be applied across different products and batches.

2. **Validation Protocols**: Standardized validation protocols to streamline the validation process for new products.

c. Data Integration:

1. **Process Analytical Technology (PAT)**: Implementing PAT tools to monitor and control critical process parameters in real-time.

2. **Manufacturing Execution Systems (MES)**: Integrating MES to track production processes, manage data, and ensure compliance with regulatory standards.

d. Quality Management:

1. **Quality by Design (QbD)**: Applying QbD principles to design robust processes that consistently produce high-quality products.

2. **Risk Management**: Implementing risk management frameworks to identify and mitigate potential issues during scale-up.

5. Challenges and Considerations

a. Initial Investment:

High Upfront Costs: The initial investment in standardized equipment and integrated systems can be high, though it is offset by long-term savings and efficiency gains.

b. Customization:

Balancing Standardization and Flexibility: While standardization is key, there must be enough flexibility to accommodate unique product requirements.

c. Regulatory Compliance:

Adapting to Regulations: Ensuring that standardized processes and equipment meet regulatory requirements for different markets and products.

d. Change Management:

Organizational Buy-In: Achieving buy-in from all stakeholders is crucial for successful implementation of platform technology.

Multiple Choice Questions (MCQs)

1. What is the primary purpose of pilot plant scale-up in process development?

    A) Product marketing

    B) Regulatory filing

    C) Transition from lab-scale to full-scale production

    D) Employee training

2. Which type of similarity ensures that equipment used in scale-up maintains the same ratios of dimensions as the lab-scale equipment?

    A) Geometric Similarity

    B) Dynamic Similarity

    C) Kinematic Similarity

    D) Thermal Similarity

3. What is the role of Computational Fluid Dynamics (CFD) in pilot plant scale-up?

    A) To monitor real-time quality of the products

    B) To simulate fluid flow and mixing in equipment

    C) To enhance the marketing of products

    D) To document process changes

4. Which factor is crucial for maintaining uniform mixing in scale-up processes?

    A) Heat transfer

    B) Particle size

    C) Mixing and flow dynamics

    D) Equipment cost

5. What is the significance of skilled personnel in the scale-up process?

    A) Only required for regulatory compliance

    B) Crucial for operating pilot plant equipment and process optimization

    C) Not necessary if automated systems are used

    D) Only required for maintenance

6. How does modular pilot plant design benefit the scale-up process?

    A) Reduces the need for skilled personnel

    B) Increases the cost of production

    C) Allows for flexibility in testing different configurations

    D) Eliminates the need for Computational Fluid Dynamics

7. What is the main challenge in scaling up related to heat and mass transfer?

    A) Decreased surface area-to-volume ratios

    B) Increased chemical reaction rates

    C) Reduced equipment costs

    D) Improved particle velocity

8. In the context of scale-up, what is the role of a regulatory affairs specialist?

    A) To design pilot plants

    B) To ensure compliance with standards and assist in documentation

    C) To market the product

    D) To oversee financial aspects

9. Which area of a pilot plant should be designed with flexibility to accommodate different processes?

    A) Quality control laboratories

B) Administrative offices

C) Facility layout

D) Raw material storage

10. What does FIFO stand for in inventory management?

    A) First In, First Out

    B) Final Inspection, First Out

    C) First In, Final Out

    D) Final Inspection, Final Out

11. Which documentation is necessary for managing changes in pilot plant scale-up processes?

    A) Marketing plans

    B) Change Control Documentation

    C) Product labels

    D) Employee training records

12. Why is raw material sourcing and quality critical in the scale-up process?

    A) To reduce marketing time

    B) To ensure consistency and quality of the product

    C) To comply with employee safety standards

    D) To enhance equipment design

13. What is the importance of a Process Development Report in pilot plant scale-up?

    A) To summarize marketing strategies

    B) To document the initial development and challenges encountered

    C) To provide financial forecasts

    D) To record employee training schedules

14. What aspect of pilot plant design ensures easy access and movement of personnel and materials?

    A) Quality assurance protocols

    B) Efficient use of space

C) Detailed process documentation

D) Advanced control strategies

15. Which type of validation is critical for new equipment during scale-up?

A) Marketing validation

B) Financial validation

C) Equipment validation

D) Employee validation

16. How does maintaining geometric similarity impact pilot plant scale-up?

A) Reduces the need for skilled personnel

B) Ensures that processes developed at lab scale work efficiently at larger scales

C) Decreases manufacturing time

D) Lowers raw material costs

17. What role do quality assurance specialists play in scale-up?

A) They oversee financial reporting

B) They ensure that processes meet quality standards and regulatory requirements

C) They handle marketing campaigns

D) They design pilot plants

18. Which strategy is essential for managing stock and reducing waste in material handling?

A) Just-In-Time (JIT) inventory

B) On-Time Delivery

C) Delayed Manufacturing Strategy

D) Long-Term Storage

19. What is critical for ensuring the safety and functionality of pilot plant operations?

A) Advanced marketing techniques

B) Regulatory documentation

C) Proper facility design and layout

D) Strategic financial planning

20. What is the primary benefit of process analytical technology (PAT) in scale-up?

A) Reduces labor costs

B) Enhances real-time monitoring and control of processes

C) Simplifies marketing strategies

D) Decreases raw material needs

Short Answer Type Questions (Subjective)

1. What is the main purpose of pilot plant scale-up in process development?
2. Explain the concept of geometric similarity in the context of scale-up.
3. How does Computational Fluid Dynamics (CFD) contribute to pilot plant scale-up?
4. Why is it important to maintain dynamic similarity across different scales of production?
5. Describe a key challenge in scaling up processes related to heat and mass transfer.
6. What role do regulatory affairs specialists play in the scale-up process?
7. How does modular design benefit the flexibility of pilot plant operations?
8. What is the significance of skilled personnel in the successful scale-up of a pilot plant?
9. What considerations should be made for space requirements when designing a pilot plant?
10. Explain the importance of sourcing high-quality raw materials in the scale-up process.
11. How does the First-In-First-Out (FIFO) method benefit inventory management during scale-up?
12. What is the purpose of process analytical technology (PAT) in scale-up?

13. Describe the role of quality assurance in maintaining standards during the scale-up process.

14. Why is maintaining detailed batch records crucial in a pilot plant scale-up?

15. How do changes in equipment design impact the scale-up process according to SUPAC guidelines?

16. Explain the process of validating new equipment in a pilot plant.

17. What are the benefits of implementing platform technology in pilot plant operations?

18. How does the integration of data management systems improve pilot plant operations?

19. Describe the impact of regulatory compliance on the design and operation of a pilot plant.

20. What is the role of stability testing in the quality assurance of raw materials?

Long Answer Type Questions (Subjective)

1. Discuss the importance of maintaining both geometric and dynamic similarity in the scale-up process and how these factors influence the success of scale-up.

2. Elaborate on the challenges and strategies involved in managing heat and mass transfer differences when scaling up from laboratory to pilot plant scale.

3. Describe the process of designing a pilot plant with considerations for modular and flexible setups, and how these designs contribute to the effectiveness of scale-up operations.

4. Analyze the critical role of personnel training and expertise in the scale-up process, detailing the types of training and knowledge essential for success.

5. Discuss the impact of raw materials management on the overall success of pilot plant operations, including sourcing, quality control, and inventory management.

6. Explain the application of Process Analytical Technology (PAT) in ensuring product quality and consistency during the scale-up process.

7. Detail the documentation requirements for a pilot plant scale-up, focusing on the importance of process development reports, batch records, and change control documentation.

8. Discuss the implications of SUPAC guidelines for scaling up pharmaceutical manufacturing, focusing on equipment changes and process adjustments.

9. Provide an in-depth analysis of the benefits and challenges of adopting platform technology in pilot plant operations, particularly focusing on cost savings and regulatory compliance.

10. Examine the role of quality by design (QbD) in pilot plant scale-up and how it can be used to ensure consistent product quality across different scales of production.

Answer Key

1. (C) Transition from lab-scale to full-scale production
2. (A) Geometric Similarity
3. (B) To simulate fluid flow and mixing in equipment
4. (C) Mixing and flow dynamics
5. (B) Crucial for operating pilot plant equipment and process optimization
6. (C) Allows for flexibility in testing different configurations
7. (A) Decreased surface area-to-volume ratios
8. (B) To ensure compliance with standards and assist in documentation
9. (C) Facility layout
10. (A) First In, First Out

11.(B) Change Control Documentation

12.(B) To ensure consistency and quality of the product

13.(B) To document the initial development and challenges encountered

14.(B) Efficient use of space

15.(C) Equipment validation

16.(B) Ensures that processes developed at lab scale work efficiently at larger scales

17.(B) They ensure that processes meet quality standards and regulatory requirements

18.(A) Just-In-Time (JIT) inventory

19.(C) Proper facility design and layout

20.(B) Enhances real-time monitoring and control of processes

CHAPTER - 2

TECHNOLOGY DEVELOPMENT AND TRANSFER

INTRODUCTION:

Technology development and transfer are crucial components of innovation, economic growth, and competitive advantage in the global market. They encompass the creation of new technologies and the processes through which these technologies are disseminated and adopted across different sectors and regions.

Technology Development

Technology development refers to the process of creating new or improved technologies through research and innovation. It involves several stages:

1. **Basic Research**: This is the initial phase where scientific knowledge is expanded. Researchers explore fundamental principles without specific applications in mind.

2. **Applied Research**: In this phase, the focus shifts to practical applications. Scientists and engineers aim to solve specific problems or develop new products.

3. **Development**: This stage involves turning research findings into tangible technologies. It includes design, prototyping, and testing.

4. **Commercialization**: Finally, the technology is prepared for market entry. This involves production scaling, marketing, and sales strategies.

Key Drivers of Technology Development:

1. **Innovation Ecosystem**: Collaboration between universities, research institutions, and industry.

2. **Funding**: Investment from government, private sector, and venture capital.

3. **Regulation and Policy**: Government policies that support research and development (R&D) through grants, tax incentives, and intellectual property protection.

4. **Market Demand**: Consumer needs and market trends that drive the development of new technologies.

Technology Transfer

Technology transfer is the process through which technology developed in one place is transferred to another. This can occur within a country or internationally. The goal is to enable widespread adoption and utilization of new technologies. Technology transfer can happen through several mechanisms:

1. **Licensing Agreements**: Companies or institutions can license their technology to others for a fee or royalties.

2. **Joint Ventures**: Two or more entities collaborate to develop and commercialize technology.

3. **Collaborative Research**: Partnerships between research institutions and companies to develop new technologies.

4. **Spin-offs and Start-ups**: New companies created to bring a technology to market.

5. **Consulting and Training**: Experts from the technology's origin provide training and consulting services to the adopters.

Challenges in Technology Transfer:

- **Intellectual Property (IP) Issues**: Protecting IP rights while sharing technology.

- **Cultural and Organizational Differences**: Variations in business practices and organizational culture.

- **Economic Barriers**: Cost of technology adoption and infrastructure requirements.

- **Regulatory Hurdles**: Compliance with different regulatory standards across regions.

Importance of Technology Development and Transfer

1. **Economic Growth**: New technologies can lead to the creation of new industries and jobs.

2. **Competitive Advantage**: Companies and nations that effectively develop and transfer technology can gain a significant edge over their competitors.

3. **Social Impact**: Technologies in healthcare, agriculture, and education can vastly improve quality of life.

4. **Sustainability**: Innovations in energy and materials can lead to more sustainable practices and reduce environmental impact.

Strategies for Effective Technology Transfer

1. **Strong IP Management**: Clear policies and practices for IP protection and licensing.

2. **Building Collaborative Networks**: Establishing partnerships between academia, industry, and government.

3. **Capacity Building**: Training and educating the workforce to handle new technologies.

4. **Market Analysis**: Understanding the needs and capabilities of the target market.

5. **Supportive Policies**: Government incentives and support for R&D and technology adoption.

WHO GUIDELINES FOR TECHNOLOGY TRANSFER(TT)

The World Health Organization (WHO) has established guidelines for technology transfer (TT) to ensure the successful development, manufacturing, and distribution of health-related technologies, particularly pharmaceuticals and medical devices. These guidelines are designed to facilitate the transfer of technology in a way that ensures quality, safety, and efficacy of health products.

Key Aspects of WHO Guidelines for Technology Transfer

1. Scope and Purpose

a. **Objective**: To provide a framework for transferring technology in the pharmaceutical sector, ensuring the quality of medicines and healthcare products.

b. **Scope:** Applicable to all types of technology transfer in the pharmaceutical industry, including manufacturing processes, analytical methods, and quality control.

2. **Planning and Preparation**

    a. **Technology Transfer Plan (TTP)**: A detailed document outlining the entire TT process, including objectives, responsibilities, timelines, and resources.

    b. **Risk Assessment**: Identify potential risks associated with the transfer process and develop mitigation strategies.

3. **Documentation**

    a. **Standard Operating Procedures (SOPs):** Detailed SOPs must be in place for each step of the TT process.

    b. **Technology Transfer Protocol (TTP):** Comprehensive documentation of the technology to be transferred, including detailed process descriptions, quality specifications, and validation requirements.

    c. **Reports and Records**: Maintain thorough records of all activities related to TT, including deviations, corrective actions, and final reports.

4. **Training and Capacity Building**

    a. **Personnel Training**: Ensure that all personnel involved in the TT process are adequately trained and competent.

    b. **Knowledge Transfer**: Facilitate the transfer of knowledge through training sessions, workshops, and hands-on practice.

5. **Communication**

a. **Effective Communication**: Establish clear and continuous communication channels between the sending and receiving parties.

b. **Regular Meetings**: Schedule regular meetings to review progress, address issues, and ensure alignment between all parties.

6. Quality Management

a. **Quality Assurance (QA)**: Integrate QA principles throughout the TT process to maintain product quality and compliance with regulatory standards.

b. **Quality Control (QC):** Implement robust QC procedures to monitor and verify the quality of the transferred technology.

7. Validation and Qualification

a. **Process Validation**: Validate all critical processes to ensure they consistently produce products meeting predetermined quality criteria.

b. **Equipment Qualification**: Ensure that all equipment used in the TT process is qualified and operates within specified parameters.

8. Regulatory Compliance

a. **Regulatory Requirements**: Adhere to all relevant regulatory requirements and guidelines throughout the TT process.

b. **Regulatory Submissions**: Prepare and submit necessary documentation to regulatory authorities to obtain approvals for the transferred technology.

9. Post-Transfer Activities

a. **Monitoring and Evaluation**: Continuously monitor the performance of the transferred technology to ensure it meets quality and performance standards.

b. **Continuous Improvement**: Identify areas for improvement and implement changes to optimize the technology and process.

Detailed Steps in WHO Technology Transfer Process

1. Initiation

a. **Feasibility Study**: Conduct a feasibility study to evaluate the potential for successful technology transfer.

b. **Gap Analysis**: Identify gaps between current capabilities and requirements for the new technology.

2. **Development**

a. **Technical Package**: Develop a comprehensive technical package that includes detailed descriptions of the technology, processes, and quality standards.

b. **Pilot Testing**: Conduct pilot tests to verify the feasibility and performance of the technology in the new setting.

3. **Transfer**

a. **Execution of TTP**: Implement the Technology Transfer Plan, ensuring all steps are followed as outlined.

b. **Trial Batches**: Produce trial batches to validate the transfer process and ensure consistency with the original technology.

4. **Validation**

a. **Full-Scale Production**: Scale up production and conduct full-scale validation to confirm the technology operates effectively at the intended scale.

b. **Performance Qualification (PQ):** Perform PQ to verify that the technology produces consistent and high-quality products.

5. **Commercialization**

a. **Launch Preparation**: Prepare for product launch, including finalizing production schedules, marketing strategies, and distribution plans.

b. **Post-Market Surveillance**: Monitor the product post-launch to ensure ongoing compliance and performance.

Terminology

Understanding the specific terminology used in the WHO guidelines for technology transfer is essential for correctly interpreting and implementing these guidelines. Below is a detailed explanation of key terms commonly found in these guidelines.

Key Terminology

1. **Technology Transfer (TT)**

   a. **Definition:** The process of transferring knowledge, skills, methodologies, and technologies between organizations or within an organization to ensure successful production and commercialization of a product.

   b. **Context:** TT can occur between research institutions and manufacturers, between different manufacturing sites, or between companies.

2. **Technology Transfer Plan (TTP)**

   a. **Definition**: A comprehensive document that outlines the objectives, scope, responsibilities, timelines, and resources required for the TT process.

   b. **Context:** The TTP ensures that all aspects of the transfer are planned and executed systematically.

3. **Technical Package**

   a. **Definition**: A detailed set of documents that describe the technology to be transferred, including process descriptions, standard operating procedures (SOPs), analytical methods, and quality specifications.

   b. **Context:** This package is crucial for the receiving party to understand and replicate the technology accurately.

4. **Sending Unit (SU)**

   a. **Definition**: The organization or site that initially developed the technology and is responsible for transferring it to another entity.

b. **Context**: The SU provides the necessary technical and documentation support to the receiving unit.

5. **Receiving Unit (RU)**

   a. **Definition**: The organization or site that receives the technology from the SU and is responsible for implementing and validating the technology in their setting.

   b. **Context:** The RU must ensure they have the necessary capabilities and resources to adopt the new technology.

6. **Standard Operating Procedures (SOPs)**

   a. **Definition**: Detailed, written instructions to achieve uniformity in the performance of specific functions.

   b. **Context:** SOPs are essential for ensuring consistent application of the transferred technology.

7. **Validation**

   a. **Definition:** The documented process of demonstrating that a procedure, process, or activity will consistently produce a result meeting predetermined criteria.

   b. **Context:** Validation ensures that the transferred technology operates effectively and meets quality standards.

8. **Qualification**

   a. **Definition:** The action of proving that any equipment or system works correctly and consistently to produce the expected results.

   b. **Context:** This includes Installation Qualification (IQ), Operational Qualification (OQ), and Performance Qualification (PQ).

9. **Risk Assessment**

   a. **Definition**: A systematic process of identifying and evaluating potential risks that could affect the TT process, followed by the implementation of measures to mitigate those risks.

b. **Context**: Risk assessments are critical for anticipating and addressing issues that could impact the success of the transfer.

10. Process Validation

a. **Definition**: The act of validating the manufacturing process to ensure it consistently produces products meeting predetermined specifications.

b. **Context:** It includes various stages such as process design, process qualification, and continued process verification.

11. Analytical Method Transfer

a. **Definition:** The process of transferring analytical methods from the SU to the RU to ensure that the RU can accurately perform the necessary tests.

b. **Context:** Analytical method transfer is crucial for maintaining product quality and compliance.

12. Pilot Scale

a. **Definition:** A smaller scale production run used to test the feasibility and performance of the technology before full-scale manufacturing.

b. **Context:** Pilot scale runs help identify potential issues and refine the process.

13. Commercial Scale

a. **Definition**: The production level at which the technology is implemented for large-scale manufacturing and commercialization.

b. **Context:** This phase follows successful validation and qualification at the pilot scale.

14. Knowledge Management

a. **Definition**: The systematic management of information and knowledge, including its creation, dissemination, and utilization.

b. **Context:** Effective knowledge management is essential for ensuring all stakeholders are informed and capable of implementing the technology.

15. **Regulatory Compliance**

    a. **Definition:** Adherence to all applicable laws, regulations, and guidelines governing the development, manufacturing, and distribution of the product.

    b. **Context:** Regulatory compliance ensures that the transferred technology meets all legal and quality requirements.

16. **Intellectual Property (IP)**

    a. **Definition**: Legal rights that protect creations and inventions, including patents, trademarks, and copyrights.

    b. **Context**: Proper management of IP is crucial for protecting the interests of both the SU and RU during the TT process.

Technology transfer protocol

The Technology Transfer Protocol (TTP) is a critical component of the WHO guidelines for technology transfer in the pharmaceutical and healthcare sectors. It serves as a comprehensive document that outlines the processes, responsibilities, and requirements for transferring technology from the sending unit (SU) to the receiving unit (RU).

Key Components of the Technology Transfer Protocol (TTP)

1. **Introduction**

    a. **Objective**: State the purpose of the technology transfer and the goals to be achieved.

    b. **Scope:** Define the scope of the transfer, including the specific technology or product involved, and the parties (SU and RU).

2. **Roles and Responsibilities**

    a. **Sending Unit (SU):** Detail the responsibilities of the SU, including providing technical documentation, training, and ongoing support.

b. **Receiving Unit (RU)**: Outline the responsibilities of the RU, including preparing facilities, training staff, and validating processes.

c. **Project Team**: Identify key personnel involved in the TT process from both the SU and RU, and define their roles.

3. **Technology Transfer Plan**

a. **Project Timeline**: Provide a detailed timeline with milestones and deadlines for each phase of the transfer.

b. **Resources and Budget**: Specify the resources required, including personnel, equipment, and financial resources, and outline the budget.

4. **Documentation and Technical Package**

a. **Technical Package**: Include detailed documentation on the technology being transferred. This should encompass:

   i. **Process Description**: Step-by-step procedures for manufacturing the product.

   ii. **Equipment Specifications**: Detailed information on equipment needed for the process.

   iii. **Analytical Methods**: Standard operating procedures (SOPs) for all analytical methods to be used.

   iv. Quality Specifications: Criteria for raw materials, intermediates, and final products.

b. **Standard Operating Procedures (SOPs)**: Provide all necessary SOPs related to the transferred technology.

5. **Training and Knowledge Transfer**

a. **Training Plan**: Outline the training programs for RU personnel, including hands-on training, workshops, and documentation reviews.

b. **Knowledge Transfer Activities**: Describe activities to ensure thorough understanding of the technology, such as seminars and Q&A sessions.

6. **Validation and Qualification**

a. **Process Validation**: Describe the process validation steps to ensure the technology works as intended at the RU.

b. **Equipment Qualification**: Outline the steps for qualifying equipment, including Installation Qualification (IQ), Operational Qualification (OQ), and Performance Qualification (PQ).

c. **Analytical Method Validation**: Detail the validation of analytical methods to ensure they perform correctly at the RU.

7. **Risk Management**

   a. **Risk Assessment**: Conduct a risk assessment to identify potential risks associated with the technology transfer.

   b. **Risk Mitigation Strategies**: Develop strategies to mitigate identified risks, including contingency plans.

8. **Regulatory Compliance**

   a. **Regulatory Requirements**: List all regulatory requirements that must be met in both the SU and RU regions.

   b. **Regulatory Submissions**: Provide guidelines for preparing and submitting necessary documentation to regulatory authorities.

9. **Monitoring and Reporting**

   a. **Progress Monitoring**: Define procedures for monitoring progress throughout the TT process, including regular updates and status reports.

   b. **Reporting**: Specify the format and frequency of reports to be submitted to stakeholders.

10. **Post-Transfer Activities**

    a. **Ongoing Support**: Outline the support provided by the SU after the transfer, such as troubleshooting and technical assistance.

    b. **Continuous Improvement**: Describe mechanisms for continuous improvement based on feedback and post-transfer performance.

Detailed Steps in Implementing the Technology Transfer Protocol

1. **Preparation Phase**
    a. **Initial Assessment**: Conduct a thorough initial assessment to evaluate the feasibility of the technology transfer.
    b. **Gap Analysis**: Identify gaps between current capabilities and those required to implement the new technology.
2. **Execution Phase**
    a. **Technical Transfer**: Implement the technical transfer according to the TTP, ensuring all steps are meticulously followed.
    b. **Training and Development**: Conduct training sessions and workshops to build the necessary skills within the RU.
    c. **Trial Production**: Perform trial production runs to validate processes and identify any issues.
3. **Validation Phase**
    a. **Full-Scale Validation**: Conduct full-scale validation to ensure the technology performs as expected.
    b. **Documentation Review**: Review all documentation to ensure compliance with regulatory standards and internal quality requirements.
4. **Commercialization Phase**
    a. **Scale-Up Production**: Scale up production to commercial levels, ensuring all validation and qualification criteria are met.
    b. **Market Launch**: Prepare for the market launch, including finalizing production schedules and distribution plans.
5. **Post-Transfer Monitoring**
    a. **Performance Monitoring**: Continuously monitor the performance of the transferred technology to ensure ongoing compliance and quality.
    b. **Feedback Mechanisms**: Implement feedback mechanisms to gather insights and make necessary adjustments.

Quality risk management

Quality Risk Management (QRM) is an integral part of the WHO guidelines for technology transfer in the pharmaceutical and healthcare sectors. It ensures that risks to product quality are systematically identified, assessed, and controlled throughout the technology transfer process. This is crucial for maintaining the integrity, safety, and efficacy of health products during and after the transfer.

Key Components of Quality Risk Management in Technology Transfer

1. **Risk Management Framework**

    a. **Objective:** To create a structured and systematic process for identifying, evaluating, and mitigating risks associated with technology transfer.

    b. **Scope**: Applies to all stages of technology transfer, from initial planning to post-transfer monitoring.

2. **Risk Assessment**

    a. **Risk Identification**: Systematically identify potential risks that could impact product quality, process performance, or regulatory compliance. Common risks include variations in raw materials, equipment differences, and human error.

    b. **Risk Analysis**: Evaluate the identified risks to understand their nature, sources, and potential impacts. This involves determining the likelihood of occurrence and the severity of the impact.

    c. Risk Evaluation: Compare the identified and analyzed risks against predefined criteria to prioritize them based on their potential impact on product quality.

3. **Risk Control**

    a. **Risk Reduction**: Implement measures to mitigate identified risks. This may include process adjustments, enhanced training, additional controls, or changes to equipment or materials.

b. **Risk Acceptance**: Determine which risks can be accepted based on their impact and the feasibility of further control measures. Document the rationale for accepting these risks.

c. **Risk Communication**: Ensure that all relevant stakeholders are informed about identified risks, control measures, and the rationale for risk acceptance.

4. Risk Review

a. **Continuous Monitoring**: Regularly monitor the identified risks and control measures to ensure their effectiveness. This includes tracking any changes in the risk profile and updating risk assessments as necessary.

b. **Periodic Review**: Conduct periodic reviews of the risk management process to identify opportunities for improvement and to ensure ongoing compliance with regulatory requirements.

5. Documentation and Reporting

a. **Risk Management Plan**: Develop and maintain a comprehensive risk management plan that outlines the processes and responsibilities for managing risks throughout the technology transfer.

b. **Risk Assessment Reports**: Document the findings of all risk assessments, including identified risks, analysis results, and control measures.

c. **Risk Management Reviews**: Record the outcomes of continuous monitoring and periodic reviews, including any changes to the risk profile or control measures.

Detailed Steps in Implementing Quality Risk Management

1. Planning and Preparation

a. **Form Risk Management Team**: Assemble a cross-functional team with expertise in various aspects of the technology and process.

b. **Develop Risk Management Plan**: Outline the objectives, scope, methodology, and responsibilities for risk management activities.

2. **Risk Assessment**

   a. **Conduct Risk Identification Workshops**: Facilitate workshops with key stakeholders to identify potential risks.

   b. **Perform Risk Analysis**: Use tools such as Failure Mode and Effects Analysis (FMEA), Hazard Analysis and Critical Control Points (HACCP), or risk matrices to analyze identified risks.

   c. **Evaluate Risks**: Prioritize risks based on their likelihood and potential impact on product quality.

3. **Risk Control**

   a. **Implement Risk Reduction Measures**: Take actions to mitigate high-priority risks, such as optimizing process parameters, upgrading equipment, or enhancing training programs.

   b. **Develop Contingency Plans**: Prepare contingency plans for managing risks that cannot be fully mitigated.

4. **Risk Communication and Documentation**

   a. **Communicate Risk Information**: Share risk assessment results and control measures with all relevant stakeholders, including production, quality assurance, regulatory affairs, and management.

   b. **Maintain Risk Documentation**: Keep comprehensive records of all risk management activities, including risk assessments, control measures, and reviews.

5. **Ongoing Monitoring and Review**

   a. **Continuous Risk Monitoring**: Track the effectiveness of risk control measures through regular process monitoring and quality audits.

   b. **Conduct Periodic Risk Reviews**: Regularly review the risk management plan and update it based on new information, changes in the process, or regulatory updates.

Tools and Techniques for Quality Risk Management

1. **Failure Mode and Effects Analysis (FMEA)**: A systematic method for evaluating processes to identify where and how they might fail and assessing the relative impact of different failures.

2. **Hazard Analysis and Critical Control Points (HACCP)**: A preventive approach to food safety and pharmaceutical quality that identifies critical points where risks could arise and implements controls to mitigate them.

3. **Risk Matrices**: A visual tool that helps in assessing and prioritizing risks by plotting them on a matrix based on their likelihood and severity.

4. **Root Cause Analysis (RCA)**: A method for identifying the underlying causes of identified risks or quality issues to implement effective corrective actions.

Transfer from R & D to production -Process

Transferring technology from Research and Development (R&D) to production is a critical phase in the technology transfer process. According to the WHO guidelines, this transfer must be carefully planned and executed to ensure the integrity, quality, and consistency of the product as it moves from a research setting to full-scale manufacturing. Below is a detailed outline of the process involved in this transfer.

Key Phases in the Transfer from R&D to Production

1. Preparation Phase

a. **Project Team Formation**: Establish a cross-functional team that includes members from R&D, production, quality assurance, regulatory affairs, and other relevant departments.

b. **Gap Analysis**: Conduct a thorough gap analysis to identify differences between the R&D environment and the production environment, including equipment, processes, and capabilities.

c. **Technology Transfer Plan (TTP)**: Develop a detailed Technology Transfer Plan that outlines the objectives, scope, timelines, responsibilities, and resources required for the transfer.

2. **Documentation and Technical Package Preparation**

   a. **Technical Package**: Assemble a comprehensive technical package that includes all necessary documentation to replicate the R&D process in the production setting. This should include:

      i. **Process Descriptions**: Detailed process flows, including step-by-step manufacturing instructions.

      ii. **Formulations**: Exact formulations used in the R&D phase, with precise measurements and materials specifications.

      iii. **Standard Operating Procedures (SOPs):** SOPs for each step of the process, including handling of raw materials, intermediate products, and final products.

      iv. **Analytical Methods**: Detailed analytical methods for quality control, including testing procedures, equipment specifications, and validation reports.

      v. **Quality Specifications**: Quality criteria for raw materials, in-process materials, and final products, including acceptance criteria.

3. **Training and Knowledge Transfer**

   a. **Training Programs**: Develop and implement training programs for production personnel. These should cover:

      i. **Process Understanding**: Detailed training on the manufacturing process and the rationale behind each step.

      ii. **Equipment Operation**: Hands-on training on the operation and maintenance of equipment used in production.

      iii. **Quality Control**: Training on analytical methods and quality control procedures.

b. **Knowledge Transfer Sessions**: Conduct knowledge transfer sessions where R&D personnel provide insights and answer questions about the process and technology.

4. **Pilot Scale Production**

   a. **Pilot Batches**: Produce pilot batches at the production site to test the transfer of the technology from R&D. This involves:

      i. **Process Verification**: Verifying that the manufacturing process can be replicated at the production scale.

      ii. **Quality Testing**: Conducting comprehensive quality testing on pilot batches to ensure they meet specified criteria.

      iii. **Troubleshooting**: Identifying and addressing any issues that arise during the pilot production.

5. **Process Validation**

   a. **Validation Protocols**: Develop and implement process validation protocols to demonstrate that the production process consistently produces products meeting predetermined quality criteria. This includes:

      i. **Installation Qualification (IQ):** Ensuring that equipment and installations comply with design specifications.

      ii. **Operational Qualification (OQ):** Confirming that the equipment operates as intended under defined conditions.

      iii. **Performance Qualification (PQ):** Verifying that the production process performs effectively and reproducibly under normal operating conditions.

   b. **Validation Batches**: Produce validation batches and conduct thorough testing to confirm process consistency and product quality.

6. **Full-Scale Production**

a. **Scale-Up**: Transition from pilot scale to full-scale production, ensuring that all equipment, materials, and processes are scaled appropriately.

b. **Ongoing** Monitoring: Implement ongoing process monitoring and control systems to maintain product quality and consistency. This includes:

   i. **In-Process Controls**: Real-time monitoring and control of critical process parameters.

   ii. **Batch Testing:** Regular testing of production batches to ensure compliance with quality specifications.

7. **Regulatory Compliance**

   a. **Regulatory Submissions**: Prepare and submit necessary documentation to regulatory authorities to obtain approval for the commercial production of the product. This includes:

      i. **Process Descriptions**: Detailed descriptions of the production process.

      ii. **Validation Data**: Comprehensive validation data demonstrating process consistency and product quality.

      iii. **Quality Control Procedures**: Documentation of quality control procedures and results.

   b. **Regulatory Inspections**: Facilitate inspections by regulatory authorities and address any observations or findings.

8. **Post-Transfer Activities**

   a. **Continuous Improvement:** Implement systems for continuous improvement based on feedback from production, quality control, and regulatory reviews. This includes:

      i. **Process Optimization**: Identifying opportunities to optimize the manufacturing process for efficiency and cost-effectiveness.

ii. **Quality Enhancements**: Implementing changes to enhance product quality based on ongoing monitoring and testing.

b. **Ongoing Support**: Provide ongoing technical support to the production team to address any issues and ensure the continued success of the technology transfer.

Transfer from R & D to production - packaging

Packaging is a crucial component of the technology transfer process from R&D to production. Proper packaging ensures the protection, stability, and integrity of pharmaceutical products, as well as compliance with regulatory requirements. The WHO guidelines emphasize the need for careful planning and execution when transferring packaging processes from R&D to production.

Key Components of the Packaging Transfer Process

1. Preparation Phase

a. **Project Team Formation**: Assemble a cross-functional team including members from R&D, packaging development, production, quality assurance, and regulatory affairs.

b. **Gap Analysis**: Conduct a gap analysis to identify differences between the packaging processes and materials used in R&D and those required for full-scale production.

c. **Packaging Transfer Plan (PTP)**: Develop a detailed Packaging Transfer Plan outlining objectives, scope, timelines, responsibilities, and resources required for the transfer.

2. Documentation and Technical Package Preparation

a. **Technical Package**: Assemble a comprehensive technical package that includes all necessary documentation to replicate the R&D packaging process in the production setting. This should include:

i. **Packaging Design**: Detailed drawings and specifications of primary, secondary, and tertiary packaging.

ii. **Material Specifications**: Specifications for all packaging materials, including suppliers, material grades, and quality standards.

iii. **Standard Operating Procedures (SOPs)**: SOPs for each packaging step, including material handling, filling, sealing, labeling, and storage.

iv. **Packaging Process Descriptions**: Detailed process flows and descriptions for all packaging operations.

v. **Quality Control Methods**: Methods for testing and verifying packaging integrity and quality.

3. **Training and Knowledge Transfer**

   a. **Training Programs**: Develop and implement training programs for production personnel. These should cover:

      i. **Packaging Process Understanding**: Detailed training on the packaging processes and the rationale behind each step.

      ii. **Equipment Operation**: Hands-on training on the operation and maintenance of packaging equipment.

      iii. **Quality Control**: Training on packaging quality control procedures and testing methods.

   b. **Knowledge Transfer Sessions**: Conduct knowledge transfer sessions where R&D personnel provide insights and answer questions about the packaging process and technology.

4. **Pilot Scale Packaging**

   a. **Pilot Batches:** Produce pilot batches at the production site to test the transfer of the packaging process from R&D. This involves:

      i. **Process Verification**: Verifying that the packaging process can be replicated at the production scale.

      ii. **Quality Testing**: Conducting comprehensive quality testing on pilot batches to ensure they meet specified criteria.

   iii. **Troubleshooting**: Identifying and addressing any issues that arise during pilot packaging.

5. **Process Validation**

  a. **Validation Protocols**: Develop and implement packaging process validation protocols to demonstrate that the packaging process consistently produces products meeting predetermined quality criteria. This includes:

    i. **Installation Qualification (IQ): Ensuring** that packaging equipment and installations comply with design specifications.

    ii. **Operational Qualification (OQ):** Confirming that the packaging equipment operates as intended under defined conditions.

    iii. **Performance Qualification (PQ):** Verifying that the packaging process performs effectively and reproducibly under normal operating conditions.

  b. **Validation Batches**: Produce validation batches and conduct thorough testing to confirm process consistency and packaging quality.

6. **Full-Scale Production**

  a. **Scale-Up:** Transition from pilot scale to full-scale packaging, ensuring that all equipment, materials, and processes are scaled appropriately.

  b. **Ongoing Monitoring**: Implement ongoing process monitoring and control systems to maintain packaging quality and consistency. This includes:

    i. **In-Process Controls**: Real-time monitoring and control of critical packaging parameters.

    ii. **Batch Testing**: Regular testing of packaging batches to ensure compliance with quality specifications.

7. **Regulatory Compliance**

a. **Regulatory Submissions**: Prepare and submit necessary documentation to regulatory authorities to obtain approval for the commercial packaging of the product. This includes:

    i. **Packaging Process Descriptions**: Detailed descriptions of the packaging process.

    ii. **Validation Data**: Comprehensive validation data demonstrating process consistency and packaging quality.

    iii. **Quality Control Procedures**: Documentation of packaging quality control procedures and results.

b. **Regulatory Inspections**: Facilitate inspections by regulatory authorities and address any observations or findings.

8. Post-Transfer Activities

a. **Continuous Improvement**: Implement systems for continuous improvement based on feedback from production, quality control, and regulatory reviews. This includes:

    i. **Process Optimization**: Identifying opportunities to optimize the packaging process for efficiency and cost-effectiveness.

    ii. **Quality Enhancements**: Implementing changes to enhance packaging quality based on ongoing monitoring and testing.

b. **Ongoing Support**: Provide ongoing technical support to the production team to address any issues and ensure the continued success of the packaging process.

Detailed Steps in the Packaging Transfer Process

1. Preparation Phase

a. **Initial Assessment**: Conduct an initial assessment to evaluate the feasibility of the packaging transfer and identify potential challenges.

b. **Develop Transfer Plan**: Create a Packaging Transfer Plan detailing all aspects of the transfer, including timelines, resource allocation, and risk management strategies.

2. **Documentation and Technical Package Preparation**

   a. **Collect and Compile Documentation**: Gather all relevant documentation from R&D, including packaging specifications, SOPs, and quality control methods.

   b. **Create Technical Package:** Compile the technical package, ensuring all information is accurate and complete.

3. **Training and Knowledge Transfer**

   a. **Conduct Training Sessions**: Provide comprehensive training for production personnel on the new packaging processes and equipment.

   b. **Facilitate Knowledge Transfer**: Ensure thorough knowledge transfer from R&D to production, addressing any questions or concerns.

4. **Pilot Scale Packaging**

   a. **Run Pilot Batches:** Execute pilot batches to test the packaging process at the production site, making adjustments as necessary.

   b. **Evaluate and Refine**: Assess the results of the pilot batches and refine the process based on findings.

5. **Process Validation**

   a. **Develop and Execute Validation Protocols**: Implement validation protocols to ensure the packaging process is reliable and consistent.

   b. **Produce Validation Batches:** Conduct validation batches, thoroughly testing them to confirm they meet all quality standards.

6. **Full-Scale Production**

   a. **Scale-Up Production**: Transition to full-scale production, ensuring all packaging processes and equipment are fully operational.

   b. **Monitor and Control**: Implement continuous monitoring and control mechanisms to maintain packaging quality.

7. **Regulatory Compliance**

   a. **Prepare Regulatory Submissions**: Compile and submit the necessary documentation to regulatory authorities for approval.

b. **Facilitate Inspections**: Support regulatory inspections and address any issues that arise.

8. Post-Transfer Activities

a. **Implement Continuous Improvement**: Establish processes for continuous improvement based on feedback and performance data.

b. **Provide Ongoing Support**: Offer ongoing technical support to ensure the packaging process remains efficient and effective.

Transfer from R & D to production -cleaning

The cleaning process is a critical aspect of technology transfer from R&D to production, particularly in the pharmaceutical and healthcare sectors. Proper cleaning ensures that equipment is free from contaminants and residues, which is essential for maintaining product quality, safety, and regulatory compliance. The WHO guidelines emphasize the importance of establishing robust cleaning procedures and validation methods during this transition.

Key Components of the Cleaning Transfer Process

1. Preparation Phase

a. **Project Team Formation**: Form a cross-functional team with members from R&D, production, quality assurance, and regulatory affairs.

b. **Gap Analysis**: Conduct a gap analysis to identify differences in cleaning requirements and practices between R&D and production environments.

c. **Cleaning Transfer Plan (CTP):** Develop a detailed Cleaning Transfer Plan outlining objectives, scope, timelines, responsibilities, and resources required for the transfer.

2. Documentation and Technical Package Preparation

a. **Technical Package**: Assemble a comprehensive technical package that includes all necessary documentation to replicate the R&D cleaning processes in the production setting. This should include:

i. **Cleaning Procedures**: Detailed standard operating procedures (SOPs) for cleaning all equipment and facilities.

ii. **Cleaning Agents and Materials**: Specifications for cleaning agents and materials, including their concentrations and usage instructions.

iii. **Cleaning Validation Protocols**: Protocols for validating cleaning processes, including acceptance criteria and testing methods.

iv. **Analytical Methods**: Methods for detecting and quantifying residues and contaminants.

3. **Training and Knowledge Transfer**

a. **Training Programs**: Develop and implement training programs for production personnel. These should cover:

   i. **Cleaning Process Understanding**: Detailed training on the cleaning procedures and the rationale behind each step.

   ii. **Equipment Cleaning**: Hands-on training on the cleaning of specific equipment used in production.

   iii. **Quality Control**: Training on cleaning validation and residue testing methods.

b. **Knowledge Transfer Sessions**: Conduct sessions where R&D personnel provide insights and answer questions about the cleaning processes and validation methods.

4. **Pilot Scale Cleaning**

a. **Pilot Cleaning Batches**: Perform cleaning on pilot batches of production equipment to test the transfer of the cleaning processes from R&D. This involves:

   i. **Process Verification**: Verifying that the cleaning process can be replicated at the production scale.

ii. **Residue Testing**: Conducting comprehensive residue testing to ensure that the cleaning processes meet specified criteria.

iii. **Troubleshooting:** Identifying and addressing any issues that arise during pilot cleaning.

5. **Cleaning Validation**

   a. **Validation Protocols**: Develop and implement cleaning validation protocols to demonstrate that the cleaning processes consistently meet predetermined quality criteria. This includes:

      i. **Installation Qualification (IQ)**: Ensuring that cleaning equipment and installations comply with design specifications.

      ii. **Operational Qualification (OQ)**: Confirming that the cleaning equipment operates as intended under defined conditions.

      iii. **Performance Qualification (PQ)**: Verifying that the cleaning process performs effectively and reproducibly under normal operating conditions.

   b. **Validation Batches**: Perform cleaning validation batches and conduct thorough testing to confirm process consistency and cleanliness.

6. **Full-Scale Production**

   a. **Scale-Up**: Transition from pilot scale to full-scale cleaning, ensuring that all equipment, materials, and processes are scaled appropriately.

   b. **Ongoing Monitoring**: Implement ongoing monitoring and control systems to maintain cleaning quality and consistency. This includes:

      i. **In-Process Controls**: Real-time monitoring and control of critical cleaning parameters.

ii. **Routine Testing**: Regular testing of cleaned equipment to ensure compliance with cleanliness specifications.

7. **Regulatory Compliance**

    a. **Regulatory Submissions:** Prepare and submit necessary documentation to regulatory authorities to obtain approval for the cleaning processes used in commercial production. This includes:

        i. **Cleaning Process Descriptions**: Detailed descriptions of the cleaning processes.

        ii. **Validation Data**: Comprehensive validation data demonstrating cleaning process consistency and effectiveness.

        iii. **Quality Control Procedures**: Documentation of cleaning quality control procedures and results.

    b. **Regulatory Inspections**: Facilitate inspections by regulatory authorities and address any observations or findings.

8. **Post-Transfer Activities**

    a. **Continuous Improvement**: Implement systems for continuous improvement based on feedback from production, quality control, and regulatory reviews. This includes:

        i. **Process Optimization**: Identifying opportunities to optimize the cleaning process for efficiency and effectiveness.

        ii. **Quality Enhancements**: Implementing changes to enhance cleaning quality based on ongoing monitoring and testing.

    b. **Ongoing Support**: Provide ongoing technical support to the production team to address any issues and ensure the continued success of the cleaning processes.

Detailed Steps in the Cleaning Transfer Process

1. Preparation Phase

a. **Initial Assessment**: Conduct an initial assessment to evaluate the feasibility of the cleaning transfer and identify potential challenges.

b. **Develop Transfer Plan**: Create a Cleaning Transfer Plan detailing all aspects of the transfer, including timelines, resource allocation, and risk management strategies.

2. **Documentation and Technical Package Preparation**

a. **Collect and Compile Documentation**: Gather all relevant documentation from R&D, including cleaning SOPs, cleaning agent specifications, and validation protocols.

b. **Create Technical Package**: Compile the technical package, ensuring all information is accurate and complete.

3. **Training and Knowledge Transfer**

a. **Conduct Training Sessions**: Provide comprehensive training for production personnel on the new cleaning processes and equipment.

b. **Facilitate Knowledge Transfer**: Ensure thorough knowledge transfer from R&D to production, addressing any questions or concerns.

4. **Pilot Scale Cleaning**

a. **Run Pilot Cleaning Batches**: Execute pilot cleaning batches to test the cleaning process at the production site, adjusting as necessary.

b. **Evaluate and Refine**: Assess the results of the pilot cleaning batches and refine the process based on findings.

5. **Cleaning Validation**

a. **Develop and Execute Validation Protocols**: Implement validation protocols to ensure the cleaning process is reliable and consistent.

b. **Perform Validation Batches**: Conduct validation batches, thoroughly testing them to confirm they meet all cleanliness standards.

6. **Full-Scale Production**

a. **Scale-Up Production**: Transition to full-scale production, ensuring all cleaning processes and equipment are fully operational.

b. **Monitor and Control**: Implement continuous monitoring and control mechanisms to maintain cleaning quality.

7. **Regulatory Compliance**

   a. **Prepare Regulatory Submissions**: Compile and submit the necessary documentation to regulatory authorities for approval.

   b. **Facilitate Inspections**: Support regulatory inspections and address any issues that arise.

8. **Post-Transfer Activities**

   a. **Implement Continuous Improvement**: Establish processes for continuous improvement based on feedback and performance data.

   b. **Provide Ongoing Support**: Offer ongoing technical support to ensure the cleaning process remains efficient and effective.

GRANULARITY OF TT PROCESS (API, EXCIPIENTS, FINISHED PRODUCTS, PACKAGING MATERIALS)

The technology transfer process involves transferring the production process from Research and Development (R&D) to full-scale manufacturing, ensuring that the product retains its intended quality, safety, and efficacy. The granularity of the TT process includes detailed steps for transferring the technology of Active Pharmaceutical Ingredients (API), excipients, finished products, and packaging materials. Each element requires meticulous planning and execution to ensure successful commercialization.

1. Active Pharmaceutical Ingredients (API)

Objective: Ensure consistent quality and reliable supply of the API during and after the transfer.

Detailed Steps:

   a. **Documentation:** Comprehensive documentation including API specifications, manufacturing process, critical quality attributes (CQAs), and critical process parameters (CPPs).

b. **Raw Material Specifications**: Define and ensure raw materials meet the required quality standards.

c. **Process Understanding**: Detailed transfer of knowledge on the API synthesis process, including chemical reactions, purification steps, and handling of intermediates.

d. **Equipment Transfer**: Identify, qualify, and validate equipment necessary for API production.

e. **Validation and Testing**: Conduct process validation and stability testing to ensure the API meets regulatory and quality requirements.

f. **Regulatory Compliance**: Prepare regulatory submissions with detailed process descriptions and validation data.

Considerations:

a. Consistency in the source and quality of raw materials.

b. Detailed SOPs for each manufacturing step.

c. Continuous monitoring and quality control during production.

2. Excipients

Objective: Maintain the functional characteristics and quality of excipients used in production.

Detailed Steps:

a. **Specification and Sourcing**: Define detailed specifications for excipients, including functional requirements and quality standards.

b. **Supplier Qualification**: Ensure suppliers are qualified and capable of providing consistent quality excipients.

c. **Material Compatibility**: Assess the compatibility of excipients with APIs and other formulation components.

d. **Process Documentation**: Provide detailed SOPs for handling, storage, and incorporation of excipients in the manufacturing process.

e. **Validation and Testing**: Validate excipients' use in the formulation and conduct stability studies to ensure they do not negatively impact the product.

Considerations:

a. Detailed assessment of excipient functionality in the final product.

b. Robust supply chain management to prevent variations in excipient quality.

c. Regular quality checks and supplier audits.

3. Finished Products

Objective: Ensure the final product is produced consistently with the same quality as in the R&D phase.

Detailed Steps:

a. **Comprehensive Documentation**: Develop detailed manufacturing instructions, including batch records, SOPs, and quality control procedures.

b. **Process Validation**: Validate the entire manufacturing process, from raw material input to final product output, ensuring all CQAs are met.

c. **Scale-Up and Pilot Batches**: Conduct pilot batches to identify and mitigate potential issues during scale-up.

d. **Quality Assurance**: Implement stringent in-process and final product quality assurance measures.

e. **Stability Testing**: Perform stability testing to ensure the product maintains its quality over its shelf life.

Considerations:

a. Thorough training of production personnel.

b. Detailed monitoring and control of critical process parameters.

c. Ensuring consistency in product appearance, efficacy, and safety.

4. Packaging Materials

Objective: Ensure packaging materials protect the product effectively and comply with regulatory requirements.

Detailed Steps:

a. **Material Specifications**: Define detailed specifications for all packaging materials, including primary, secondary, and tertiary packaging.

b. **Supplier Qualification**: Qualify suppliers to ensure they can consistently provide materials that meet specifications.

c. **Compatibility Testing**: Test the compatibility of packaging materials with the product to prevent interactions that could affect product quality.

d. **Packaging Process Documentation**: Develop detailed SOPs for packaging processes, including handling, filling, sealing, and labeling.

e. **Validation and Testing**: Validate the packaging process and conduct tests to ensure packaging integrity and performance.

Considerations:

a. Ensuring packaging materials do not compromise product stability.

b. Compliance with local and international packaging regulations.

c. Detailed training of personnel on packaging procedures and quality control measures.

DOCUMENTATION

Documentation plays a crucial role in technology development and transfer, ensuring transparency, consistency, and compliance throughout the process. It serves as a repository of critical information, guiding stakeholders and facilitating seamless transitions from research to full-scale production. Here's a detailed look at the documentation involved:

1. Technology Transfer Plan (TTP)

Purpose: The TTP outlines the overarching strategy for transferring technology from R&D to production.

Content:

a. **Objectives and Scope**: Clearly define the goals and scope of the technology transfer.

b. **Timelines**: Establish timelines for each phase of the transfer process.

c. **Responsibilities**: Assign roles and responsibilities to individuals or teams involved in the transfer.

d. **Resources**: Identify the resources required, including personnel, equipment, and materials.

e. **Risk Assessment**: Evaluate potential risks and mitigation strategies.

2. Standard Operating Procedures (SOPs)

Purpose: SOPs provide detailed instructions for performing specific tasks or processes involved in technology development and transfer.

Content:

a. **Process Description**: Describe each step of the process in sequential order.

b. **Equipment Setup and Operation**: Provide instructions for setting up and operating equipment.

c. **Safety Precautions**: Outline safety measures to be followed during the process.

d. **Quality Control Checks**: Specify quality control checks to ensure product quality and consistency.

e. **Record Keeping**: Define procedures for documenting process parameters, observations, and results.

3. Technical Documentation

Purpose: Technical documentation provides detailed information about the technology being transferred, including specifications, procedures, and validation data.

Content:

a. **Product Specifications**: Define the specifications for raw materials, intermediates, and finished products.

b. **Manufacturing Procedures**: Document the step-by-step manufacturing process, including critical process parameters.

c. **Validation Protocols and Reports**: Detail protocols for process validation and provide validation reports demonstrating process robustness and reliability.

d. **Analytical Methods**: Describe analytical methods used for testing product quality and performance.

e. **Stability Studies**: Document stability studies conducted to assess product shelf life and degradation profiles.

4. Regulatory Documentation

Purpose: Regulatory documentation ensures compliance with regulatory requirements in different jurisdictions.

Content:

a. **Drug Master Files (DMFs):** Submit DMFs containing detailed information about the manufacturing process, controls, and specifications to regulatory authorities.

b. **Regulatory Submissions**: Prepare and submit applications for regulatory approval or marketing authorization, including INDs, NDAs, or MAAs.

c. **Compliance Documentation**: Maintain records of regulatory inspections, audits, and corrective actions taken to address any deficiencies.

5. Training Materials

Purpose: Training materials ensure personnel involved in the technology transfer are adequately trained to perform their roles effectively.

Content:

a. **Training Manuals**: Provide comprehensive manuals covering all aspects of the technology transfer process.

b. **Training Presentations**: Develop presentations to deliver training sessions on specific topics or procedures.

c. **Hands-On Demonstrations**: Conduct hands-on training sessions to familiarize personnel with equipment operation and process techniques.

d. **Assessments:** Administer assessments to evaluate personnel's understanding and competency in performing transfer-related tasks.

6. Change Control Documentation

Purpose: Change control documentation manages changes to processes, procedures, or specifications during technology transfer.

Content:

a. **Change Request Forms**: Use forms to document proposed changes and justification for the change.

b. **Change Control Procedures**: Define procedures for evaluating, approving, and implementing changes.

c. **Change Records**: Maintain records of all approved changes, including the rationale and impact of the change.

d. **Change Impact Assessments**: Assess the potential impact of proposed changes on product quality, safety, and regulatory compliance.

PREMISES AND EQUIPMENT'S

Premises and equipment are integral components of technology development and transfer, providing the infrastructure and tools necessary for research, development, and production processes. Proper design, qualification, and maintenance of premises and equipment are essential to ensure product quality, safety, and regulatory compliance throughout the technology transfer process. Here's a detailed overview:

1. Premises

Purpose: Premises encompass the physical facilities where technology development and transfer activities take place, including laboratories, manufacturing plants, and storage areas.

Considerations:

a. **Design and Layout**: Premises should be designed to facilitate efficient workflow and minimize the risk of contamination or cross-contamination.

b. **Environmental Controls**: Maintain appropriate environmental conditions, including temperature, humidity, and cleanliness, to support the intended processes and protect product integrity.

c. **Safety and Security**: Implement measures to ensure the safety of personnel and the security of assets, including emergency response procedures and access control systems.

d. **Compliance:** Ensure premises comply with regulatory requirements, including zoning, building codes, and Good Manufacturing Practice (GMP) standards.

2. Equipment

Purpose: Equipment encompasses the machinery, instruments, and tools used in technology development, manufacturing, and testing processes.

Considerations:

a. **Selection and Qualification**: Select equipment appropriate for the intended use and ensure it is qualified and validated before use in production.

b. **Installation and Calibration**: Properly install and calibrate equipment to ensure accuracy, precision, and reliability in measurement and operation.

c. **Maintenance and Calibration**: Establish a schedule for routine maintenance and calibration to ensure equipment remains in optimal working condition and complies with regulatory requirements.

d. **Cleaning and Sanitization**: Develop procedures for cleaning and sanitizing equipment to prevent contamination and cross-contamination.

e. **Documentation**: Maintain comprehensive documentation for each piece of equipment, including operating manuals, maintenance records, and calibration certificates.

f. **Training:** Provide training to personnel on the proper use, maintenance, and troubleshooting of equipment to minimize downtime and ensure safety.

3. Technology Transfer Considerations

During technology transfer, specific considerations arise regarding premises and equipment:

a. **Compatibility**: Ensure that premises and equipment at the receiving site are compatible with the transferred technology and capable of achieving the desired outcomes.

b. **Validation**: Validate premises and equipment at the receiving site to demonstrate that they meet the requirements for the intended use.

c. **Scale-Up:** Evaluate the scalability of premises and equipment to accommodate larger production volumes or different manufacturing processes.

d. **Regulatory Compliance**: Ensure that premises and equipment comply with regulatory requirements at both the transferring and receiving sites, including environmental, safety, and GMP standards.

e. **Documentation Transfer**: Transfer relevant documentation related to premises and equipment, including SOPs, validation protocols, and maintenance records, to the receiving site to support technology transfer and ongoing operations.

QUALIFICATION AND VALIDATION

Qualification and validation are essential processes in technology development and transfer, ensuring that equipment, facilities, processes, and systems meet predefined requirements and consistently produce products of desired quality. These processes are critical for maintaining regulatory compliance, product safety, and efficacy throughout the technology transfer lifecycle. Here's a detailed overview:

1. Equipment Qualification

Purpose: Equipment qualification verifies that equipment is properly installed, operates as intended, and produces results within acceptable parameters.

Steps:

a. **Installation Qualification (IQ):** Verify that equipment is correctly installed according to manufacturer specifications and site requirements.

b. **Operational Qualification (OQ):** Demonstrate that equipment operates within defined parameters and produces accurate and reliable results.

c. **Performance Qualification (PQ):** Confirm that equipment consistently produces results that meet predetermined acceptance criteria under actual operating conditions.

Documentation: Maintain documentation of qualification protocols, test results, and equipment maintenance records.

2. Facility Qualification

Purpose: Facility qualification ensures that premises meet regulatory requirements and provide a suitable environment for product manufacturing and storage.

Steps:

a. **Design Qualification (DQ):** Assess facility design to ensure it meets intended use, regulatory, and safety requirements.

b. **Installation Qualification (IQ):** Verify that facility systems and utilities are installed correctly and operate as intended.

c. **Operational Qualification (OQ):** Confirm that facility systems, such as HVAC, utilities, and environmental controls, operate within specified parameters.

d. **Performance Qualification (PQ):** Evaluate facility performance under simulated or actual operating conditions to ensure consistent product quality and safety.

Documentation: Maintain documentation of facility design specifications, installation records, qualification protocols, and performance test results.

3. Process Validation

Purpose: Process validation demonstrates that manufacturing processes consistently produce products that meet predefined quality attributes and specifications.

Steps:

    a. **Process Design**: Define and optimize manufacturing processes based on scientific principles and risk assessment.

    b. **Process Qualification (PQ):** Conduct trials to confirm that the manufacturing process consistently produces products that meet quality requirements.

    c. **Continued Process Verification**: Implement ongoing monitoring and control measures to ensure that the manufacturing process remains in a state of control.

Documentation: Maintain documentation of process development studies, validation protocols, validation reports, and ongoing monitoring data.

4. Analytical Method Validation

Purpose: Analytical method validation verifies that analytical methods used to test product quality are accurate, reliable, and suitable for their intended purpose.

Steps:

    a. **Method Development**: Develop and optimize analytical methods based on scientific principles and regulatory requirements.

    b. **Method Qualification**: Evaluate method performance characteristics, such as specificity, accuracy, precision, linearity, and robustness.

    c. **Method Validation**: Conduct validation studies to demonstrate that analytical methods consistently produce accurate and reliable results.

Documentation: Maintain documentation of method development studies, method qualification protocols, validation reports, and ongoing method performance monitoring data.

5. Computer System Validation (CSV)

Purpose: Computer system validation ensures that computerized systems used in technology development and transfer, such as laboratory information management systems (LIMS) and manufacturing execution systems (MES), operate reliably and securely.

Steps:

a. **User Requirements Specification (URS):** Define user requirements for the computerized system based on intended use and regulatory requirements.

b. **Functional Requirements Specification (FRS):** Specify functional requirements of the system based on user requirements.

c. **Installation Qualification (IQ):** Verify that the system is installed correctly and configured according to specifications.

d. **Operational Qualification (OQ):** Confirm that the system operates according to functional requirements.

e. **Performance Qualification (PQ):** Demonstrate that the system performs reliably and consistently under actual operating conditions.

Documentation: Maintain documentation of user requirements, functional specifications, validation protocols, test results, and system change control records.

QUALITY CONTROL, ANALYTICAL METHOD TRANSFER

Quality control (QC) plays a vital role in technology development and transfer by ensuring that products meet predefined quality standards and specifications throughout the development and manufacturing process. It involves a range of activities aimed at monitoring and evaluating product quality, identifying deviations, and implementing corrective actions to maintain consistency and compliance. Here's a detailed overview:

1. Quality Control Activities

a. **Incoming Material Inspection**: QC personnel inspect incoming raw materials, components, and packaging materials to ensure they meet specified quality standards before being used in production.

b. **In-Process Monitoring**: QC monitors critical process parameters and conducts in-process testing to verify that manufacturing processes are operating within defined parameters and producing products of desired quality.

c. **Finished Product Testing**: QC performs comprehensive testing on finished products to evaluate their quality attributes, such as identity, strength, purity, and stability, before release for distribution or use.

d. **Environmental Monitoring**: QC conducts environmental monitoring to ensure that manufacturing facilities and cleanrooms meet specified cleanliness levels and regulatory requirements.

e. **Stability Testing**: QC conducts stability studies to evaluate the long-term stability of products under various storage conditions and to determine product shelf life.

2. Analytical Method Transfer (AMT)

Analytical method transfer (AMT) is the process of transferring analytical methods from one laboratory or site to another while ensuring that the methods remain robust, accurate, and reliable. It is a critical aspect of technology transfer, particularly in pharmaceutical development and manufacturing. Here's how it's done:

a. **Method Evaluation**: The receiving laboratory evaluates the transferred analytical method to ensure it is suitable for the intended use and meets regulatory requirements.

b. **Protocol Development**: A transfer protocol is developed outlining the procedures, acceptance criteria, responsibilities, and timelines for the method transfer process.

c. **Method Verification**: The receiving laboratory verifies the transferred method by performing validation experiments, comparing results with the transferring laboratory, and assessing method performance criteria.

d. **Training and Documentation**: Personnel in the receiving laboratory are trained on the transferred method, and comprehensive documentation is maintained, including the transfer protocol, validation reports, and training records.

e. **Ongoing Performance Monitoring**: The receiving laboratory continues to monitor the performance of the transferred method through routine testing, method validation, and proficiency testing programs.

3. Considerations for Quality Control and Analytical Method Transfer

a. **Regulatory Compliance**: QC activities and AMT must comply with relevant regulatory guidelines and requirements, such as Good Manufacturing Practice (GMP) and Good Laboratory Practice (GLP) regulations.

b. **Risk Assessment**: Conduct risk assessments to identify potential risks associated with QC activities and AMT and implement appropriate mitigation strategies.

c. **Data Integrity**: Ensure that all QC data and AMT records are accurate, complete, and reliable, with appropriate controls in place to prevent data manipulation or loss.

d. **Personnel Training**: Provide comprehensive training to QC personnel and analysts involved in AMT to ensure they have the necessary knowledge, skills, and competencies to perform their duties effectively.

e. **Continuous Improvement**: Continuously monitor and evaluate QC processes and AMT procedures to identify areas for improvement and implement corrective and preventive actions to enhance efficiency and effectiveness.

APPROVED REGULATORY BODIES AND AGENCIES

In technology development and transfer, especially in industries like pharmaceuticals, biotechnology, and medical devices, regulatory bodies and agencies play a crucial role in ensuring the safety, efficacy, and quality of products. These organizations establish and enforce regulations, guidelines, and standards that govern various aspects of technology development, manufacturing, and transfer. Here's a detailed overview of some of the prominent regulatory bodies and agencies involved:

1. Food and Drug Administration (FDA)

Location: United States

Role:

a. The FDA is responsible for protecting public health by regulating food, drugs, vaccines, medical devices, biologics, cosmetics, dietary supplements, and tobacco products.

b. It oversees various aspects of technology development and transfer, including product approvals, manufacturing processes, quality control, labeling, and advertising.

Key Functions:

a. Review and approval of new drug applications (NDAs), abbreviated new drug applications (ANDAs), and biologics license applications (BLAs).

b. Inspection of manufacturing facilities to ensure compliance with Good Manufacturing Practice (GMP) regulations.

c. Evaluation of clinical trial data to assess the safety and efficacy of investigational products.

d. Issuance of guidance documents and regulations to provide industry guidance on technology development and transfer processes.

2. European Medicines Agency (EMA)

Location: European Union (EU)

Role:

a. The EMA is responsible for the evaluation, supervision, and safety monitoring of medicines in the EU.

b. It coordinates the evaluation and approval of medicinal products across EU member states and ensures consistent regulatory standards are maintained.

Key Functions:

a. **Centralized procedure**: Evaluation and approval of medicinal products for use in the EU.

b. **Mutual recognition procedure (MRP) and decentralized procedure (DCP):** Facilitation of regulatory approval for medicines in multiple EU member states.

c. **Scientific advice**: Provision of scientific guidance and advice to pharmaceutical companies on drug development and regulatory requirements.

d. **Pharmacovigilance**: Monitoring and assessment of the safety of medicines throughout their lifecycle.

3. Pharmaceuticals and Medical Devices Agency (PMDA)

Location: Japan

Role:

a. The PMDA is Japan's regulatory agency responsible for the evaluation and approval of pharmaceuticals and medical devices.

b. It ensures the safety, efficacy, and quality of products marketed in Japan.

Key Functions:

a. Review and approval of new drug applications, medical device applications, and marketing authorization applications.

b. Post-market surveillance and pharmacovigilance activities to monitor the safety of marketed products.

c. Collaboration with international regulatory agencies and participation in regulatory harmonization initiatives.

4. Medicines and Healthcare products Regulatory Agency (MHRA)

Location: United Kingdom

Role:

a. The MHRA is the regulatory agency responsible for regulating medicines, medical devices, and blood components for transfusion in the UK.

b. It ensures that products meet applicable standards of safety, quality, and efficacy.

Key Functions:

a. Evaluation and approval of marketing authorization applications for medicines and medical devices.

b. Inspection of manufacturing facilities to ensure compliance with GMP regulations.

c. Post-market surveillance and pharmacovigilance activities to monitor the safety of products on the market.

d. Provision of guidance and advice to industry stakeholders on regulatory requirements.

5. World Health Organization (WHO)

Location: International

Role:

a. The WHO is a specialized agency of the United Nations responsible for international public health.

b. It provides leadership on global health matters, sets norms and standards, and promotes technical cooperation among member states.

Key Functions:

a. Establishment of international standards and guidelines for the quality, safety, and efficacy of medicines and vaccines.

b. Prequalification of medicines, vaccines, and diagnostics for procurement by United Nations agencies and other international organizations.

c. Technical assistance and capacity-building support to member states to strengthen regulatory systems and improve access to quality healthcare products.

COMMERCIALIZATION - PRACTICAL ASPECTS AND PROBLEMS (CASE STUDIES)

Commercialization is a critical phase in technology development and transfer where innovations are brought to market, generating value and fulfilling their intended purpose. However, this phase often comes with practical challenges and problems that can hinder success. Here, we'll explore some common practical aspects and problems encountered during commercialization, along with case studies illustrating these challenges:

Practical Aspects and Problems in Commercialization:

1. Market Assessment and Validation:

a. **Problem:** Insufficient market research and validation can lead to products that do not meet market needs or fail to gain traction.

b. **Case Study**: Kodak's failure to adapt to the digital camera market despite having invented the technology highlights the importance of understanding market dynamics and consumer preferences.

2. Intellectual Property (IP) Protection:

a. **Problem:** Inadequate protection of intellectual property rights can result in competitors replicating or infringing upon innovations, reducing market exclusivity and profitability.

b. **Case Study**: In the pharmaceutical industry, companies like Pfizer invest heavily in patent protection for blockbuster drugs like Viagra to maintain market exclusivity and profitability.

3. Regulatory Compliance:

a. **Problem**: Non-compliance with regulatory requirements can delay market entry, incur significant costs, and even result in product recalls or sanctions.

b. **Case Study**: The Boeing 737 MAX aircraft faced regulatory scrutiny and grounding following two fatal crashes, highlighting the importance of rigorous regulatory compliance in safety-critical industries.

4. Manufacturing Scalability:

a. **Problem:** Scaling up production from R&D to commercial scale can pose challenges related to process optimization, equipment scalability, and supply chain management.

b. **Case Study**: Tesla faced production bottlenecks and quality control issues when scaling up production of its Model 3 electric vehicle, resulting in delays and quality concerns.

5. Distribution and Market Access:

a. **Problem**: Limited distribution networks and access to target markets can hinder market penetration and revenue generation.

b. **Case Study**: In emerging markets, companies like Coca-Cola and PepsiCo face challenges in establishing distribution networks and adapting products to local preferences while maintaining global brand consistency.

6. Pricing and Revenue Generation:

a. **Problem:** Setting the right pricing strategy is crucial for achieving profitability while remaining competitive in the market.

b. **Case Study**: Gilead Sciences faced public backlash and scrutiny over the high pricing of its hepatitis C drug, Sovaldi, despite its significant therapeutic value, highlighting the ethical and practical considerations in pricing life-saving medications.

7. Technology Adoption and User Acceptance:

a. **Problem:** User resistance, lack of awareness, or inadequate training can impede technology adoption and limit market penetration.

b. **Case Study**: Google Glass failed to gain widespread adoption due to privacy concerns, social stigma, and limited use cases, despite its innovative technology and potential applications.

TT agencies in India - APCTD, NRDC, TIFAC, BCIL, TBSE / SIDBI

In India, several agencies and organizations play key roles in facilitating technology development and transfer across various sectors, including government bodies, research institutions, and industry associations. Here, we'll delve into some of the prominent technology transfer (TT) agencies in India, their roles, and contributions:

1. Andhra Pradesh Centre for Technology Development (APCTD)

Role:

a. APCTD, established by the Government of Andhra Pradesh, aims to promote technology development and commercialization in the state.

b. It facilitates collaboration between research institutions, industries, and entrepreneurs to foster innovation and technology transfer.

Contributions:

a. Provides support for technology commercialization through incubation, funding, and networking opportunities.

b. Facilitates technology licensing and transfer agreements between research institutions and industry partners.

c. Offers guidance and assistance to startups and entrepreneurs in navigating the technology transfer process.

2. National Research Development Corporation (NRDC)

Role:

a. NRDC is an autonomous organization under the Department of Scientific and Industrial Research (DSIR), Ministry of Science and Technology, Government of India.

b. It promotes, develops, and commercializes indigenous technologies developed by Indian scientists and researchers.

Contributions:

a. Facilitates technology transfer through licensing agreements, joint ventures, and technology partnerships between public and private sector entities.

b. Provides technical and financial assistance to inventors, innovators, and entrepreneurs for technology commercialization.

c. Manages a portfolio of patents, copyrights, and trademarks to protect and monetize intellectual property.

3. Technology Information, Forecasting and Assessment Council (TIFAC)

Role:

a. TIFAC is an autonomous organization under the Department of Science and Technology (DST), Government of India.

b. It serves as a think tank and technology forecasting agency, identifying emerging technology trends and facilitating technology transfer and diffusion.

Contributions:

a. Conducts technology foresight studies to identify priority areas for research and development.

b. Facilitates technology transfer through collaborative research projects, technology missions, and industry-academia partnerships.

c. Provides policy advice and recommendations to government agencies on technology development, transfer, and adoption.

4. Biotech Consortium India Limited (BCIL)

Role:

a. BCIL is a public sector enterprise under the Department of Biotechnology (DBT), Ministry of Science and Technology, Government of India.

b. It promotes and facilitates technology transfer and commercialization in the biotechnology sector.

Contributions:

a. Facilitates technology licensing, technology transfer agreements, and technology partnerships between biotechnology research institutions, startups, and industry players.

b. Provides support for entrepreneurship development, incubation, and funding through initiatives like the Biotechnology Industry Partnership Programme (BIPP).

c. Promotes international collaboration and market access for Indian biotechnology companies through initiatives like the Biotechnology Industry Research Assistance Council (BIRAC).

5. Technology Development Board (TDB) / Small Industries Development Bank of India (SIDBI)

Role:

a. TDB is a statutory body under the Department of Science and Technology (DST), Government of India, responsible for promoting technology development and commercialization.

b. SIDBI is a financial institution that provides financial and technical assistance to small and medium-sized enterprises (SMEs) in India.

Contributions:

a. TDB provides financial support through grants, soft loans, and equity participation to SMEs and startups for technology development and commercialization.

b. SIDBI offers financial assistance, including venture capital, debt financing, and project finance, to SMEs for technology adoption, modernization, and expansion.

c. Collaboratively, TDB and SIDBI support technology-driven entrepreneurship and innovation through funding schemes like the Technology Development and Demonstration Programme (TDDP) and the Venture Capital Fund for Technology Development (VCF-TD).

TT RELATED DOCUMENTATION - CONFIDENTIALITY AGREEMENT, LICENSING, MOUS, LEGAL ISSUES

Technology development and transfer involve various types of documentation to formalize agreements, protect intellectual property, and address legal issues. Here's a detailed overview of key documentation used in technology transfer, including confidentiality agreements, licensing agreements, memorandums of understanding (MoUs), and associated legal considerations:

1. Confidentiality Agreement (Non-Disclosure Agreement - NDA):

Purpose:

a. A confidentiality agreement is a legally binding contract that protects confidential information shared between parties during technology transfer discussions and negotiations.

b. It ensures that sensitive information, such as proprietary technology, trade secrets, and business strategies, remains confidential and is not disclosed to third parties without authorization.

Contents:

a. **Definition of Confidential Information**: Clearly define what constitutes confidential information under the agreement.

b. **Obligations of Parties**: Specify the obligations of the disclosing and receiving parties regarding the handling, use, and protection of confidential information.

c. **Duration of Confidentiality**: Define the duration for which confidentiality obligations remain in effect.

d. **Exceptions**: Outline exceptions to confidentiality, such as information already in the public domain or disclosed with prior written consent.

e. **Remedies for Breach**: Specify remedies, such as injunctive relief or monetary damages, in the event of a breach of confidentiality.

2. Licensing Agreement:

Purpose:

a. A licensing agreement grants permission to another party (licensee) to use, manufacture, sell, or distribute intellectual property owned by the licensor in exchange for royalties or other financial considerations.

b. It allows for the commercialization of technologies developed by research institutions, universities, or private companies.

Contents:

a. **License Grant**: Define the scope of the license, including the rights granted to the licensee and any restrictions or limitations.

b. **Financial Terms**: Specify royalty rates, upfront fees, milestone payments, and other financial terms associated with the license.

c. **Intellectual Property Rights**: Identify the intellectual property being licensed, including patents, copyrights, trademarks, and know-how.

d. **Term and Termination**: Define the duration of the license agreement and circumstances under which it may be terminated.

e. **Representations and Warranties**: Provide assurances regarding the validity of the licensed intellectual property and the licensor's authority to grant the license.

3. Memorandum of Understanding (MoU):

Purpose:

a. A Memorandum of Understanding (MoU) is a non-binding agreement that outlines the terms and intentions of parties entering into a technology transfer arrangement.

b. It serves as a preliminary step in negotiations, establishing a framework for future collaboration and formal agreements.

Contents:

a. **Objectives and Scope:** Clearly define the goals, objectives, and scope of the collaboration or technology transfer initiative.

b. **Roles and Responsibilities**: Specify the roles, responsibilities, and contributions of each party involved in the MoU.

c. **Terms and Conditions**: Outline key terms and conditions that parties intend to include in formal agreements, such as confidentiality, licensing, and dispute resolution.

d. **Duration and Termination**: Define the duration of the MoU and circumstances under which it may be terminated or extended.

e. **Governing Law:** Specify the governing law and jurisdiction for resolving disputes arising from the MoU.

4. Legal Issues in Technology Development and Transfer:

a. **Intellectual Property Protection**: Ensure that intellectual property rights, including patents, copyrights, and trademarks, are properly protected through registration, licensing agreements, and confidentiality measures.

b. **Contractual Disputes**: Address potential disputes arising from technology transfer agreements by including dispute resolution mechanisms, such as arbitration or mediation, in contractual terms.

c. **Export Control and Regulatory Compliance**: Comply with export control regulations and regulatory requirements governing the transfer of sensitive technologies, particularly in industries like aerospace, defense, and biotechnology.

d. **Antitrust and Competition Law**: Avoid antitrust violations by ensuring that technology transfer agreements do not result in anti-competitive behavior, such as price-fixing or market allocation.

e. **International Considerations**: Take into account international laws and regulations governing technology transfer when engaging in cross-border collaborations or licensing arrangements.

Multiple Choice Questions (MCQs)

1. What is the primary purpose of a Technology Transfer Plan (TTP)?

    A) To detail the budget of a project

B) To outline the entire technology transfer process

C) To provide a framework for regulatory submissions

D) To establish the training protocols for new employees

2. Which stage of technology development involves turning research findings into tangible technologies?

A) Basic Research

B) Applied Research

C) Development

D) Commercialization

3. What is a key component of the Technology Transfer Protocol (TTP) regarding documentation?

A) Risk assessment report

B) Financial analysis

C) Equipment specification

D) Analytical methods

4. Which of the following is NOT a method of technology transfer?

A) Licensing Agreements

B) Direct sales

C) Joint Ventures

D) Consulting and Training

5. What does the WHO emphasize in its guidelines for technology transfer in the pharmaceutical sector?

A) Marketing strategies

B) Ensuring quality, safety, and efficacy of health products

C) Investment returns

D) Social media promotion strategies

6. Which document defines the responsibilities and procedures for a technology transfer?

A) Memorandum of Understanding (MoU)

B) Technology Transfer Plan (TTP)

C) Licensing Agreement

D) Non-Disclosure Agreement (NDA)

7. What is a critical aspect of Quality Risk Management (QRM) in technology transfer?

    A) Budget planning

    B) Marketing assessment

    C) Risk identification and control

    D) Sales forecasting

8. Which agency is responsible for evaluating and approving medicines within the European Union?

    A) FDA

    B) EMA

    C) WHO

    D) PMDA

9. What role does the 'Sending Unit' (SU) play in technology transfer?

    A) Receives the technology

    B) Develops initial prototypes

    C) Transfers the technology to another entity

    D) Provides financial support

10. What is the purpose of Pilot Scale production in the technology transfer process?

    A) To finalize the commercial product

    B) To test the feasibility and performance of the technology

    C) To train production staff

    D) To market the product

11. Which quality control activity involves inspecting incoming materials to ensure they meet quality standards?

    A) In-Process Monitoring

B) Finished Product Testing

C) Incoming Material Inspection

D) Stability Testing

12. Which document is crucial for protecting confidential information shared during technology transfer negotiations?

A) Technology Transfer Plan (TTP)

B) Licensing Agreement

C) Non-Disclosure Agreement (NDA)

D) Operational Manual

13. What is the main objective of 'Process Validation' in technology transfer?

A) To ensure that all processes are cost-effective

B) To confirm that the processes produce consistent results meeting quality criteria

C) To verify that all employees are adequately trained

D) To document all processes for legal purposes

14. What is emphasized in the 'Gap Analysis' phase of technology transfer?

A) Identifying skills gaps in employees

B) Identifying differences between current capabilities and requirements

C) Analyzing market gaps for product sales

D) Estimating financial gaps in funding

15. Which of the following best describes 'Regulatory Compliance' in technology transfer?

A) Ensuring all marketing materials are approved

B) Ensuring the technology meets legal and quality standards

C) Confirming that all staff have legal clearances

D) Ensuring all products are patented

16. What does 'Performance Qualification' (PQ) aim to verify in the technology transfer process?

A) Employee performance levels

B) The technology produces consistent and high-quality products

C) Financial performance of the technology

D) Marketing strategies effectiveness

17. Which entity is responsible for regulating medicines, medical devices, and blood components in the UK?

A) FDA

B) EMA

C) MHRA

D) WHO

18. What is a 'Technical Package' in the context of technology transfer?

A) A compilation of financial reports

B) Detailed documentation describing the technology to be transferred

C) A set of marketing materials for the technology

D) An employee training program

19. What role does 'Quality Assurance' (QA) play in the technology transfer process?

A) Ensures all marketing strategies are effective

B) Integrates principles throughout the process to maintain product quality

C) Oversees financial transactions

D) Manages employee relations

20. Which of the following is NOT typically a focus of a 'Feasibility Study' in technology transfer?

A) Technical feasibility

B) Economic viability

C) Employee job satisfaction

D) Market demand

Short Answer Type Questions

1. What is the primary goal of technology transfer?

2. Define the role of a Technology Transfer Plan (TTP).

3. What are key considerations in a Gap Analysis during technology transfer?

4. List three mechanisms through which technology transfer can occur.

5. How do Licensing Agreements facilitate technology transfer?

6. Describe the concept of 'Pilot Scale' in technology transfer.

7. What is the importance of Quality Risk Management in technology transfer?

8. Explain the role of 'Process Validation' in ensuring effective technology transfer.

9. How do Standard Operating Procedures (SOPs) support technology transfer?

10. What is the purpose of the 'Technical Package' in the technology transfer documentation?

11. Define the 'Receiving Unit' in the context of technology transfer.

12. What is meant by 'Regulatory Compliance' in technology transfer?

13. How does 'Performance Qualification' (PQ) aid in technology transfer?

14. List the types of risk assessments important in technology transfer.

15. Describe the function of 'Analytical Method Transfer' in quality control.

16. What challenges might arise in transferring technology from R&D to production?

17. What is the significance of training and knowledge transfer in technology adoption?

18. Why is 'Commercial Scale' production critical in technology transfer?

19. What are some potential legal issues in technology transfer agreements?

20. How do Intellectual Property (IP) rights impact technology transfer?

Long Answer Type Questions

1. Discuss the role of the World Health Organization (WHO) in establishing guidelines for technology transfer, specifically in the pharmaceutical sector.

2. Explain the step-by-step process involved in transferring technology from a 'Sending Unit' to a 'Receiving Unit', according to WHO guidelines.

3. Analyze the importance of maintaining robust Quality Assurance practices throughout the technology transfer process.

4. Describe the key components of a Technology Transfer Protocol (TTP) and their significance in the overall process.

5. Discuss how Quality Risk Management (QRM) integrates into the technology transfer process to ensure product safety and compliance.

6. Examine the critical steps involved in the scale-up from pilot production to full-scale manufacturing during technology transfer.

7. Detail the role and impact of regulatory compliance on technology transfer in international markets.

8. Evaluate the challenges and solutions in managing intellectual property during technology transfer between multinational entities.

9. Describe the steps involved in transferring packaging processes from R&D to production, according to WHO guidelines.

10. Analyze the implications of cultural and organizational differences in the technology transfer process across global locations.

Answer Key

1. (B) To outline the entire technology transfer process
2. (C) Development
3. (D) Analytical methods
4. (B) Direct sales
5. (B) Ensuring quality, safety, and efficacy of health products
6. (B) Technology Transfer Plan (TTP)

7. (C) Risk identification and control

8. (B) EMA

9. (C) Transfers the technology to another entity

10. (B) To test the feasibility and performance of the technology

11. (C) Incoming Material Inspection

12. (C) Non-Disclosure Agreement (NDA)

13. (B) To confirm that the processes produce consistent results meeting quality criteria

14. (B) Identifying differences between current capabilities and requirements

15. (B) Ensuring the technology meets legal and quality standards

16. (B) The technology produces consistent and high-quality products

17. (C) MHRA

18. (B) Detailed documentation describing the technology to be transferred

19. (B) Integrates principles throughout the process to maintain product quality

20. (C) Employee job satisfaction

CHAPTER - 3

REGULATORY AFFAIRS

INTRODUCTION:

Regulatory affairs is a critical field in industries like pharmaceuticals, biotechnology, medical devices, cosmetics, and food, encompassing the processes and activities related to ensuring that products meet all regulatory requirements in the markets where they are sold. This multifaceted discipline is integral to the development, approval, marketing, and post-marketing surveillance of products. It involves strategic, tactical, and operational activities to ensure compliance with regulations and laws to protect public health and safety.

Key Responsibilities of Regulatory Affairs

1. **Regulatory Strategy and Planning:**
   a. Developing regulatory strategies for product development and approval.
   b. Anticipating regulatory obstacles and opportunities throughout the product lifecycle.
   c. Ensuring alignment of regulatory strategies with business goals.

2. **Regulatory Submissions and Approvals:**
   a. Preparing and submitting documentation required for the approval of products, such as Investigational New Drug (IND) applications, New Drug Applications (NDA), and Marketing Authorization Applications (MAA).
   b. Interacting with regulatory agencies such as the FDA (U.S. Food and Drug Administration), EMA (European Medicines Agency), and others to facilitate product approval.

3. **Compliance and Quality Assurance:**

a. Ensuring products and processes comply with current regulations, guidelines, and standards.

b. Overseeing quality assurance practices to meet Good Manufacturing Practice (GMP), Good Clinical Practice (GCP), and Good Laboratory Practice (GLP) requirements.

4. Labeling and Advertising:

a. Reviewing and approving product labeling, advertising, and promotional materials to ensure compliance with regulatory standards.

b. Ensuring that product information is truthful, not misleading, and provides necessary information for safe and effective use.

5. Post-Marketing Surveillance and Reporting:

a. Monitoring the safety and efficacy of products after they reach the market.

b. Managing adverse event reporting and conducting post-market studies if required.

c. Facilitating recalls and product withdrawals when necessary.

Regulatory Affairs in Different Sectors

1. Pharmaceuticals and Biotechnology:

a. Involves drug development from preclinical trials through clinical trials to market approval.

b. Engages with complex regulatory frameworks, such as the FDA's regulations in the U.S. and the EMA's guidelines in Europe.

2. Medical Devices:

a. Covers the classification of devices, pre-market approval (PMA), and 510(k) clearances.

b. Focuses on the risk-based approach to regulatory submissions and post-market surveillance.

3. Cosmetics and Personal Care Products:

a. Ensures products meet safety standards and labeling requirements.

b. Involves compliance with regulations like the EU Cosmetics Regulation and FDA's requirements for cosmetics.

4. Food and Dietary Supplements:

a. Involves compliance with food safety standards and nutritional labeling regulations.

b. Covers the approval process for novel food ingredients and additives.

Regulatory Agencies and Global Perspective

a. **U.S. Food and Drug Administration (FDA):** Governs pharmaceuticals, medical devices, food, and cosmetics in the United States.

b. **European Medicines Agency (EMA):** Regulates medicinal products in the European Union.

c. **International Conference on Harmonisation (ICH):** Provides guidelines to harmonize regulatory requirements across different regions.

Importance of Regulatory Affairs

Regulatory affairs professionals play a pivotal role in ensuring that products are safe, effective, and of high quality. They bridge the gap between regulatory bodies and the industries, facilitating the development and approval of innovative products while maintaining compliance with all applicable regulations. This field requires a deep understanding of regulatory science, excellent project management skills, and the ability to navigate complex legal and scientific information.

HISTORICAL OVERVIEW OF REGULATORY AFFAIRS

The field of regulatory affairs has evolved significantly over the past century, driven by public health crises, scientific advancements, and the increasing complexity of global markets. This evolution has shaped the regulatory landscape and established the framework for the rigorous oversight of products today. Here is a detailed historical overview of regulatory affairs:

Early Beginnings and Foundations (1800s - Early 1900s)

During the 1800s and early 1900s, the foundations of regulatory affairs were laid as a response to the emerging challenges posed by industrialization, urbanization, and mass production. This period witnessed a growing recognition of the need for governmental oversight to protect public health and safety. Here's an in-depth look at the early beginnings and foundations of regulatory affairs during this time:

1. Industrial Revolution and Public Health Concerns

    a. **Rapid Industrialization**: The Industrial Revolution led to the mass production of food, drugs, and consumer goods, resulting in increased accessibility but also raising concerns about product safety and quality.

    b. **Adulteration and Contamination**: Lack of regulation led to widespread adulteration and contamination of food, drugs, and other consumer products, posing significant risks to public health.

2. Early Regulatory Efforts

    a. **19th Century Regulations**: Governments began enacting early regulatory measures to address public health concerns. For example:

        i. **United States**: Various states passed laws regulating the sale and labeling of food and drugs, such as the Pure Food and Drug Acts enacted by individual states.

        ii. **United Kingdom**: Legislation such as the Sale of Food and Drugs Act 1875 aimed to regulate the quality and sale of food and drugs.

3. Establishment of Initial Regulatory Bodies

    a. **1902 - Biologics Control Act (United States):**

        i. **Significance**: One of the earliest regulatory laws targeting biological products, prompted by incidents of contaminated vaccines.

ii.   **Provisions**: Required licensing for establishments manufacturing biological products and provided for inspections to ensure compliance with quality standards.

b. 1906 - Pure Food and Drug Act (United States):

i.   **Landmark Legislation**: Marked a significant milestone in regulatory history, addressing concerns about food and drug safety.

ii.   **Key Provisions**: Prohibited interstate commerce of adulterated or misbranded food and drugs, and established the Bureau of Chemistry, the precursor to the U.S. Food and Drug Administration (FDA), to enforce the law.

4. Early Regulatory Challenges and Progress

a.   **Limited Scope**: Early regulatory efforts primarily focused on addressing immediate threats to public health, such as adulteration and contamination of food and drugs.

b.   **Challenges**: Enforcement of regulations faced challenges due to limited resources, lack of standardized testing methods, and resistance from industry stakeholders.

c.   **Progressive Legislation**: Despite limitations, regulatory efforts laid the groundwork for future regulatory frameworks, emphasizing the importance of governmental oversight in ensuring product safety and quality.

5. Evolutionary Significance

a.   **Foundation for Regulatory Frameworks**: The early regulatory efforts established foundational principles and frameworks that paved the way for the development of more comprehensive regulatory systems in the future.

b.   **Public Awareness**: Increased public awareness about product safety and quality prompted governments to prioritize regulatory reforms, reflecting a growing recognition of the role of regulation in safeguarding public health.

Expansion and Formalization (1930s - 1960s)

The period from the 1930s to the 1960s witnessed significant expansion and formalization of regulatory affairs, driven by public health crises, scientific advancements, and the recognition of the need for more comprehensive regulatory oversight. During this time, regulatory frameworks were strengthened, and regulatory agencies gained greater authority to ensure the safety, efficacy, and quality of products. Here's a detailed overview of the expansion and formalization of regulatory affairs during this period:

1. Strengthening Regulatory Frameworks

    a. 1938 - Federal Food, Drug, and Cosmetic Act (FFDCA):

        i. **Landmark Legislation**: Replaced the earlier Pure Food and Drug Act and significantly expanded the authority of the U.S. FDA.

        ii. **Key Provisions**: Required new drugs to be proven safe before marketing, introduced requirements for drug labeling, and established the distinction between prescription and over-the-counter drugs.

    b. 1951 - Durham-Humphrey Amendment:

        i. **Prescription Drug Regulation**: Defined the categories of drugs that could only be dispensed with a prescription and those that could be sold over-the-counter.

2. Response to Public Health Crises

    a. Sulfanilamide Tragedy (1937):

        i. **Motivation for Legislation**: The deaths caused by elixir sulfanilamide, a toxic drug formulation, highlighted the need for stronger regulatory oversight of pharmaceuticals, leading to the passage of the FFDCA.

    b. Thalidomide Tragedy (Early 1960s):

i.   **Kefauver-Harris Amendments (1962):**

    i. **Response to Crisis**: Enacted in response to the thalidomide tragedy, where a drug caused birth defects in thousands of infants.

    ii. **Strengthened Regulations**: Required drug manufacturers to provide proof of effectiveness and safety before approval, mandated informed consent for clinical trials, and established Good Manufacturing Practices (GMP) standards.

3. Advancements in Regulatory Science

a. Introduction of Good Manufacturing Practices (GMP):

    i. **Quality Standards**: GMP regulations set standards for the manufacturing processes of drugs, ensuring quality, purity, and consistency.

    ii. **Adoption:** Regulatory agencies worldwide began adopting GMP regulations to ensure the quality and safety of pharmaceutical products.

b. Standardization of Testing Methods:

    i. **Pharmacopoeias**: Pharmacopoeial organizations, such as the United States Pharmacopeia (USP) and the British Pharmacopoeia (BP), played a crucial role in standardizing testing methods for drugs and pharmaceutical ingredients.

4. International Cooperation and Harmonization

a. Formation of the World Health Organization (WHO):

    i. **1948:** Established to promote international public health, the WHO facilitated cooperation among member states in setting global health standards and guidelines.

b. 1960s - Formation of International Regulatory Bodies:

    i. **International Conference on Harmonisation (ICH):** Established in the 1990s, but its roots can be traced back to initiatives in the

1960s to harmonize regulatory requirements across different regions, promoting efficiency and reducing duplication in drug development.

5. Evolution of Regulatory Agencies

a. Expansion of Regulatory Authority:

i. Regulatory agencies like the FDA in the United States and similar bodies in other countries gained expanded authority and resources to enforce new regulations and standards.

Global Harmonization and Advances (1970s - 1990s)

The period from the 1970s to the 1990s witnessed significant strides in global harmonization and advancements in regulatory affairs. This era was characterized by efforts to harmonize regulatory requirements across different regions, promote international cooperation, and respond to emerging challenges in the regulation of pharmaceuticals and medical products. Here's a detailed overview:

1. International Conference on Harmonisation (ICH)

a. **Formation:** The International Conference on Harmonisation of Technical Requirements for Registration of Pharmaceuticals for Human Use (ICH) was established in 1990.

b. **Purpose**: The ICH aimed to bring together regulatory authorities and the pharmaceutical industry from Europe, Japan, and the United States to harmonize technical requirements for drug registration.

c. **Key Achievements**: The ICH developed guidelines covering various aspects of drug development, including quality, safety, efficacy, and multidisciplinary topics, promoting consistency and efficiency in the regulatory review process.

2. Harmonization of Regulatory Requirements

a. **Alignment of Standards**: Regulatory agencies worldwide worked to align their standards and requirements for pharmaceuticals and medical devices.

b. **Mutual Recognition Agreements (MRAs):** Some regions established MRAs to recognize regulatory decisions made by other competent authorities, facilitating the acceptance of data and approvals across borders.

c. **Transatlantic Cooperation**: Efforts were made to harmonize regulations between the United States and the European Union, including initiatives to streamline the drug approval process and eliminate unnecessary duplication of efforts.

3. Advancements in Regulatory Science

a. **Risk-Based Approach**: Regulatory agencies began adopting a risk-based approach to evaluate and manage risks associated with pharmaceuticals and medical devices, focusing resources on areas of highest concern.

b. **Technology and Innovation**: Advances in technology, such as computer modeling and simulation, contributed to the development of innovative regulatory strategies for product evaluation and approval.

4. Implementation of Good Practices

a. **Good Clinical Practice (GCP):** Standards for conducting clinical trials were established, ensuring the ethical conduct of trials and the reliability of trial data.

b. **Good Manufacturing Practice (GMP):** GMP standards were refined and updated to ensure the quality and consistency of pharmaceutical manufacturing processes.

5. Regulatory Reform and Legislation

a. **United States**: The Prescription Drug User Fee Act (PDUFA) and subsequent reauthorizations were enacted to provide additional resources to the FDA for the timely review of new drug applications.

b. **European Union**: The creation of the European Medicines Agency (EMA) in 1995 centralized the regulation of pharmaceuticals in the EU, streamlining the approval process for new medicines.

6. Impact of Technological Advances

a. **Biotechnology and Genomics**: Advances in biotechnology and genomics presented new regulatory challenges and opportunities, leading to the development of specialized regulatory frameworks for biopharmaceuticals and gene therapies.

b. **Digital Health**: The emergence of digital health technologies prompted regulatory agencies to adapt existing frameworks to address issues related to software as a medical device (SaMD), mobile health applications, and telemedicine.

Modern Era and Increasing Complexity (2000s - Present)

The period from the 2000s to the present marks the modern era of regulatory affairs, characterized by rapid advancements in technology, globalization of markets, and the emergence of novel therapeutic modalities. Regulatory agencies have faced the challenge of adapting to a rapidly evolving landscape while ensuring the safety, efficacy, and quality of products. Here's an in-depth overview:

1. Rapid Technological Advancements

a. **Biotechnology and Gene Therapy**: The rise of biotechnology and gene therapy has presented new regulatory challenges, requiring specialized frameworks to evaluate the safety and efficacy of innovative therapies.

b. **Advanced Medical Devices**: Technological innovations in medical devices, including digital health technologies and wearable devices, have necessitated updates to regulatory frameworks to ensure their safety and effectiveness.

2. Globalization and International Collaboration

a. **Harmonization Efforts**: Continued efforts in global harmonization, building upon earlier initiatives such as the ICH, have aimed to streamline regulatory processes and promote consistency across regions.

b. **International Cooperation**: Regulatory agencies worldwide have strengthened collaborations and information-sharing mechanisms to address global challenges such as pandemics, drug shortages, and counterfeit medicines.

3. Regulatory Challenges and Complexities

a. **Personalized Medicine**: The advent of personalized medicine, including pharmacogenomics and precision therapies, has raised questions about regulatory pathways for individualized treatments and companion diagnostics.

b. **Regulation of Digital Health**: The proliferation of digital health technologies, mobile applications, and artificial intelligence in healthcare has led to regulatory complexities surrounding data privacy, security, and software as a medical device (SaMD).

4. Adaptive Regulatory Frameworks

a. **Flexible Regulations**: Regulatory agencies have implemented more flexible and adaptive regulatory frameworks, including expedited pathways for breakthrough therapies, fast-track designations, and accelerated approval programs.

b. **Real-World Evidence (RWE)**: Emphasis on the use of real-world data and evidence to supplement traditional clinical trial data, informing regulatory decision-making and post-market surveillance.

5. Regulatory Response to Public Health Crises

COVID-19 Pandemic: The COVID-19 pandemic underscored the importance of regulatory agility and collaboration in responding to public health emergencies. Regulatory agencies expedited review processes, implemented Emergency Use Authorizations (EUAs), and facilitated international cooperation to expedite the development and deployment of vaccines and treatments.

6. Emerging Regulatory Frontiers

a. **Gene Editing and Cell Therapies**: Advances in gene editing technologies (e.g., CRISPR) and cell-based therapies have prompted regulatory agencies to develop specialized frameworks to evaluate their safety, efficacy, and ethical implications.

b. **Nano-medicine and Advanced Materials**: Regulatory agencies are grappling with the regulatory challenges posed by nanotechnology and advanced materials in drug delivery systems and medical devices, ensuring their safety and effectiveness.

Key Milestones in Regulatory Affairs

Regulatory affairs have evolved significantly over time, shaped by historical events, scientific advancements, and changes in societal needs. Here are some key milestones that have marked the development of regulatory affairs:

1. Establishment of Early Regulatory Laws and Agencies (19th - Early 20th Century)

i. **Pure Food and Drug Act (1906):**

   a. **Significance:** One of the earliest regulatory laws in the United States aimed at preventing the manufacture, sale, and transportation of adulterated or misbranded foods and drugs.

   b. **Foundation:** Established the Bureau of Chemistry, the precursor to the U.S. Food and Drug Administration (FDA), to enforce the law.

ii. **Biologics Control Act (1902):**

   a. **Significance:** Introduced regulatory oversight for biological products after incidents of contaminated vaccines.

   b. **Foundation:** Laid the groundwork for future regulation of biologics and vaccines.

2. Strengthening of Regulatory Frameworks (1930s - 1960s)

i. **Federal Food, Drug, and Cosmetic Act (1938):**

   a. **Significance:** Expanded the authority of the FDA and introduced requirements for pre-market safety evaluations of drugs.

   b. **Foundation**: Laid the foundation for modern drug regulation in the United States.

ii. **Kefauver-Harris Amendments (1962):**

   a. **Significance**: Enacted in response to the thalidomide tragedy, mandated proof of effectiveness and safety for drug approval and introduced informed consent for clinical trials.

   b. **Foundation:** Established key principles for drug safety and efficacy regulation.

3. Global Harmonization Efforts (1990s - Present)

i. **International Conference on Harmonisation (ICH):**

   a. **Significance:** Formed to harmonize technical requirements for drug registration among regulatory authorities from Europe, Japan, and the United States.

   b. **Impact**: Facilitated global harmonization of regulatory standards, reducing duplication and promoting efficiency in drug development.

ii. **European Medicines Agency (EMA) Establishment (1995):**

   a. **Significance:** Centralized regulatory oversight of pharmaceuticals in the European Union, streamlining the approval process for new medicines.

   b. **Impact:** Standardized regulatory procedures across EU member states, enhancing access to medicines for European citizens.

4. Response to Emerging Challenges (2000s - Present)

i. **Prescription Drug User Fee Act (PDUFA) (1992):**

a. **Significance**: Authorized the FDA to collect fees from drug manufacturers to expedite the review process for new drug applications.

b. **Impact**: Accelerated drug approvals and increased resources for regulatory review.

ii. **COVID-19 Pandemic Response (2020):**

a. **Significance:** Highlighted the importance of regulatory agility and international collaboration in responding to public health emergencies.

b. **Impact**: Expedited regulatory processes, facilitated emergency use authorizations for vaccines and treatments, and underscored the need for global cooperation in healthcare.

5. Advancements in Regulatory Science and Technology

i. **Introduction of Good Manufacturing Practices (GMP):**

a. **Significance**: Set standards for the manufacturing processes of drugs, ensuring quality, purity, and consistency.

b. **Impact**: Ensured the quality and safety of pharmaceutical products worldwide.

ii. **Regulation of Biotechnology and Advanced Therapies:**

a. **Significance:** Developed specialized regulatory frameworks for biopharmaceuticals, gene therapies, and cell-based therapies.

b. **Impact:** Enabled the evaluation and approval of innovative therapeutic modalities, fostering advancements in healthcare.

HISTORICAL OVERVIEW OF REGULATORY AUTHORITIES

The development of regulatory authorities has been a crucial aspect of the evolution of regulatory affairs, shaping how products are evaluated, approved, and monitored to ensure public safety. This historical overview provides a detailed account of the formation and evolution of major regulatory bodies around the world.

Early Beginnings and the Formation of Initial Regulatory Bodies

The emergence of initial regulatory bodies marks the early stages of formalized oversight in various industries, responding to growing concerns about product safety, efficacy, and quality. Here's an in-depth look at the early beginnings and formation of some of the initial regulatory bodies:

1. United States:

   a. Pure Food and Drug Act (1906):

      i. **Formation of Regulatory Authority**: Established the Bureau of Chemistry, later renamed the Food and Drug Administration (FDA), as the primary regulatory authority for ensuring the safety and efficacy of foods, drugs, and cosmetics.

      ii. **Role:** The FDA was tasked with enforcing the Pure Food and Drug Act, prohibiting the interstate commerce of adulterated or misbranded food and drugs.

2. United Kingdom:

   a. Sale of Food and Drugs Act (1875):

      i. **Early Legislation**: Introduced regulatory controls on the sale of food and drugs in the United Kingdom, addressing concerns about adulteration and contamination.

      ii. **Formation of Regulatory Oversight:** Led to the establishment of regulatory bodies such as the Medicines and Healthcare products Regulatory Agency (MHRA) in modern times to oversee the safety and efficacy of medicines and medical devices.

3. Canada:

   a. Food and Drugs Act (1920):

      i. **Origins:** Canada's first comprehensive legislation addressing the safety and quality of food and drugs.

      ii. **Evolution**: Over time, regulatory oversight expanded, leading to the formation of Health Canada, which oversees various aspects of health regulation, including pharmaceuticals, medical devices, and food safety.

4. European Union:

  a. Formation of European Medicines Agency (EMA) (1995):

    i. **Centralized Regulation**: Established the EMA to centralize the regulation of medicines across European Union (EU) member states.

    ii. **Harmonization Efforts**: Aimed to harmonize regulatory standards and procedures for pharmaceuticals, facilitating the approval and marketing authorization process for medicines within the EU.

5. International Collaboration:

  a. World Health Organization (WHO):

    i. **Global Health Oversight**: Established by the United Nations in 1948 to address global health challenges and promote international cooperation in health regulation.

    ii. **Regulatory Guidance**: Provides technical guidance and support to member states in establishing and strengthening regulatory frameworks for medicines and healthcare products.

Formation of Key Regulatory Authorities

The formation of key regulatory authorities has been instrumental in shaping the regulatory landscape across various industries, ensuring compliance with standards and safeguarding public health. Here's a detailed overview of the formation of some key regulatory authorities:

1. United States Food and Drug Administration (FDA)

  a. **Establishment:** The FDA traces its origins to the passage of the Pure Food and Drug Act in 1906, which created the Bureau of Chemistry within the Department of Agriculture. In 1927, it was transferred to the Department of Health, Education, and Welfare, where it became the FDA in 1930.

b. **Role:** The FDA is responsible for protecting and promoting public health by regulating food safety, pharmaceuticals, medical devices, cosmetics, and other products. It oversees product approval, manufacturing, labeling, and post-market surveillance to ensure safety and efficacy.

2. European Medicines Agency (EMA)

a. **Formation:** The EMA was established in 1995 as a centralized regulatory agency for medicines in the European Union (EU). It was created to harmonize regulatory processes across EU member states and facilitate the approval and oversight of medicines.

b. **Role:** The EMA evaluates and supervises medicines throughout their lifecycle, from preclinical development to post-market surveillance. It assesses marketing authorization applications, monitors safety, and provides scientific guidance to promote public health.

3. Medicines and Healthcare products Regulatory Agency (MHRA) - United Kingdom

a. **Origins:** The MHRA was formed in 2003 through the merger of the Medicines Control Agency (MCA) and parts of the Medical Devices Agency (MDA) and the Veterinary Medicines Directorate (VMD).

b. **Role:** The MHRA regulates medicines, medical devices, and blood components for transfusion in the UK. It assesses the safety, quality, and efficacy of healthcare products, licenses medicines and devices, and monitors their safety in the market.

4. Health Canada

a. **Establishment:** Health Canada was formed in 1996 through the merger of the Department of National Health and Welfare with Health and Welfare Canada.

b. **Role:** Health Canada regulates health products, including pharmaceuticals, medical devices, and natural health products. It assesses

the safety, efficacy, and quality of products, issues licenses and
authorizations, and monitors their safety in the market.

5. Pharmaceuticals and Medical Devices Agency (PMDA) - Japan

    a. **Formation:** The PMDA was established in 2004 as an independent
administrative agency under the Ministry of Health, Labour, and Welfare
(MHLW) in Japan.

    b. **Role:** The PMDA evaluates the safety, efficacy, and quality of
pharmaceuticals and medical devices in Japan. It reviews marketing
authorization applications, conducts post-marketing surveillance, and
provides scientific guidance to ensure public health and safety.

International Harmonization and Cooperation

International harmonization and cooperation in regulatory affairs have been
critical in addressing global health challenges, promoting efficiency in product
development, and facilitating access to safe and effective healthcare products
worldwide. Here's a detailed overview of international harmonization and
cooperation efforts:

1. Formation of International Regulatory Bodies:

    a. **International Conference on Harmonisation (ICH):**

        i. **Establishment:** Formed in 1990 by regulatory authorities and
industry representatives from the United States, Europe, and Japan.

        ii. **Objective:** Harmonize technical requirements for the registration
of pharmaceuticals to streamline the global drug development and
regulatory review process.

        iii. **Achievements:** Developed guidelines covering various aspects of
drug development, including quality, safety, efficacy, and
multidisciplinary topics, fostering consistency and efficiency in
regulatory submissions and reviews.

    b. **World Health Organization (WHO):**

    i.   **Role:** Established in 1948 as a specialized agency of the United Nations responsible for international public health.

    ii.   **Functions:** Provides leadership on global health matters, sets norms and standards, provides technical support to countries, and coordinates international health responses.

    iii.   **Impact**: Offers technical assistance to member states in establishing and strengthening regulatory systems, facilitating capacity building and information sharing to enhance regulatory practices worldwide.

2. Harmonization Initiatives and Mutual Recognition Agreements (MRAs):

a. Transatlantic Cooperation:

    i.   **United States-European Union (EU) Cooperation**: Collaborative efforts between the FDA and the European Medicines Agency (EMA) to align regulatory requirements, share information, and facilitate mutual recognition of inspections and regulatory decisions.

    ii.   **Impact:** Reduces duplication of efforts, accelerates regulatory processes, and promotes access to medicines for patients in the United States and the EU.

b. Mutual Recognition Agreements (MRAs):

    i.   **Purpose:** Enable regulatory authorities to recognize inspections, approvals, and certifications conducted by other competent authorities.

    ii.   **Examples**: MRAs between regulatory agencies of different countries or regions, such as the EU's MRAs with Switzerland, Canada, Japan, and the United States, promote the acceptance of inspection outcomes and regulatory decisions, enhancing global regulatory cooperation and efficiency.

3. Standardization of Regulatory Requirements and Processes:

a. **Harmonized Guidelines and Standards:**

  i. **ICH Guidelines**: Provide internationally accepted standards and guidelines for pharmaceutical development, facilitating the submission and review of regulatory applications across regions.

  ii. **Pharmacopoeial Standards**: Organizations such as the United States Pharmacopeia (USP) and the European Pharmacopoeia (Ph. Eur.) develop and promote standards for pharmaceuticals, ensuring consistency in quality and testing methods worldwide.

4. Global Collaboration in Public Health Emergencies:

a. **COVID-19 Pandemic Response:**

  i. **International Cooperation**: Regulatory authorities worldwide collaborated to expedite the development, review, and approval of COVID-19 vaccines, treatments, and diagnostics.

  ii. **Emergency Use Authorizations (EUAs):** Regulatory agencies issued EUAs to facilitate timely access to critical healthcare products, balancing the urgency of the pandemic response with safety and efficacy considerations.

  iii. **Sharing of Information**: Regulatory agencies shared data, scientific expertise, and regulatory best practices to support global efforts to control the spread of the virus and mitigate the impact of the pandemic on public health.

Modern Regulatory Authorities and Advances

In the modern era, regulatory authorities have adapted to evolving technologies, globalization, and emerging challenges in healthcare to ensure the safety, efficacy, and quality of products. Here's a comprehensive overview of modern regulatory authorities and the advances in regulatory affairs:

1. United States Food and Drug Administration (FDA):

a. **Adaptation to Technological Advances:**

i. **Embracing Digital Health**: The FDA has developed regulatory frameworks to oversee digital health technologies, including software as a medical device (SaMD), mobile health applications, and artificial intelligence (AI) algorithms.

ii. **Regulation of Advanced Therapies**: With the emergence of gene therapies, cell-based therapies, and regenerative medicine products, the FDA has established specialized review processes and expedited pathways to facilitate their development and approval.

b. **Enhanced Collaboration and Innovation:**

i. **FDA Innovation Pathway**: Introduced initiatives such as the Breakthrough Therapy Designation and the Priority Review Program to expedite the development and review of innovative drugs for serious diseases, fostering collaboration between the FDA and industry stakeholders.

ii. **Regulatory Science Initiatives**: Invested in regulatory science research to enhance the understanding of product safety and efficacy, promote the development of novel methodologies, and support evidence-based regulatory decision-making.

2. European Medicines Agency (EMA):

a. **Promotion of Regulatory Science:**

i. **Innovation Task Force**: Established to support the development of innovative medicines and technologies, providing scientific advice, guidance, and regulatory support to stakeholders.

ii. **Priority Medicines (PRIME) Scheme**: Facilitates early dialogue and accelerated evaluation of promising medicines to address unmet medical needs, supporting innovation and expedited access to therapies for patients.

b. **Adaptation to Global Challenges:**

i.   **Brexit Preparedness**: Implemented measures to ensure continuity and minimize disruption to regulatory processes following the United Kingdom's withdrawal from the European Union, including relocation of the EMA headquarters to Amsterdam.

ii. **Response to Public Health Emergencies**: Enhanced coordination with global partners to address public health emergencies such as the COVID-19 pandemic, expediting regulatory processes for vaccines, therapeutics, and diagnostics.

3. Health Canada:

a. Modernization of Regulatory Frameworks:

i.   **Regulatory Review Modernization**: Implemented initiatives to streamline regulatory processes, reduce review timelines, and enhance efficiency in the evaluation and approval of drugs, medical devices, and biologics.

ii. **Access to Investigational Products**: Introduced pathways such as the Special Access Program and the Emergency Drug Release Program to facilitate access to investigational drugs for patients with serious or life-threatening conditions.

b. Harnessing Data and Technology:

i.   **Real-World Evidence (RWE)**: Leveraging real-world data to support regulatory decision-making, complementing traditional clinical trial data and providing insights into product effectiveness and safety in real-world settings.

ii. **Digital Health Regulation:** Developed guidance and frameworks to regulate digital health products, including software, wearables, and telemedicine platforms, ensuring their safety, effectiveness, and privacy compliance.

Recent Developments and Future Directions

Recent developments in regulatory affairs have been shaped by advancements in technology, globalization, and emerging healthcare challenges. Looking ahead, regulatory authorities are poised to address new opportunities and challenges in a rapidly evolving landscape. Here's an overview of recent developments and future directions:

1. Embracing Digital Transformation:

    a. Digital Health Regulations:

        i. **Software as a Medical Device (SaMD)**: Regulatory authorities are refining frameworks to regulate SaMD, including artificial intelligence (AI) algorithms, mobile health apps, and digital therapeutics, ensuring safety, effectiveness, and data privacy.

        ii. **Telemedicine and Remote Monitoring**: Guidance is being developed to oversee telemedicine platforms, remote monitoring devices, and virtual healthcare services, facilitating access to care and improving patient outcomes.

2. Enhanced Data Utilization and Regulatory Science:

    a. Real-World Evidence (RWE):

        i. **Integration into Regulatory Decision-making**: Regulatory authorities are increasingly leveraging RWE to complement traditional clinical trial data, informing regulatory decisions on product safety, effectiveness, and post-market surveillance.

        ii. **Evidence Generation Platforms**: Investments in data infrastructure and interoperability are enabling the development of evidence generation platforms to facilitate the collection, analysis, and utilization of real-world data for regulatory purposes.

3. Addressing Emerging Therapies and Technologies:

    a. Advanced Therapies:

        i. **Gene and Cell Therapies**: Regulatory frameworks are evolving to accommodate the unique challenges posed by gene editing technologies, cell-based therapies, and regenerative medicine products, ensuring their safety, efficacy, and ethical use.

ii. **Nano-medicine and Biomaterials**: Regulatory agencies are exploring specialized approaches to evaluate nanotechnology-based drug delivery systems, biomaterials, and advanced medical devices, addressing their unique characteristics and potential risks.

4. Strengthening International Collaboration:

a. Global Harmonization:

i. **Continued Collaboration:** Regulatory authorities are strengthening partnerships and information-sharing mechanisms to harmonize regulatory requirements, streamline processes, and facilitate access to healthcare products across borders.

ii. **Mutual Recognition Agreements (MRAs)**: Efforts to expand MRAs and mutual reliance on inspections and regulatory decisions are promoting regulatory convergence and reducing duplication of efforts.

5. Adaptive Regulatory Approaches:

a. Agility in Response to Public Health Emergencies:

i. **Pandemic Preparedness:** Regulatory agencies are enhancing preparedness and response mechanisms to address public health emergencies such as pandemics, facilitating rapid review and approval of vaccines, treatments, and diagnostics.

ii. **Emergency Use Authorizations (EUAs):** Streamlined pathways for EUAs enable expedited access to critical healthcare products during emergencies while ensuring appropriate safety and efficacy assessments.

6. Ethical and Social Considerations:

a. Ethical Use of Healthcare Technologies:

i. **AI and Data Privacy**: Regulatory frameworks are incorporating principles of transparency, fairness, and accountability to address ethical concerns surrounding AI algorithms, data privacy, and algorithmic bias in healthcare decision-making.

ii. **Equity and Access**: Efforts are underway to ensure equitable access to healthcare products and services, addressing disparities in healthcare access, affordability, and health outcomes across diverse populations.

ROLE OF REGULATORY AFFAIRS DEPARTMENT

The Regulatory Affairs (RA) department plays a pivotal role in industries such as pharmaceuticals, biotechnology, medical devices, cosmetics, and food. This department is responsible for ensuring that products comply with all regulations and laws pertaining to their market. Here's an in-depth look at the functions and responsibilities of the RA department.

Regulatory Strategy Development

The Regulatory Affairs (RA) department plays a critical role in developing and executing regulatory strategies to ensure compliance with regulations and facilitate the timely approval of healthcare products. Here's an in-depth overview of regulatory strategy development within the RA department:

1. Understanding Regulatory Landscape:

a. Comprehensive Regulatory Intelligence:

i. **Monitoring**: The RA department continuously monitors changes in regulatory requirements, guidelines, and legislation relevant to the company's products and markets.

ii. **Analysis: It** assesses the impact of regulatory changes on product development, registration, and commercialization strategies.

2. Collaboration with Cross-Functional Teams:

a. Integration with Product Development:

i. **Early Involvement**: RA professionals collaborate closely with R&D and product development teams to integrate regulatory considerations into the design and development of new products or modifications to existing products.

ii. **Risk Assessment**: Conducting risk assessments to identify potential regulatory challenges and mitigation strategies at each stage of product development.

3. Strategic Planning and Execution:

a. Developing Regulatory Strategies:

i. **Tailored Approaches**: Based on regulatory intelligence and product specifics, the RA department develops customized regulatory strategies aligned with business objectives and regulatory requirements.

ii. **Pathway Selection**: Evaluating and selecting the most appropriate regulatory pathways for product approval or clearance, considering factors such as intended use, therapeutic area, and regulatory precedent.

b. Submission Planning and Management:

i. **Timely Preparation**: Planning and coordinating the preparation of regulatory submissions, including investigational new drug applications (INDs), new drug applications (NDAs), marketing authorization applications (MAAs), and premarket notifications (510(k)s).

ii. **Quality Assurance**: Ensuring the completeness, accuracy, and compliance of regulatory submissions with regulatory requirements and company standards.

4. Communication with Regulatory Authorities:

a. Engagement with Regulatory Agencies:

    i.   **Proactive Interaction**: Establishing productive relationships with regulatory authorities through pre-submission meetings, regulatory consultations, and scientific advice procedures to seek guidance and resolve regulatory issues.

    ii. **Negotiation Skills**: Advocating for the company's interests while maintaining compliance with regulatory requirements during interactions with regulatory agencies.

5. Post-Market Compliance and Lifecycle Management:

a. Post-Market Surveillance:

    i.   **Vigilance Reporting**: Monitoring and reporting adverse events, complaints, and safety issues to regulatory authorities in compliance with post-market surveillance requirements.

    ii. **Lifecycle Management**: Developing strategies for post-approval changes, variations, and product maintenance activities to ensure ongoing compliance with regulatory requirements and product quality standards.

6. Training and Continuous Improvement:

a. Employee Training and Development:

    i.   **Regulatory Education**: Providing training and education to employees across functions on regulatory requirements, processes, and updates to enhance regulatory awareness and compliance.

    ii. **Continuous Improvement**: Evaluating and refining regulatory processes, SOPs, and systems based on feedback, lessons learned, and industry best practices to optimize regulatory performance and efficiency.

Regulatory Submissions and Approvals

The Regulatory Affairs (RA) department is responsible for preparing, managing, and facilitating regulatory submissions to obtain approvals or clearances for healthcare products from regulatory authorities. Here's a detailed overview of the role of the RA department in regulatory submissions and approvals:

1. Submission Planning and Preparation:

  a. Regulatory Strategy Development:

    i. Collaborating with cross-functional teams to develop regulatory strategies aligned with business objectives and regulatory requirements.

    ii. Identifying the most appropriate regulatory pathways for product approval or clearance based on product characteristics, intended use, and regulatory precedent.

  b. Submission Planning:

    i. Developing a comprehensive submission plan outlining the regulatory requirements, timelines, milestones, and responsibilities for each submission.

    ii. Conducting gap analyses to identify any missing data or documentation required for regulatory submissions.

  c. Document Preparation:

    i. Coordinating the preparation of regulatory documents, including investigational new drug applications (INDs), new drug applications (NDAs), marketing authorization applications (MAAs), premarket notifications (510(k)s), and technical files for medical devices.

    ii. Ensuring the accuracy, completeness, and compliance of regulatory submissions with regulatory requirements and company standards.

2. Regulatory Submission Management:

  a. Submission Compilation:

    i. Compiling and organizing the required documentation, including clinical data, nonclinical data, manufacturing information, quality control data, and labeling, into a submission-ready format.

ii. Managing the assembly and version control of regulatory submissions, including electronic submissions where applicable.

b. Regulatory Agency Interactions:

i. Coordinating and facilitating interactions with regulatory agencies, including pre-submission meetings, regulatory consultations, and responses to agency inquiries or deficiency letters.

ii. Serving as the primary point of contact between the company and regulatory authorities throughout the submission and review process.

3. Submission Tracking and Monitoring:

a. Timely Submission:

i. Tracking submission timelines and milestones to ensure timely submission of regulatory documents according to planned schedules.

ii. Addressing any potential delays or issues that may impact submission timelines and communicating with stakeholders to mitigate risks.

b. Regulatory Intelligence:

i. Monitoring regulatory developments, guidelines, and updates related to submission requirements, processes, and timelines.

ii. Keeping abreast of changes in regulatory requirements that may affect submission strategies or content.

4. Regulatory Review and Approval:

a. Regulatory Review Process:

i. Facilitating the review of regulatory submissions by regulatory authorities, including the FDA, EMA, Health Canada, and other relevant agencies.

ii. Addressing any questions, requests for clarification, or deficiencies raised by regulatory agencies during the review process.

b. Approval Coordination:

   i. Coordinating activities related to regulatory approvals or clearances, including label negotiations, post-approval commitments, and product launch preparations.

   ii. Ensuring compliance with regulatory conditions and requirements imposed as part of the approval or clearance process.

Compliance and Quality Assurance

The Regulatory Affairs (RA) department plays a crucial role in ensuring compliance with regulatory requirements and maintaining high-quality standards throughout the lifecycle of healthcare products. Here's an in-depth overview of the RA department's involvement in compliance and quality assurance:

1. Interpretation and Implementation of Regulations:

a. Regulatory Compliance Monitoring:

   i. Continuously monitoring changes in regulations, guidelines, and standards relevant to the company's products and markets.

   ii. Interpreting regulatory requirements and providing guidance to internal stakeholders to ensure compliance with applicable regulations.

b. Gap Analysis and Remediation:

   i. Conducting gap analyses to identify areas of non-compliance or potential risks.

   ii. Developing and implementing corrective and preventive actions (CAPAs) to address identified gaps and ensure compliance with regulatory requirements.

2. Documentation and Record Keeping:

a. Document Control:

i. Establishing and maintaining systems for document control, including versioning, archival, and retrieval of regulatory documents.

ii. Ensuring that regulatory documentation, including submissions, approvals, and correspondence with regulatory agencies, is accurate, complete, and up-to-date.

b. **Regulatory Dossier Management:**

i. Managing regulatory dossiers and technical files for healthcare products, ensuring they contain all required documentation to support regulatory submissions and approvals.

ii. Maintaining documentation in compliance with Good Documentation Practices (GDP) and regulatory requirements for record keeping.

3. Audits and Inspections:

a. **Internal Audits:**

i. Conducting internal audits to assess compliance with regulatory requirements, quality management systems (QMS), and standard operating procedures (SOPs).

ii. Identifying areas for improvement and implementing corrective actions to address findings from internal audits.

b. **Regulatory Inspections:**

i. Coordinating and facilitating regulatory inspections conducted by regulatory authorities, such as the FDA, EMA, and Health Canada.

ii. Preparing the organization for regulatory inspections, ensuring readiness, and providing support during inspections to address inquiries and observations.

4. Change Control and Risk Management:

a. **Change Control Processes:**

i. Implementing change control processes to manage changes to products, processes, facilities, or documentation.

ii. Assessing the impact of proposed changes on regulatory compliance and product quality and obtaining regulatory approvals or notifications as required.

b. Risk Management:

i. Conducting risk assessments to identify and mitigate risks related to regulatory compliance, product quality, and patient safety.

ii. Implementing risk management processes, such as Failure Mode and Effects Analysis (FMEA) or Hazard Analysis and Critical Control Points (HACCP), to proactively manage risks throughout the product lifecycle.

5. Training and Continuous Improvement:

a. Employee Training:

i. Providing training and education to employees on regulatory requirements, quality standards, and compliance expectations.

ii. Ensuring that employees are knowledgeable and competent in performing their regulatory and quality-related responsibilities.

b. Continuous Improvement Initiatives:

i. Establishing a culture of continuous improvement to drive enhancements to regulatory processes, quality systems, and compliance practices.

ii. Implementing metrics and key performance indicators (KPIs) to monitor compliance effectiveness and identify opportunities for improvement.

Labeling and Advertising

The Regulatory Affairs (RA) department plays a critical role in ensuring that the labeling and advertising of healthcare products comply with regulatory requirements and accurately convey product information to healthcare professionals and consumers. Here's a detailed overview of the RA department's involvement in labeling and advertising:

1. Labeling Compliance:

a. Regulatory Review and Approval:

i. Conducting regulatory reviews of product labeling, including package inserts, labels, and prescribing information, to ensure compliance with applicable regulations, standards, and guidelines.

ii. Obtaining regulatory approvals or clearances for labeling changes, updates, or new product launches from regulatory authorities, such as the FDA, EMA, or Health Canada.

b. Labeling Content and Accuracy:

i. Ensuring that labeling content accurately reflects product characteristics, indications, dosages, warnings, precautions, contraindications, and instructions for use.

ii. Verifying the accuracy of labeling information through review of clinical data, product specifications, and regulatory submissions.

2. Advertising Compliance:

a. Promotional Material Review:

i. Reviewing and approving promotional materials, including advertisements, brochures, websites, and sales aids, to ensure compliance with regulatory requirements and company policies.

ii. Assessing promotional claims for accuracy, substantiation, balance, and fair presentation of product benefits and risks.

b. Promotional Labeling Review:

i. Reviewing promotional labeling, such as product packaging, product inserts, and promotional literature distributed to healthcare professionals, to ensure compliance with regulatory requirements and guidelines.

ii. Ensuring that promotional labeling contains appropriate indications, limitations, and warnings consistent with approved product labeling.

3. Regulatory Submissions and Notifications:

a. Labeling Submissions:

i. Coordinating the preparation and submission of labeling supplements or variations to regulatory authorities to update product labeling in response to changes in product information, regulations, or labeling guidelines.

ii. Managing the regulatory review process for labeling submissions, including addressing inquiries or requests for additional information from regulatory agencies.

b. Adverse Event Reporting:

i. Monitoring and reporting adverse events or complaints related to product labeling, such as medication errors or off-label use, to regulatory authorities in compliance with pharmacovigilance requirements.

ii. Ensuring timely and accurate reporting of labeling-related adverse events to regulatory agencies and internal stakeholders.

4. Compliance Monitoring and Training:

a. Regulatory Compliance Monitoring:

i. Monitoring changes in labeling and advertising regulations, guidelines, and enforcement trends to ensure ongoing compliance.

ii. Conducting internal audits or assessments of labeling and advertising practices to identify areas for improvement and ensure adherence to regulatory requirements.

b. Employee Training and Education:

i. Providing training and education to employees involved in labeling and advertising activities on regulatory requirements, compliance expectations, and best practices.

ii. Ensuring that employees understand their roles and responsibilities in maintaining compliant labeling and advertising practices.

Clinical Trials and Research Support

The Regulatory Affairs (RA) department plays a crucial role in facilitating clinical trials and supporting research activities by ensuring compliance with regulatory requirements and ethical standards. Here's a detailed overview of the RA department's involvement in clinical trials and research support:

1. Regulatory Strategy Development:

a. Clinical Development Planning:

i. Collaborating with cross-functional teams, including clinical development, medical affairs, and research and development, to develop regulatory strategies for clinical trial programs.

ii. Identifying regulatory requirements, pathways, and considerations for the design, conduct, and submission of clinical trials in different jurisdictions.

2. Regulatory Submissions and Approvals:

a. Clinical Trial Applications (CTAs):

i. Preparing and submitting CTAs, investigational new drug applications (INDs), or equivalent regulatory submissions to obtain approvals from regulatory authorities to initiate clinical trials.

ii. Managing interactions with regulatory agencies, including responding to inquiries, providing additional information, and addressing regulatory concerns during the review process.

3. Compliance and Quality Assurance:

a. GxP Compliance:

i. Ensuring compliance with Good Clinical Practice (GCP) guidelines, International Council for Harmonisation of Technical Requirements for Pharmaceuticals for Human Use (ICH) guidelines, and applicable regulations throughout the conduct of clinical trials.

ii. Conducting audits and inspections of clinical trial sites, vendors, and internal processes to verify compliance with regulatory requirements and quality standards.

4. Ethics and Patient Safety:

a. Ethical Review and Oversight:

i. Facilitating ethical review and approval of clinical trial protocols by institutional review boards (IRBs) or ethics committees to ensure the protection of human subjects' rights, safety, and welfare.

ii. Addressing ethical considerations, informed consent requirements, and protocol deviations in compliance with ethical standards and regulatory requirements.

5. Regulatory Reporting and Documentation:

a. Safety Reporting:

i. Managing the reporting of adverse events, serious adverse events (SAEs), and unanticipated problems to regulatory authorities, IRBs, and other stakeholders in compliance with pharmacovigilance requirements.

ii. Ensuring timely and accurate submission of safety reports, periodic safety updates, and other regulatory documentation related to clinical trial safety monitoring.

6. Post-Trial Activities:

a. Clinical Trial Results Reporting:

i. Facilitating the preparation and submission of clinical trial results, including clinical study reports (CSRs), to regulatory authorities, clinical trial registries, and scientific publications in compliance with transparency requirements.

ii. Ensuring that clinical trial results are accurately reported and disseminated to support evidence-based decision-making and public health.

7. Training and Education:

a. Staff Training:

i. Providing training and education to internal staff involved in clinical trials on regulatory requirements, GCP guidelines, study protocols, and study-specific procedures.

ii. Ensuring that clinical trial personnel understand their roles and responsibilities in maintaining compliance with regulatory and ethical standards.

Post-Market Surveillance and Reporting

Post-market surveillance (PMS) and reporting are essential components of regulatory affairs, aimed at monitoring the safety, performance, and effectiveness of healthcare products after they are marketed. The Regulatory Affairs (RA) department plays a crucial role in post-market surveillance activities to ensure compliance with regulatory requirements and to protect public health. Here's an in-depth overview of the RA department's involvement in post-market surveillance and reporting:

1. Establishing Post-Market Surveillance Systems:

a. System Development:

i. Collaborating with cross-functional teams, including pharmacovigilance, quality assurance, and medical affairs, to establish post-market surveillance systems and processes.

ii. Implementing systems for the collection, evaluation, and reporting of post-market data, including adverse events, product complaints, and quality issues.

b. **Compliance with Regulations:**

    i. Ensuring that post-market surveillance systems and processes comply with regulatory requirements, including Good Pharmacovigilance Practices (GVP), Medical Device Reporting (MDR), and adverse event reporting regulations.

2. Adverse Event Monitoring and Reporting:

a. Adverse Event Identification:

    i. Monitoring and assessing adverse event reports, product complaints, and other safety-related information received from healthcare professionals, consumers, and regulatory authorities.

    ii. Investigating and evaluating adverse events to determine causality, severity, and potential impact on patient safety.

b. Regulatory Reporting:

    i. Ensuring timely and accurate reporting of adverse events to regulatory authorities in compliance with pharmacovigilance regulations, including periodic safety update reports (PSURs), individual case safety reports (ICSRs), and expedited reporting requirements for serious or unexpected events.

3. Product Quality Monitoring and Reporting:

a. Quality Surveillance:

    i. Monitoring product quality-related issues, including manufacturing deviations, defects, recalls, and non-conformances, through post-market surveillance activities.

    ii. Investigating product quality issues to identify root causes, implement corrective and preventive actions (CAPAs), and prevent recurrence.

b. Regulatory Notifications:

    i. Reporting product quality-related issues to regulatory authorities, including field safety corrective actions (FSCAs), recalls, and Field

Safety Notices (FSNs), in compliance with regulatory requirements and timelines.

4. Signal Detection and Risk Management:

a. Signal Detection:

    i. Conducting signal detection activities to identify potential safety signals or emerging risks associated with healthcare products based on post-market data analysis, literature review, and safety surveillance findings.

    ii. Investigating and evaluating safety signals to determine the need for further risk assessment and management actions.

b. Risk Management:

    i. Implementing risk management strategies to mitigate identified risks or safety concerns associated with healthcare products, including changes to product labeling, risk minimization measures, and communication strategies.

5. Continuous Improvement and Communication:

a. Process Optimization:

    i. Evaluating post-market surveillance processes, systems, and performance metrics to identify opportunities for improvement and efficiency gains.

    ii. Implementing continuous improvement initiatives to enhance the effectiveness, timeliness, and quality of post-market surveillance activities.

b. Stakeholder Communication:

    i. Communicating post-market surveillance findings, safety updates, and regulatory actions to internal stakeholders, including senior management, product development teams, and commercialization teams.

ii. Collaborating with external stakeholders, including healthcare professionals, patients, and regulatory authorities, to exchange information, address safety concerns, and promote public health.

Risk Management

Risk management is a crucial aspect of regulatory affairs, encompassing activities aimed at identifying, assessing, mitigating, and monitoring risks associated with healthcare products throughout their lifecycle. The Regulatory Affairs (RA) department plays a pivotal role in coordinating risk management efforts to ensure compliance with regulatory requirements and to safeguard patient safety. Here's an in-depth overview of the RA department's involvement in risk management:

1. Risk Identification:

   a. Regulatory Requirements:

      i. Understanding and interpreting regulatory requirements related to risk management, including Good Manufacturing Practice (GMP), Good Clinical Practice (GCP), and ISO standards for medical devices.

      ii. Identifying specific risk management requirements outlined by regulatory authorities, such as risk management plans (RMPs) for pharmaceuticals or risk management files (RMFs) for medical devices.

   b. Cross-Functional Collaboration:

      i. Collaborating with cross-functional teams, including product development, quality assurance, and pharmacovigilance, to identify potential risks associated with product design, manufacturing processes, clinical use, and post-market surveillance.

2. Risk Assessment:

   a. Risk Analysis Techniques:

    i.   Utilizing risk analysis techniques such as Failure Mode and Effects Analysis (FMEA), Hazard Analysis and Critical Control Points (HACCP), and fault tree analysis to assess potential hazards, failure modes, and their associated risks.

    ii.   Conducting risk assessments to evaluate the severity, probability, and detectability of identified risks and to prioritize risk mitigation efforts.

b. Regulatory Impact Assessment:

    i.   Assessing the regulatory impact of identified risks on product development, registration, marketing authorization, and post-market surveillance activities.

    ii.   Determining whether identified risks meet the criteria for reporting to regulatory authorities and initiating appropriate risk management actions.

3. Risk Mitigation:

a. Risk Control Strategies:

    i.   Developing risk control strategies to mitigate identified risks and reduce their impact on product safety, efficacy, and quality.

    ii.   Implementing risk mitigation measures, such as design changes, process improvements, quality controls, or labeling updates, to address identified hazards and minimize associated risks.

b. Regulatory Compliance:

    i.   Ensuring that risk mitigation measures comply with regulatory requirements and standards, including documentation of risk management activities, implementation of CAPAs, and incorporation of risk reduction strategies into regulatory submissions.

4. Risk Communication:

a. Stakeholder Engagement:

i. Communicating risk assessment findings, risk control measures, and risk management decisions to internal stakeholders, including senior management, project teams, and regulatory affairs colleagues.

ii. Facilitating communication with external stakeholders, such as regulatory authorities, healthcare professionals, patients, and consumers, to provide transparency and ensure understanding of risk management efforts.

5. Risk Monitoring and Review:

a. Post-Market Surveillance:

i. Monitoring post-market data, including adverse event reports, product complaints, and quality issues, to identify emerging risks or changes in risk profiles.

ii. Conducting periodic reviews of risk management plans, risk registers, and risk control measures to evaluate their effectiveness and make adjustments as necessary.

b. Continuous Improvement:

i. Implementing a process for continuous improvement of risk management practices, including feedback mechanisms, lessons learned from risk events, and updates to risk management tools and methodologies.

ii. Incorporating feedback from regulatory authorities, industry guidelines, and best practices to enhance risk management capabilities and ensure alignment with evolving regulatory requirements.

Liaison and Advocacy

Liaison and advocacy are essential functions of the Regulatory Affairs (RA) department, involving interaction with regulatory authorities, industry associations, and other stakeholders to influence regulatory policies, shape industry standards, and advance the interests of the organization. Here's a detailed overview of the RA department's involvement in liaison and advocacy:

1. Regulatory Agency Interaction:

a. Regulatory Submissions and Communications:

i. Serving as the primary point of contact between the organization and regulatory authorities, such as the FDA, EMA, Health Canada, and other regulatory agencies.

ii. Facilitating regulatory submissions, including marketing authorization applications, investigational new drug applications, and post-market notifications, and addressing regulatory inquiries or requests for information.

b. Regulatory Meetings and Consultations:

i. Organizing and participating in regulatory meetings, including pre-submission meetings, scientific advice procedures, and regulatory consultations, to seek guidance, address regulatory issues, and resolve challenges.

ii. Advocating for the organization's interests and positions while maintaining compliance with regulatory requirements and fostering constructive relationships with regulatory agencies.

2. Industry Collaboration:

a. Partnerships and Alliances:

i. Collaborating with industry associations, professional societies, and trade organizations to advocate for regulatory policies, standards, and initiatives that support the organization's objectives.

ii. Participating in industry working groups, committees, and task forces to contribute expertise, share best practices, and influence the development of regulatory guidelines and industry standards.

b. Information Sharing and Networking:

i.   Sharing regulatory intelligence, updates, and insights with industry peers and stakeholders through conferences, seminars, webinars, and industry events.

ii. Networking with regulatory professionals, industry experts, and key opinion leaders to exchange knowledge, build relationships, and stay informed about emerging regulatory trends and issues.

3. Legislative Affairs:

a. Monitoring Regulatory Legislation:

i.   Tracking proposed regulatory legislation, policy changes, and government initiatives that may impact the organization's business operations, product portfolio, or regulatory environment.

ii. Analyzing the potential implications of legislative developments and advocating for positions that align with the organization's interests and regulatory compliance objectives.

b. Engagement with Policymakers:

i.   Engaging with policymakers, legislators, and government officials to provide input on regulatory matters, share perspectives on industry challenges, and advocate for policies that support innovation, patient access, and public health.

ii. Participating in advocacy campaigns, public hearings, and comment periods to influence regulatory decision-making and shape the regulatory landscape.

4. Internal Advocacy and Education:

a. Internal Stakeholder Engagement:

i.   Advocating for regulatory compliance, quality standards, and best practices within the organization by providing guidance, training, and support to internal stakeholders, including senior management, product development teams, and commercialization teams.

ii. Building awareness of regulatory requirements, expectations, and implications across functional areas to foster a culture of regulatory excellence and accountability.

b. Risk Communication:

i. Communicating regulatory developments, policy changes, and compliance requirements to internal stakeholders in a timely and transparent manner to ensure understanding and alignment with organizational goals and priorities.

ii. Providing strategic guidance and recommendations to senior management on regulatory strategies, risk management, and compliance initiatives to support informed decision-making and business continuity.

Training and Education

Training and education are vital components of the Regulatory Affairs (RA) department's responsibilities, aimed at ensuring that employees across the organization possess the necessary knowledge, skills, and understanding of regulatory requirements to support compliance and successful regulatory outcomes. Here's a comprehensive overview of training and education in the role of the RA department:

1. Regulatory Requirements Training:

1. Regulatory Fundamentals:

a. Providing foundational training on key regulatory concepts, principles, and requirements applicable to the organization's products, markets, and regulatory pathways.

b. Covering topics such as Good Manufacturing Practices (GMP), Good Clinical Practice (GCP), Good Laboratory Practice (GLP), and relevant regulations from regulatory authorities such as the FDA, EMA, and Health Canada.

2. Product-Specific Training:

a. Offering specialized training on regulatory requirements specific to the organization's product portfolio, including pharmaceuticals, biologics, medical devices, diagnostics, and combination products.

b. Tailoring training content to address the unique regulatory considerations, approval processes, and lifecycle stages of different product categories.

2. Regulatory Processes and Procedures:

1. Regulatory Submissions:

a. Training employees on the preparation, compilation, and submission of regulatory documents, including marketing authorization applications, investigational new drug applications, and post-market notifications.

b. Providing guidance on regulatory submission timelines, formatting requirements, and documentation standards to ensure compliance with regulatory authorities' expectations.

2. Change Management:

a. Educating employees on change control processes and procedures for managing changes to products, processes, facilities, or documentation in compliance with regulatory requirements.

b. Ensuring that employees understand their roles and responsibilities in documenting and assessing changes, implementing appropriate controls, and obtaining regulatory approvals or notifications as necessary.

3. Quality and Compliance Training:

1. Quality Management Systems (QMS):

a. Training employees on QMS principles, practices, and procedures to support compliance with quality standards, such as ISO 13485 for medical devices or ISO 9001 for pharmaceuticals.

b. Providing instruction on document control, record keeping, deviation management, corrective and preventive actions (CAPAs), and internal audit processes to maintain regulatory compliance and product quality.

2. Compliance Awareness:

a. Raising awareness of regulatory compliance expectations and ethical standards among employees through training sessions, workshops, and communication campaigns.

b. Emphasizing the importance of adherence to regulatory requirements, data integrity principles, and ethical conduct in all activities related to product development, manufacturing, and commercialization.

4. Role-Specific Training:

1. Functional Training:

a. Offering role-specific training to employees involved in regulatory affairs, quality assurance, clinical development, manufacturing, supply chain, and other relevant functions.

b. Customizing training content to address the specific regulatory responsibilities, tasks, and challenges faced by employees in their respective roles.

2. Leadership Development:

a. Providing leadership and management training to regulatory affairs managers, team leaders, and senior executives to enhance their regulatory knowledge, decision-making skills, and strategic acumen.

b. Equipping leaders with the tools and resources needed to effectively lead regulatory teams, drive regulatory initiatives, and navigate complex regulatory issues.

5. Continuous Learning and Professional Development:

1. **Regulatory Updates:**
   a. Keeping employees informed about regulatory updates, changes in legislation, guidance documents, and best practices through regular communication, newsletters, and training sessions.
   b. Encouraging employees to stay abreast of regulatory developments by participating in industry conferences, seminars, webinars, and continuing education programs.
2. **Certifications and Qualifications:**
   a. Supporting employees in pursuing relevant certifications, qualifications, and professional memberships in regulatory affairs, quality management, and related disciplines.
   b. Providing resources and opportunities for employees to enhance their regulatory expertise, skills, and credentials to support career advancement and organizational success.

Key Skills and Attributes for Regulatory Affairs Professionals

Regulatory Affairs (RA) professionals play a critical role in navigating the complex regulatory landscape and ensuring compliance with regulatory requirements across the lifecycle of healthcare products. To excel in this role, individuals need a combination of technical knowledge, regulatory expertise, and interpersonal skills. Here's a detailed overview of the key skills and attributes required for success in regulatory affairs:

1. Regulatory Knowledge:
   a. **Understanding of Regulations**: A solid grasp of regulatory frameworks, guidelines, and requirements issued by regulatory authorities such as the FDA, EMA, and Health Canada.
   b. **Product-Specific Expertise**: In-depth knowledge of regulations applicable to specific product categories, including pharmaceuticals, biologics, medical devices, and diagnostics.

c. **Global Perspective**: Familiarity with international regulations and standards to support global product development, registration, and market access.

2. Technical Competence:

a. **Scientific Background**: A strong foundation in scientific principles, including biology, chemistry, pharmacology, or engineering, depending on the product type.

b. **Data Interpretation**: Ability to interpret scientific and clinical data, including study protocols, clinical trial results, and technical specifications, to support regulatory submissions and compliance activities.

c. **Quality Management Systems**: Understanding of quality management principles, including Good Manufacturing Practices (GMP), Good Laboratory Practices (GLP), and ISO standards for medical devices.

3. Regulatory Strategy Development:

a. **Analytical Thinking**: The capacity to analyze regulatory requirements, assesses risks, and develops strategic approaches to achieve regulatory objectives effectively.

b. **Problem-Solving Skills**: Ability to identify regulatory challenges, addresses issues, and develops creative solutions to overcome obstacles in product development and market access.

c. **Project Management**: Skills in project planning, coordination, and execution to manage regulatory timelines, resources, and deliverables effectively.

4. Communication and Interpersonal Skills:

a. **Written Communication**: Proficiency in writing regulatory documents, including submissions, reports, and correspondence, with clarity, accuracy, and compliance with regulatory standards.

b. **Verbal Communication**: Strong presentation and negotiation skills to communicate effectively with regulatory authorities, internal stakeholders, and external partners.

c. **Stakeholder Management**: Ability to build and maintain positive relationships with regulatory agencies, cross-functional teams, and industry partners to facilitate regulatory interactions and achieve common objectives.

5. Attention to Detail and Compliance:

a. **Attention to Detail**: Meticulousness in reviewing documentation, data, and regulatory requirements to ensure accuracy, completeness, and compliance.

b. **Ethical Integrity**: Commitment to upholding ethical standards, data integrity principles, and regulatory compliance in all aspects of regulatory affairs activities.

c. **Adaptability and Resilience**: Flexibility to adapt to changing regulatory environments, regulations, and priorities while maintaining focus on achieving regulatory goals and objectives.

6. Continuous Learning and Professional Development:

a. **Curiosity and Learning Orientation**: Eagerness to stay updated on regulatory developments, industry trends, and best practices through continuous learning, professional development, and networking opportunities.

b. **Professional Certifications**: Pursuit of relevant certifications, qualifications, and memberships in regulatory affairs organizations to enhance skills, credibility, and career advancement prospects.

RESPONSIBILITY OF REGULATORY AFFAIRS PROFESSIONALS

Regulatory Affairs (RA) professionals are crucial in ensuring that products comply with all relevant laws and regulations throughout their lifecycle. They work across various industries, including pharmaceuticals, biotechnology, medical devices, cosmetics, and food. Here's a detailed look at the responsibilities of RA professionals:

1. Regulatory Strategy and Planning

  a. **Regulatory Landscape Analysis**: RA professionals analyze the regulatory environment to develop strategies that align with product development and commercialization plans.

  b. **Strategic Planning**: They devise regulatory strategies for new products, including identifying the most efficient pathways for obtaining market approval.

  c. **Lifecycle Management**: They plan for regulatory compliance from product conception through post-market surveillance, ensuring ongoing adherence to regulations.

2. Regulatory Submissions and Documentation

  a. **Preparation of Submissions**: Preparing and compiling regulatory submission dossiers, including Investigational New Drug (IND) applications, New Drug Applications (NDA), Marketing Authorization Applications (MAA), and other relevant documentation.

  b. **Quality Control**: Ensuring that all submissions are accurate, complete, and meet the specific requirements of regulatory authorities.

  c. **Filing and Tracking**: Filing submissions with regulatory agencies and tracking the progress of these submissions through the review process.

3. Compliance and Quality Assurance

  a. **Regulatory Compliance**: Ensuring that company practices, product manufacturing, and testing comply with applicable regulations, guidelines, and standards such as GMP, GCP, and GLP.

  b. **Audit Preparation**: Preparing for and managing regulatory inspections and audits, addressing any findings or compliance issues identified by regulatory agencies.

c. **Internal Audits**: Conducting internal audits to proactively identify and correct compliance issues.

4. Labeling and Advertising Review

a. **Labeling Compliance**: Reviewing and approving product labeling to ensure it meets regulatory requirements for content, format, and accuracy.

b. **Promotional Materials**: Evaluating advertising and promotional materials to ensure they are truthful, not misleading, and comply with regulatory standards.

5. Clinical Trials and Research Oversight

a. **Trial Documentation**: Preparing regulatory documentation for clinical trial applications and amendments, ensuring compliance with regulatory requirements.

b. **Ethical Compliance**: Ensuring that clinical trials adhere to ethical standards, including informed consent and patient safety.

c. **Trial Monitoring**: Overseeing the conduct of clinical trials to ensure compliance with regulatory and ethical standards.

6. Post-Market Surveillance and Reporting

a. **Pharmacovigilance**: Monitoring the safety and efficacy of products after they reach the market, collecting and analyzing adverse event reports.

b. **Safety Reporting**: Submitting periodic safety update reports (PSURs) and other required post-market surveillance documents to regulatory agencies.

c. **Recall Management**: Managing product recalls or withdrawals when necessary, including communication with regulatory agencies and stakeholders.

7. Risk Management

a. **Risk Assessment**: Identifying potential risks associated with product development and commercialization, and developing strategies to mitigate these risks.

b. **Crisis Management**: Responding to regulatory issues or crises, such as product recalls or compliance breaches, and implementing corrective actions.

8. Liaison and Advocacy

a. **Regulatory Liaison**: Acting as the primary point of contact between the company and regulatory authorities, facilitating clear and effective communication.

b. **Internal Communication**: Coordinating with internal departments, such as R&D, manufacturing, and marketing, to ensure regulatory requirements are understood and met.

c. **Industry Advocacy**: Participating in industry groups and advocating for regulatory policies that support innovation and public health.

9. Training and Development

a. **Employee Training:** Educating and training company employees on regulatory requirements and compliance practices.

b. **Professional Development**: Staying current with changes in regulations, guidelines, and industry standards through continuous learning and professional development.

10. Documentation and Record Keeping

a. **Regulatory Records**: Maintaining detailed records of all regulatory submissions, communications with regulatory authorities, and compliance activities.

b. **Document Management**: Ensuring that all regulatory documents are organized, up-to-date, and accessible for audit and inspection purposes.

Key Skills and Attributes for RA Professionals

1. **Analytical Skills**: Ability to interpret complex regulations and guidelines accurately.

2. **Communication Skills**: Proficient in communicating with regulatory authorities and internal stakeholders effectively.

3. **Attention to Detail**: Ensuring precision and accuracy in documentation and submissions.

4. **Problem-Solving**: Capable of anticipating regulatory challenges and developing strategic solutions.

5. **Project Management**: Managing multiple projects and timelines efficiently.

Multiple-Choice Questions (MCQs)

1. What does the Regulatory Affairs department ensure in industries like pharmaceuticals and medical devices?

    A) Marketing strategies

    B) Compliance with regulatory requirements

    C) Sales targets are met

    D) Production efficiency

2. Which applications is part of the documentation required for product approval in regulatory submissions?

    A) Business development plans

    B) Investigational New Drug (IND) applications

    C) Human resource policies

    D) Financial statements

3. What is the primary role of the FDA?

    A) Funding pharmaceutical companies

    B) Regulating food and drug safety in the United States

    C) Managing hospital administrations

    D) Direct sales of medical products

4. Which of the following is a focus of medical devices regulation?

    A) Risk-based approach to regulatory submissions

    B) Celebrity endorsements

    C) Product pricing strategies

    D) Advertising on social media

5. What are Good Manufacturing Practice (GMP) requirements intended to ensure?

   A) Environmental protection

   B) Employee safety only

   C) Marketing strategies

   D) Product quality and safety

6. Which agency regulates medicinal products within the European Union?

   A) CDC

   B) EMA

   C) WHO

   D) UNESCO

7. The International Conference on Harmonisation (ICH) provides guidelines to harmonize:

   A) Educational standards

   B) Taxation in pharmaceutical sales

   C) Regulatory requirements across different regions

   D) Employment laws across countries

8. Which amendment defined the categories of drugs that could only be dispensed with a prescription?

   A) Kefauver-Harris Amendment

   B) Durham-Humphrey Amendment

   C) Federal Food, Drug, and Cosmetic Act

   D) Pure Food and Drug Act

9. What is a primary purpose of post-market surveillance?

   A) Monitor product placement in stores

   B) Evaluate ongoing product promotions

   C) Monitor the safety and efficacy of products aftermarket release

   D) Assess customer satisfaction through surveys

10. Which act requires new drugs to be proven safe before marketing in the United States?

A) Biologics Control Act

B) Federal Food, Drug, and Cosmetic Act

C) Durham-Humphrey Amendment

D) Pure Food and Drug Act

11. What does the Kefauver-Harris Amendment require from drug manufacturers?

A) Proof of drug popularity

B) Advertisement approvals

C) Proof of effectiveness and safety before approval

D) Investment in government bonds

12. The Prescription Drug User Fee Act (PDUFA) was enacted to:

A) Decrease the cost of prescription drugs

B) Provide additional resources for the FDA to review new drug applications quickly

C) Ban certain drugs from the market

D) Increase pharmaceutical companies' profits

13. Which agency was established to promote international public health?

A) FDA

B) EMA

C) WHO

D) ICH

14. What significant regulatory aspect does the Federal Food, Drug, and Cosmetic Act (1938) cover?

A) Prohibiting the interstate commerce of adulterated foods

B) Expanding FDA's authority and requiring pre-market safety evaluations

C) Establishing USDA

D) Requiring cosmetic products to have detailed ingredient labels

15. The formation of the EMA in 1995 was primarily to:

    A) Oversee non-European medicinal markets

    B) Centralize the regulation of medicines across EU member states

    C) Supervise the agricultural sector in Europe

    D) Develop new medical education programs

16. In the context of regulatory affairs, what is GCP primarily concerned with?

    A) Investment and finance regulations

    B) Ensuring proper clinical trial conduct and participant safety

    C) Supervising post-marketing campaigns

    D) Managing healthcare facility operations

17. Which document is essential for starting clinical trials involving new drugs?

    A) IND (Investigational New Drug application)

    B) PDUFA documentation

    C) FDA annual report

    D) WHO certification

18. Good Laboratory Practice (GLP) standards are primarily established to ensure:

    A) The environmental sustainability of laboratories

    B) The integrity and quality of nonclinical laboratory studies

    C) Employee benefits in pharmaceutical companies

    D) Effective product distribution channels

19. The role of pharmacovigilance is to:

    A) Oversee financial auditing in pharmaceuticals

    B) Monitor the safety of drugs post-market release

    C) Manage pharmacy retail chains

    D) Conduct global marketing strategies

20. What is the main function of risk management in the context of regulatory affairs?

A) To ensure all marketing activities are risk-free

B) To identify, assess, and mitigate risks associated with healthcare products

C) To eliminate financial risks in drug development

D) To manage insurance claims in medical facilities

Short Answer Type Questions

1. What is the primary role of the Regulatory Affairs department in a pharmaceutical company?

2. How does the Regulatory Affairs department ensure compliance with Good Manufacturing Practices (GMP)?

3. What are the responsibilities of Regulatory Affairs in the lifecycle management of a product?

4. What is involved in the preparation of an Investigational New Drug (IND) application?

5. Describe the importance of the European Medicines Agency (EMA) in regulatory affairs.

6. How do regulatory affairs professionals stay updated on changes in regulatory standards and guidelines?

7. What role does the Regulatory Affairs department play in post-market surveillance?

8. Explain the significance of risk management in the Regulatory Affairs department.

9. What are the main functions of the Regulatory Affairs department during a product recall?

10. How does the Regulatory Affairs department interact with regulatory agencies?

11. What is the process of obtaining a New Drug Application (NDA) approval?

12. Describe the role of Good Clinical Practice (GCP) in clinical trials.

13. What is involved in the labeling and advertising compliance process?

14. How does the Regulatory Affairs department support clinical trial operations?

15. What are the consequences of non-compliance with regulatory requirements?

16. Explain the process of pharmacovigilance in post-market surveillance.

17. What methods do Regulatory Affairs professionals use to perform risk assessments?

18. How do regulatory affairs professionals contribute to the strategic planning for new products?

19. Describe the process of preparing and submitting marketing authorization applications.

20. What is the role of the Regulatory Affairs department in managing product quality issues?

Long Answer Type Questions

1. Discuss the impact of international regulatory harmonization on the pharmaceutical industry and how it affects regulatory affairs strategies.

2. Describe the role and importance of the International Conference on Harmonisation (ICH) in global pharmaceutical development.

3. Explain the process and significance of Good Manufacturing Practice (GMP) in ensuring product quality and safety in the pharmaceutical industry.

4. Discuss the challenges faced by the Regulatory Affairs department in managing the lifecycle of a medical device from conception to market release.

5. Describe how the Regulatory Affairs department interacts with the Food and Drug Administration (FDA) during the drug approval process.

6. Explain the significance of post-market surveillance in maintaining the safety and efficacy of pharmaceutical products.

7. Describe the steps involved in developing and executing a regulatory strategy for a new biologic product.

8. Discuss the role of the Regulatory Affairs department in ensuring compliance with Good Clinical Practice (GCP) during clinical trials.

9. Explain how advancements in digital health technologies have impacted regulatory affairs and what challenges they present.

10. Discuss the role of risk management in regulatory affairs and how it helps in mitigating potential issues throughout the product lifecycle.

Answer Key

1. (B) Compliance with regulatory requirements

2. (B) Investigational New Drug (IND) applications

3. (B) Regulating food and drug safety in the United States

4. (A) Risk-based approach to regulatory submissions

5. (D) Product quality and safety

6. (B) EMA

7. (C) Regulatory requirements across different regions

8. (B) Durham-Humphrey Amendment

9. (C) Monitor the safety and efficacy of products after market release

10. (B) Federal Food, Drug, and Cosmetic Act

11. (C) Proof of effectiveness and safety before approval

12. (B) Provide additional resources for the FDA to review new drug applications quickly

13. (C) WHO

14. (B) Expanding FDA's authority and requiring pre-market safety evaluations

15. (B) Centralize the regulation of medicines across EU member states

16.(B) Ensuring proper clinical trial conduct and participant safety

17.(A) IND (Investigational New Drug application)

18.(B) The integrity and quality of nonclinical laboratory studies

19.(B) Monitor the safety of drugs post-market release

20.(B) To identify, assess, and mitigate risks associated with healthcare products

CHAPTER - 4

REGULATORY REQUIREMENTS FOR DRUG APPROVAL

INTRODUCTION:

The regulatory requirements for drug approval are a complex and rigorous set of guidelines established to ensure that new pharmaceuticals are safe and effective for human use. These requirements vary by country but generally follow similar principles. Here's a detailed introduction to the process:

1. Preclinical Testing

Before a drug can be tested in humans, it must undergo extensive laboratory and animal studies to evaluate its safety and biological activity. This phase includes:

a. **In vitro studies**: Laboratory tests on cell cultures to assess the drug's biological activity.

b. **In vivo studies**: Animal testing to evaluate the pharmacokinetics (how the drug is absorbed, distributed, metabolized, and excreted) and pharmacodynamics (the biological effects of the drug) as well as toxicity.

2. Investigational New Drug Application (IND)

After preclinical testing, a pharmaceutical company must file an IND application with the regulatory authority (e.g., the FDA in the United States). This application includes:

a. Results of preclinical studies

b. Manufacturing information

c. Clinical trial protocols for human testing

d. Investigator information to ensure they are qualified

e. An IRB (Institutional Review Board) approval

The regulatory body reviews the IND to ensure that the proposed studies do not place human subjects at unreasonable risk.

3. Clinical Trials

Clinical trials are conducted in three phases to assess the drug's safety and efficacy in humans:

a. **Phase I:** Small group (20-100 healthy volunteers or patients) to evaluate the drug's safety, determine a safe dosage range, and identify side effects.

b. **Phase II:** Larger group (100-300 patients) to determine the drug's efficacy and further evaluate its safety.

c. **Phase III:** Large group (1,000-3,000 patients) to confirm its effectiveness, monitor side effects, compare it to commonly used treatments, and collect information that will allow the drug to be used safely.

4. New Drug Application (NDA)

If clinical trials demonstrate that the drug is safe and effective, the company submits an NDA to the regulatory authority. The NDA includes:

a. Comprehensive data from preclinical and clinical trials

b. Proposed labeling

c. Information on drug manufacturing

d. Data on stability and shelf-life

The regulatory authority reviews the NDA to determine if the drug should be approved for marketing. This process includes detailed reviews by medical and scientific experts.

5. Regulatory Review and Approval

During the review process, the regulatory authority may:

a. Request additional studies or data

b. Hold advisory committee meetings

c. Inspect manufacturing facilities

If the drug is approved, the regulatory authority will issue an approval letter. If not, they will provide a complete response letter detailing the reasons for the decision and the steps required for approval.

6. Post-Marketing Surveillance

After a drug is approved, it enters the post-marketing surveillance phase (Phase IV). This phase involves:

a. Ongoing monitoring of the drug's safety and effectiveness in the general population

b. Reporting of adverse events and side effects

c. Additional studies as required by the regulatory authority to further assess long-term effects or specific populations

7. Regulatory Authorities Around the World

Different countries have their own regulatory bodies and processes:

a. **United States**: Food and Drug Administration (FDA)

b. **European Union**: European Medicines Agency (EMA)

c. **Japan:** Pharmaceuticals and Medical Devices Agency (PMDA)

d. **China**: National Medical Products Administration (NMPA)

Each of these bodies has its own guidelines and requirements, but they often collaborate to harmonize standards through organizations like the International Council for Harmonisation of Technical Requirements for Pharmaceuticals for Human Use (ICH).

DRUG DEVELOPMENT TEAMS

The development and approval of a new drug involve a multidisciplinary team working together to navigate the complex regulatory requirements. Each team plays a critical role in ensuring that the drug meets the necessary standards for safety, efficacy, and quality. Here's a detailed look at the key teams involved in the drug development process:

1. Research and Development (R&D) Team

Roles and Responsibilities:

a. **Discovery Scientists**: Focus on identifying potential drug candidates through various techniques, including high-throughput screening, molecular biology, and medicinal chemistry.

b. **Preclinical Researchers**: Conduct laboratory and animal studies to evaluate the drug's safety, pharmacokinetics, and pharmacodynamics.

2. Regulatory Affairs Team

Roles and Responsibilities:

a. **Regulatory Strategists**: Develop strategies to ensure compliance with regulatory requirements and to facilitate the approval process.

b. **Regulatory Writers**: Prepare and submit regulatory documents, including IND applications, NDAs, and Clinical Study Reports (CSRs).

c. **Liaisons**: Act as intermediaries between the company and regulatory authorities, ensuring clear and effective communication.

3. Clinical Development Team

Roles and Responsibilities:

a. **Clinical Trial Managers**: Oversee the planning, execution, and management of clinical trials.

b. **Clinical Research Associates (CRAs)**: Monitor clinical trial sites to ensure compliance with protocols and regulatory requirements.

c. **Biostatisticians**: Design clinical trials and analyze data to determine the drug's efficacy and safety.

4. Quality Assurance (QA) Team

Roles and Responsibilities:

a. **QA Specialists**: Ensure that all aspects of the drug development process comply with Good Laboratory Practice (GLP), Good Clinical Practice (GCP), and Good Manufacturing Practice (GMP).

b. **Auditors:** Conduct internal audits and inspections to verify compliance and identify areas for improvement.

5. Manufacturing and Supply Chain Team

Roles and Responsibilities:

a. **Process Engineers**: Develop and optimize the manufacturing process to ensure consistent drug quality.

b. **Supply Chain Managers**: Coordinate the sourcing of raw materials and the distribution of the finished product.

c. **Production Supervisors**: Oversee the day-to-day operations of the manufacturing facility.

6. Medical Affairs Team

Roles and Responsibilities:

a. **Medical Directors**: Provide medical expertise and oversight during the drug development process.

b. **Medical Science Liaisons (MSLs)**: Communicate scientific information to healthcare professionals and gather insights from the medical community.

c. **Pharmacovigilance Specialists**: Monitor and report adverse events and side effects to ensure the drug's ongoing safety.

7. Marketing and Commercial Team

Roles and Responsibilities:

a. **Market Analysts**: Conduct market research to understand the competitive landscape and identify potential market opportunities.

b. **Product Managers**: Develop marketing strategies and materials to support the drug's launch and commercialization.

c. **Sales Representatives**: Educate healthcare providers about the new drug and its benefits.

8. Legal and Compliance Team

Roles and Responsibilities:

a. **Legal Advisors**: Provide legal counsel on intellectual property, contracts, and regulatory compliance.

b. **Compliance Officers**: Ensure adherence to all applicable laws, regulations, and ethical standards throughout the drug development process.

9. Health Economics and Outcomes Research (HEOR) Team

Roles and Responsibilities:

a. **HEOR Analysts**: Conduct studies to evaluate the economic value of the drug and its impact on patient outcomes.

b. **Health Policy Experts**: Work on strategies to gain reimbursement and market access from healthcare payers and policymakers.

NON-CLINICAL DRUG DEVELOPMENT

Non-clinical drug development, also known as preclinical development, is a critical phase in the drug development process that involves laboratory and animal studies to evaluate a new drug candidate's safety and biological activity before it can be tested in humans. Here's a detailed look at the non-clinical drug development phase and its regulatory requirements:

Objectives of Non-Clinical Drug Development

1. **Safety Assessment**: To identify potential toxic effects and determine a safe starting dose for clinical trials.

2. **Pharmacokinetics (PK)**: To understand how the drug is absorbed, distributed, metabolized, and excreted in the body.

3. **Pharmacodynamics (PD)**: To study the biological effects of the drug and its mechanism of action.

4. **Efficacy Assessment**: To provide initial evidence that the drug has the desired therapeutic effect.

Key Components of Non-Clinical Drug Development

1. Pharmacological Studies

a. **Primary Pharmacodynamics**: Studies to determine the mechanism of action and therapeutic potential of the drug.

b. **Secondary Pharmacodynamics**: Studies to identify any unintended effects on physiological functions.

2. Toxicology Studies

a. **Acute Toxicity:** Assessment of toxic effects after a single dose or multiple doses within 24 hours.

b. **Sub-chronic Toxicity**: Studies that involve repeated dosing over a period of up to 90 days to identify potential toxic effects.

c. **Chronic Toxicity**: Long-term studies, typically lasting six months to two years, to observe any prolonged toxic effects.

d. **Genotoxicity**: Tests to determine if the drug can cause genetic mutations or chromosomal damage.

e. **Carcinogenicity:** Long-term studies to evaluate if the drug has the potential to cause cancer.

f. **Reproductive and Developmental Toxicity**: Studies to assess the drug's impact on fertility, embryonic development, and postnatal development.

3. Pharmacokinetics (PK) and Pharmacodynamics (PD)

a. **Absorption**: How the drug is absorbed into the bloodstream.

b. **Distribution:** How the drug is distributed throughout the body's tissues.

c. **Metabolism**: How the drug is metabolized by the body, typically in the liver.

d. **Excretion:** How the drug and its metabolites are excreted from the body, usually via urine or feces.

4. Other Safety Studies

a. **Immunotoxicity**: Assessment of the drug's potential to affect the immune system.

b. **Safety Pharmacology**: Studies to investigate the drug's effects on vital functions, particularly the cardiovascular, respiratory, and central nervous systems.

Regulatory Requirements and Guidelines

1. Good Laboratory Practice (GLP)

a. **GLP Standards**: Ensuring that all non-clinical studies are conducted according to standardized procedures to ensure quality and integrity of the data.

b. **Documentation**: Comprehensive documentation of study protocols, procedures, and results.

2. Regulatory Submissions

a. **Investigational New Drug (IND) Application**: Submission to regulatory authorities, such as the FDA in the United States, including all non-clinical study data, to obtain permission to start clinical trials in humans.

b. **Common Technical Document (CTD):** A standardized format for regulatory submissions in the European Union, Japan, and other regions, including a section dedicated to non-clinical study reports.

3. International Guidelines

International Council for Harmonisation (ICH) Guidelines: Harmonized guidelines that provide a unified standard for the European Union, Japan, and the United States. Key guidelines relevant to non-clinical development include:

a. **ICH M3(R2):** Guidance on non-clinical safety studies for the conduct of human clinical trials and marketing authorization.

b. **ICH S1-S9:** Specific guidelines covering various aspects of non-clinical safety testing, including carcinogenicity (S1), genotoxicity (S2), and reproductive toxicity (S5).

PHARMACOLOGY

Pharmacology plays a crucial role in the regulatory requirements for drug approval, encompassing the study of a drug's biological effects, mechanisms of action, and therapeutic potential. Understanding pharmacology is essential for assessing a new drug's efficacy and safety. Here's a detailed examination of the pharmacological aspects within the drug approval process:

Objectives of Pharmacology in Drug Development

1. **Determine Mechanism of Action**: Understand how the drug interacts with biological targets to produce its effects.
2. **Assess Therapeutic Potential**: Evaluate the drug's potential to treat or prevent a disease.
3. **Identify Side Effects**: Determine any adverse effects the drug may cause.
4. **Optimize Drug Dosing**: Find the appropriate dose that maximizes efficacy while minimizing side effects.

Key Components of Pharmacology in Drug Development

1. Primary Pharmacodynamics

a. **Target Identification and Validation**: Identifying the biological target (e.g., receptor, enzyme) that the drug interacts with and validating its role in the disease process.
b. **Mechanism of Action Studies**: Investigating how the drug interacts with its target to produce a therapeutic effect. This includes receptor binding studies, enzyme inhibition assays, and pathway analysis.
c. **Efficacy Studies**: Assessing the drug's effectiveness in disease models, often using in vitro (cell cultures) and in vivo (animal models) systems to demonstrate therapeutic potential.

2. Secondary Pharmacodynamics

a. **Off-Target Effects**: Evaluating the drug's effects on other biological targets that are not intended but may produce therapeutic or adverse effects.

b. **Safety Pharmacology**: Investigating potential effects on major organ systems, particularly cardiovascular, respiratory, and central nervous systems, to ensure the drug does not have harmful off-target effects.

Pharmacokinetics (PK) and Pharmacodynamics (PD) Integration

1. Pharmacokinetics (PK)

a. **Absorption:** How the drug enters the bloodstream from the site of administration.

b. **Distribution**: How the drug disperses throughout the body's tissues and organs.

c. **Metabolism: How** the drug is chemically altered by the body, often in the liver.

d. **Excretion:** How the drug and its metabolites are eliminated from the body, typically through urine or feces.

2. Pharmacodynamics (PD)

a. **Dose-Response Relationship**: The relationship between drug concentration and its effects, determining the minimum effective dose and the dose that produces maximum response without adverse effects.

b. **Therapeutic Index**: The ratio between the toxic dose and the effective dose, providing an indication of the drug's safety margin.

Regulatory Requirements and Guidelines

1. Preclinical Pharmacology Studies

a. **Good Laboratory Practice (GLP):** Ensuring that all pharmacological studies adhere to standardized procedures to produce reliable and reproducible results.

b. **ICH Guideli**nes: Key guidelines from the International Council for Harmonisation that pertain to pharmacological studies include:

    a. **ICH S7A:** Safety Pharmacology Studies for Human Pharmaceuticals, outlining the evaluation of drug effects on vital organ systems.

b. **ICH M3(R2): Non**-clinical Safety Studies for the Conduct of Human Clinical Trials and Marketing Authorization for Pharmaceuticals, which includes pharmacological testing requirements.

2. Clinical Pharmacology Studies

a. **Phase I Clinical Trials**: Initial human studies focusing on pharmacokinetics, pharmacodynamics, safety, and tolerability in healthy volunteers.

b. **Phase II and III Clinical Trials**: Further evaluation of efficacy and safety in patients, with continued assessment of PK and PD to optimize dosing regimens.

c. **Population Pharmacokinetics**: Analysis of PK data from diverse populations to understand how different factors (e.g., age, gender, disease state) affect drug behavior.

Documentation and Submission

1. Investigational New Drug (IND) Application

a. **Preclinical Pharmacology Data**: Detailed reports on primary and secondary pharmacodynamics, safety pharmacology, and PK/PD studies.

b. **Study Protocols**: Plans for clinical pharmacology studies, including rationale, objectives, and methodology.

2. New Drug Application (NDA)

a. **Clinical Pharmacology Section**: Comprehensive analysis of PK/PD data, dose-response relationships, therapeutic index, and safety margins.

b. **Integrated Summary**: Summary of pharmacological findings integrated with clinical data to support the overall assessment of the drug's efficacy and safety.

DRUG METABOLISM

Drug metabolism is a crucial aspect of the drug development process, providing essential insights into how a drug is processed within the body.

Understanding drug metabolism helps in predicting drug interactions, potential side effects, and the drug's overall efficacy and safety. Here's a detailed overview of the role of drug metabolism in regulatory requirements for drug approval:

Objectives of Drug Metabolism Studies

1. **Identify Metabolic Pathways**: Determine how the drug is metabolized in the body.
2. **Characterize Metabolites**: Identify and characterize the metabolites formed during drug metabolism.
3. **Understand Pharmacokinetics**: Understand how the drug is absorbed, distributed, metabolized, and excreted (ADME).
4. **Assess Drug-Drug Interactions**: Evaluate potential interactions with other drugs.
5. **Determine Safety and Efficacy**: Ensure that the drug and its metabolites are safe and effective.

Key Components of Drug Metabolism Studies

1. In Vitro Metabolism Studies

a. **Liver Microsomes and Hepatocytes**: Use of human and animal liver microsomes and hepatocytes to study the metabolic pathways and the role of liver enzymes, primarily cytochrome P450 enzymes.
b. **Recombinant Enzymes**: Utilization of specific enzymes to identify which ones are responsible for the metabolism of the drug.
c. **Metabolite Identification**: Determination of the chemical structure of metabolites formed during in vitro studies.

2. In Vivo Metabolism Studies

a. **Animal Studies**: Conducting studies in animals to understand how the drug is metabolized and to identify major metabolites.
b. **Human Studies**: Clinical studies to characterize the drug's metabolism in humans, often performed during Phase I trials.

Pharmacokinetics and Pharmacodynamics (PK/PD)

a. **Absorption**: Studying how the drug enters the bloodstream.

b. **Distribution**: Understanding how the drug spreads through the body's tissues.

c. **Metabolism**: Investigating how the drug is broken down, primarily by the liver.

d. **Excretion**: Analyzing how the drug and its metabolites are eliminated from the body, typically via urine or feces.

Regulatory Requirements and Guidelines

1. Good Laboratory Practice (GLP)

i. **GLP Compliance**: Ensuring that all drug metabolism studies adhere to GLP standards to guarantee the quality and integrity of the data.

2. Regulatory Submissions

i. **Investigational New Drug (IND) Application**: Submission includes detailed reports on preclinical metabolism studies to obtain permission for clinical trials.

ii. **New Drug Application (NDA)**: Includes comprehensive data on drug metabolism and pharmacokinetics from both preclinical and clinical studies.

3. International Guidelines

i. **ICH Guidelines**: Key guidelines from the International Council for Harmonisation (ICH) relevant to drug metabolism include:

a. **ICH M3(R2)**: Non-clinical Safety Studies for the Conduct of Human Clinical Trials and Marketing Authorization for Pharmaceuticals.

b. **ICH S3A**: Toxicokinetics: The Assessment of Systemic Exposure in Toxicity Studies.

c. **ICH S3B**: Pharmacokinetics: Guidance for Repeated Dose Tissue Distribution Studies.

d. **ICH M4Q**: The Common Technical Document (CTD) - Quality, which includes a section on drug metabolism and pharmacokinetics.

Specific Studies and Assessments

1. Metabolic Pathway Identification

   a. **Enzyme Identification**: Determining which enzymes are involved in the drug's metabolism, with a focus on cytochrome P450 enzymes.

   b. **Pathway Elucidation**: Mapping the metabolic pathways and identifying primary and secondary metabolites.

2. Drug-Drug Interaction Studies

   a. **In Vitro Interaction Studies**: Testing how the drug affects the metabolism of other drugs and vice versa using liver microsomes and hepatocytes.

   b. **Clinical Interaction Studies**: Conducting clinical studies to assess potential interactions with commonly co-administered drugs.

3. Metabolite Characterization

   a. **Toxicology of Metabolites**: Evaluating the safety of major metabolites, including those that may have different pharmacological or toxicological properties compared to the parent drug.

   b. **Pharmacological Activity**: Determining the pharmacological activity of metabolites, including efficacy and potential side effects.

Documentation and Reporting

   a. **Comprehensive Reporting**: Detailed documentation of all metabolic studies, including methodologies, results, and interpretation of data.

   b. **Integrated Summaries**: Summarizing metabolism data in regulatory submissions such as the IND and NDA, ensuring that regulatory authorities can thoroughly assess the drug's metabolic profile.

TOXICOLOGY

Toxicology is a critical aspect of drug development, focusing on assessing the potential adverse effects of a new drug. Toxicology studies are designed to ensure that a drug is safe for human use and to identify any potential risks before the drug is administered to humans in clinical trials. Here's a detailed look at the role of toxicology in the regulatory requirements for drug approval:

Objectives of Toxicology Studies

1. **Identify Toxic Effects**: Determine the adverse effects and toxic potential of the drug.

2. **Establish Safe Doses:** Identify the dose levels that are safe for initial human trials and therapeutic use.

3. **Understand Mechanisms of Toxicity**: Elucidate the mechanisms by which the drug causes toxicity.

4. **Assess Long-Term Safety**: Evaluate the potential for long-term or chronic toxic effects.

5. **Support Regulatory Submissions**: Provide essential data to support regulatory applications for clinical trials and marketing approval.

Key Components of Toxicology Studies

1. General Toxicology

i. **Acute Toxicity:** Evaluation of toxic effects following a single dose or multiple doses within a short period (typically 24 hours).

   a. **Single-Dose Studies**: Determine the lethal dose (LD50) and observe any immediate toxic effects.

ii. **Sub-chronic Toxicity**: Studies involving repeated dosing over a period of up to 90 days to identify any cumulative toxic effects.

   a. **28-Day Studies**: Short-term repeated dose studies to identify target organs of toxicity and establish a no observed adverse effect level (NOAEL).

b. **90-Day Studies**: Intermediate-term studies to further characterize the toxicological profile and refine the NOAEL.

iii. **Chronic Toxicity**: Long-term studies, typically lasting 6 months to 2 years, to observe any chronic toxic effects and support long-term safety.

   a. **6-Month Rodent Studies**: Assess potential chronic effects in rodents.

   b. **9-Month Non-Rodent** Studies: Evaluate chronic effects in non-rodent species (e.g., dogs or monkeys).

2. Genotoxicity

i. **In Vitro Genotoxicity Tests**: Assess the potential of the drug to cause genetic mutations or chromosomal damage.

   a. **Ames Test:** Bacterial reverse mutation assay to detect mutagenicity.

   b. **Micronucleus Test**: Evaluates chromosomal damage in cultured cells.

   c. **Chromosomal Aberration Test**: Detects structural chromosomal changes in mammalian cells.

ii. **In Vivo Genotoxicity Tests**: Confirm the findings from in vitro tests and assess the potential for genotoxicity in live animals.

   a. **Rodent Bone Marrow Micronucleus Test:** Measures chromosomal damage in bone marrow cells.

   b. **Comet Assay**: Detects DNA strand breaks in cells from various tissues.

3. Reproductive and Developmental Toxicity

i. **Fertility Studies**: Assess the impact of the drug on reproductive performance in male and female animals.

ii. **Embryo-Fetal Development Studies**: Evaluate the effects on embryo development during organogenesis.

a. **Segment II Studies**: Assess the potential for teratogenic effects and developmental toxicity.

iii. **Pre- and Postnatal Development Studies**: Investigate the effects on offspring following exposure during late pregnancy and lactation.

a. **Segment III Studies**: Evaluate the effects on development and behavior of offspring.

4. Carcinogenicity

i. **Long-Term Carcinogenicity Studies**: Assess the potential of the drug to cause cancer following long-term exposure.

a. **2-Year Rodent Studies**: Standard studies in mice and rats to evaluate carcinogenic potential.

ii. **Short-Term Carcinogenicity Studies**: Alternative models and methodologies to provide early insights into carcinogenic risks.

a. **Transgenic Mouse Models**: Utilize genetically modified mice that are more prone to developing tumors.

5. Other Toxicology Studies

i. **Immunotoxicity**: Evaluate the potential impact on the immune system, including hypersensitivity and immunosuppression.

ii. **Safety Pharmacology**: Focus on identifying any adverse effects on vital physiological functions, particularly cardiovascular, respiratory, and central nervous systems.

iii. **Toxicokinetics**: Study the absorption, distribution, metabolism, and excretion (ADME) of the drug to correlate exposure with toxic effects.

Regulatory Requirements and Guidelines

1. Good Laboratory Practice (GLP)

i. **GLP Standards**: Ensuring all toxicology studies adhere to GLP to ensure the reliability and integrity of the data.

ii. **Documentation**: Comprehensive records of study protocols, procedures, and results.

2. Regulatory Submissions

i.   **Investigational New Drug (IND) Application**: Submission to regulatory authorities (e.g., FDA, EMA) including detailed toxicology data to support the initiation of clinical trials.

ii. **New Drug Application (NDA)**: Submission includes comprehensive toxicology data from preclinical and clinical studies to support marketing approval.

3. International Guidelines

i.   **ICH Guidelines**: Key guidelines from the International Council for Harmonisation (ICH) relevant to toxicology studies include:

   a. **ICH S1A-S1C**: Carcinogenicity Studies.

   b. **ICH S2(R1):** Genotoxicity Testing and Data Interpretation.

   c. **ICH S3A-S3B:** Toxicokinetics and Tissue Distribution.

   d. **ICH S5(R3)**: Reproductive and Developmental Toxicity.

   e. **ICH S6(R1):** Preclinical Safety Evaluation of Biotechnology-Derived Pharmaceuticals.

   f. **ICH S7A**: Safety Pharmacology Studies.

   g. **ICH M3(R2):** Nonclinical Safety Studies for the Conduct of Human Clinical Trials and Marketing Authorization.

GENERAL CONSIDERATIONS OF INVESTIGATIONAL NEW DRUG (IND) APPLICATION

The Investigational New Drug (IND) application is a critical regulatory step in the drug development process. It serves as a request to the regulatory authority, typically the FDA in the United States, for permission to start clinical trials of a new drug in humans. Here's a detailed look at the general considerations and requirements for an IND application:

Objectives of an IND Application

1. **Ensure Safety and Rights of Participants**: Protect the safety and rights of human subjects involved in clinical trials.

2. **Provide Scientific Evidence**: Demonstrate that the preclinical data supports the initial testing of the drug in humans.

3. **Outline Clinical Trial Plans**: Present detailed plans for clinical studies, including protocols and methodologies.

Key Components of an IND Application

1. Preclinical Study Data

a. **Pharmacology and Toxicology Studies**: Detailed reports on pharmacological effects, mechanism of action, and toxicology studies in animals.

   i. **Pharmacodynamics (PD):** Information on how the drug affects the biological system.

   ii. **Pharmacokinetics (PK)**: Data on absorption, distribution, metabolism, and excretion (ADME) in animal models.

   iii. **Toxicology**: Results from acute, sub-chronic, and chronic toxicity studies, Genotoxicity, reproductive toxicity, and carcinogenicity studies.

2. Chemistry, Manufacturing, and Controls (CMC)

a. **Drug Substance and Product Information**: Detailed information on the drug's chemical composition, manufacturing process, and quality control measures.

   i. **Identification and Characterization**: Chemical structure, physical and chemical properties, and methods of synthesis or extraction.

   ii. **Manufacturing Process**: Description of the manufacturing process, including raw materials, intermediates, and final product specifications.

   iii. **Quality Control: Procedures** for ensuring batch-to-batch consistency, stability testing, and validation of analytical methods.

3. Clinical Protocols

a. **Study Design**: Detailed description of the study design, including objectives, methodology, endpoints, and statistical analysis plan.

  I. **Phase I Trials**: Initial human studies focusing on safety, tolerability, pharmacokinetics, and pharmacodynamics in healthy volunteers or patients.

  II. **Phase II and III Trials**: Subsequent studies to evaluate efficacy, optimal dosing, and longer-term safety in patient populations.

b. **Informed Consent**: Process for obtaining informed consent from study participants, including information on the risks and benefits of participation.

c. **Investigator Information**: Qualifications and experience of the principal investigators and study staff.

4. Previous Human Experience

a. **Prior Clinical Data**: If the drug has been tested previously in humans, a summary of the data and any observed adverse effects.

b. **Foreign Clinical Trials**: Data from clinical trials conducted outside the United States, if applicable.

Regulatory Requirements and Guidelines

1. Good Clinical Practice (GCP)

1. **GCP Standards**: Ensuring that clinical trials are conducted ethically and according to established standards to protect the rights and well-being of participants.

2. **Documentation**: Detailed documentation of study protocols, informed consent forms, and investigator credentials.

2. Regulatory Submission

1. **Submission Format**: The IND application must be submitted in a standardized format, often using the Common Technical Document (CTD) structure.

  a. **Module 1:** Administrative and prescribing information.

b. **Module 2:** Summaries of the quality, safety, and efficacy information.

c. **Module 3:** Quality information (CMC).

d. **Module 4:** Non-clinical study reports.

e. **Module 5:** Clinical study reports.

2. **Electronic Submissions:** Many regulatory agencies, including the FDA, require or encourage electronic submission of IND applications.

3. Review and Approval

1. **Regulatory Review:** The regulatory authority reviews the IND application to ensure the proposed clinical trial is safe and scientifically sound.

2. **30-Day Review Period:** In the United States, the FDA has 30 days to review the IND application. If there are no objections, the clinical trial may proceed.

3. **Clinical Hold:** If the regulatory authority identifies safety concerns or deficiencies in the application, the IND may be placed on clinical hold, delaying the start of the trial until issues are resolved.

Post-Submission Requirements

1. **Safety Reporting:** Ongoing reporting of adverse events and safety data during the clinical trial.

   a. **Serious Adverse Events (SAEs):** Immediate reporting of any serious adverse events to the regulatory authority.

2. **Annual Reports:** Submission of annual progress reports summarizing the clinical trial status, safety data, and any significant findings.

3. **Amendments: Submitting** amendments to the IND for any changes to the clinical protocol, manufacturing process, or other critical aspects of the trial.

INVESTIGATOR'S BROCHURE (IB) AND NEW DRUG APPLICATION (NDA)

The Investigator's Brochure (IB) and New Drug Application (NDA) are critical documents in the regulatory pathway for drug approval. The IB is used primarily during clinical trials, while the NDA is submitted to obtain marketing approval for a new drug. Below is a detailed overview of each document, their purpose, and the regulatory requirements associated with them.

Investigator's Brochure (IB)

Purpose

The IB is a comprehensive document that provides clinical investigators and regulatory authorities with detailed information on the investigational product. It is designed to ensure the safe and ethical conduct of clinical trials by providing essential information on the drug's properties, preclinical data, and clinical experience.

Key Components

1. **Introduction**
   a. Overview of the drug and its intended therapeutic use.
   b. Summary of the rationale for conducting clinical trials.

2. **Physical, Chemical, and Pharmaceutical Properties**
   a. Description of the drug's chemical structure, physical properties, and formulation.
   b. Information on the drug's stability and storage conditions.

3. **Non-Clinical Studies**
   a. **Pharmacology**: Detailed description of primary and secondary pharmacodynamic studies, including the mechanism of action and therapeutic potential.
   b. **Pharmacokinetics**: Data on absorption, distribution, metabolism, and excretion (ADME) in animal models.

c. **Toxicology**: Results from toxicology studies, including acute, sub-chronic, and chronic toxicity, genotoxicity, reproductive toxicity, and carcinogenicity.

4. **Effects in Humans**

   a. Summary of clinical data, including results from Phase I, II, and III clinical trials.

   b. Information on the drug's safety, pharmacokinetics, pharmacodynamics, and efficacy.

   c. Details of any adverse effects observed in clinical trials.

5. **Summary of Data and Guidance for the Investigator**

   a. Integrated summary of preclinical and clinical data.

   b. Guidelines for the safe administration of the drug to trial participants.

   c. Risk mitigation strategies and monitoring requirements.

Regulatory Requirements

1. **Good Clinical Practice (GCP):** The IB must comply with GCP standards, ensuring it provides accurate and comprehensive information to investigators.

2. **ICH E6 (R2) Guidelines**: The International Council for Harmonisation (ICH) provides guidelines on the content and structure of the IB, emphasizing the importance of clear and concise information to ensure the safety of trial participants.

New Drug Application (NDA)

Purpose

The NDA is submitted to regulatory authorities, such as the FDA in the United States, to request approval to market a new drug. The NDA must provide substantial evidence of the drug's safety, efficacy, and quality.

Key Components

1. **Administrative Information**

a. **Application Form**: Detailed information about the applicant and the drug product.

b. **Patent Information**: Details of any patents covering the drug.

c. **User Fee**: Payment of applicable fees for the NDA review.

2. **Summary Documents**

   a. **Overall Summary**: A high-level summary of the entire application.

   b. **Quality Summary**: Overview of the chemistry, manufacturing, and controls (CMC) data.

   c. **Non-Clinical Summary**: Summary of pharmacology, toxicology, and pharmacokinetics data.

   d. **Clinical Summary**: Summary of clinical efficacy and safety data.

3. **Chemistry, Manufacturing, and Controls (CMC)**

   a. **Drug Substance and Product**: Detailed information on the drug's composition, manufacturing process, and specifications.

   b. **Quality Control**: Description of analytical methods and validation data to ensure product quality.

   c. **Stability Data**: Information on the stability of the drug under various conditions.

4. **Non-Clinical Study Reports**

   a. Comprehensive reports on pharmacology, toxicology, and pharmacokinetics studies.

   b. Data from genotoxicity, carcinogenicity, and reproductive toxicity studies.

5. **Clinical Study Reports**

   a. Efficacy Data: Detailed results from Phase I, II, and III clinical trials, including statistical analyses.

b. Safety Data: Information on adverse events, laboratory abnormalities, and other safety concerns observed during clinical trials.

c. Integrated Summary of Efficacy and Safety: Combined analysis of all clinical data to support the overall assessment of the drug's benefit-risk profile.

6. Labeling and Package Insert

a. Proposed labeling for the drug product, including indications, dosing instructions, contraindications, warnings, and precautions.

7. Risk Management Plan

a. Strategies for post-marketing surveillance and risk mitigation to ensure ongoing safety monitoring after the drug is approved.

Regulatory Requirements

1. **FDA Guidelines**: The FDA provides detailed guidance on the content and format of the NDA, including requirements for each section of the application.

2. **Common Technical Document (CTD)**: The NDA must be submitted in the CTD format, which is divided into five modules:

   a. **Module** 1: Administrative and prescribing information (region-specific).

   b. **Module 2**: Summaries of the quality, safety, and efficacy information.

   c. **Module 3**: Quality information (CMC).

   d. **Module 4**: Non-clinical study reports.

   e. **Module 5:** Clinical study reports.

3. **Review and Approval Process**: The NDA undergoes a rigorous review by the regulatory authority, which evaluates the data to determine whether the drug's benefits outweigh its risks. The review process includes:

a. **Filing Review**: Initial assessment to ensure the application is complete.

b. **Scientific Review**: Detailed evaluation by multidisciplinary review teams (clinical, pharmacology/toxicology, chemistry/manufacturing, statistics).

c. **Advisory Committee Meetings**: Independent expert panels may be convened to provide additional input on the drug's safety and efficacy.

d. **Approval Decision**: Based on the review findings, the regulatory authority decides whether to approve the drug for marketing.

CLINICAL RESEARCH / BE STUDIES

Clinical research and bioequivalence (BE) studies are fundamental components of the drug development process, playing crucial roles in demonstrating the safety, efficacy, and comparability of new and generic drug products. Below is a detailed overview of these studies and their regulatory requirements.

Clinical Research

Clinical research involves a series of phases designed to test the investigational drug in humans to assess its safety, efficacy, pharmacokinetics, and pharmacodynamics. The regulatory requirements for clinical research ensure that studies are conducted ethically, scientifically, and in compliance with established standards.

Key Phases of Clinical Trials

1. **Phase I Trials**

   a. **Objective**: Assess safety, tolerability, pharmacokinetics (PK), and pharmacodynamics (PD) in healthy volunteers or patients.

   b. **Design**: Small sample size (20-100 participants), typically open-label or dose-escalation studies.

c. **Regulatory Requirements:**

1. **IND Application**: Must be filed and approved by regulatory authorities (e.g., FDA) before initiating Phase I trials.
2. **Good Clinical Practice (GCP)**: Trials must adhere to GCP guidelines to ensure participant safety and data integrity.
3. **Informed Consent**: Participants must provide informed consent before enrolling in the study.

2. **Phase II Trials**

a. **Objective**: Evaluate efficacy, optimal dosing, and further assess safety.

b. **Design**: Medium-sized sample (100-300 participants), randomized and controlled.

c. **Regulatory Requirements:**

1. **Clinical Protocols**: Detailed study protocols must be submitted to regulatory authorities.
2. **Interim Data Monitoring**: Ongoing monitoring of safety and efficacy data.

3. **Phase III Trials**

a. **Objective**: Confirm efficacy, monitor side effects, and compare the drug to standard treatments.

b. **Design**: Large sample size (300-3,000 participants), randomized, double-blind, and controlled.

c. **Regulatory Requirements:**

1. **NDA Submission:** Successful Phase III trials form the basis for the New Drug Application (NDA) to seek marketing approval.
2. **Regulatory Review:** Detailed review by regulatory authorities to assess benefit-risk profile.

4. **Phase IV (Post-Marketing) Trials**

a. **Objective**: Monitor long-term safety and effectiveness, identify any rare or long-term adverse effects.

b. **Design: Post**-approval studies involving larger patient populations.

c. **Regulatory Requirements:**

1. **Post-Marketing Surveillance**: Ongoing safety monitoring and reporting to regulatory authorities.

Bioequivalence (BE) Studies

Bioequivalence studies are critical for the approval of generic drugs, ensuring that they are therapeutically equivalent to their brand-name counterparts. BE studies focus on comparing the bioavailability of the generic drug to that of the innovator drug.

Key Aspects of BE Studies

1. **Objective**

   a. Demonstrate that the generic drug has the same bioavailability as the reference (brand-name) drug.

   b. Ensure that the generic drug is absorbed into the bloodstream at the same rate and extent as the reference drug.

2. **Design**

   a. **Crossover Design**: Subjects receive both the test (generic) and reference (innovator) drug in a randomized sequence.

   b. **Parameters Measured**: Key pharmacokinetic parameters include peak plasma concentration (Cmax), time to reach peak concentration (Tmax), and area under the plasma concentration-time curve (AUC).

   c. **Study Population**: Typically healthy volunteers to minimize variability.

3. **Regulatory Requirements**

a. **ANDA Submission**: Abbreviated New Drug Application (ANDA) must be filed for generic drug approval, including results from BE studies.

b. **FDA Guidelines**: Follow FDA's guidance for industry on bioavailability and bioequivalence studies.

c. **Acceptance Criteria**: The 90% confidence intervals for the ratio of the test to reference drug must fall within the bioequivalence range of 80-125% for Cmax and AUC.

Regulatory Requirements and Guidelines

1. Good Clinical Practice (GCP)

a. **ICH E6 (R2) Guidelines**: Internationally accepted standards for conducting clinical trials, ensuring ethical and scientific quality.

b. **Informed Consent:** Process for obtaining voluntary participation of subjects with full awareness of the study's risks and benefits.

2. Regulatory Submissions

a. **IND (Investigational New Drug) Application**: Required before initiating clinical trials. Must include preclinical data, study protocols, investigator information, and manufacturing data.

b. **NDA (New Drug Application)**: Comprehensive document submitted to regulatory authorities to obtain marketing approval. Includes clinical data from all phases of trials, safety and efficacy data, and CMC information.

c. **ANDA (Abbreviated New Drug Application)**: Specific to generic drugs, focusing on bioequivalence studies to demonstrate that the generic product performs similarly to the brand-name product.

3. Ethical and Safety Monitoring

a. **Institutional Review Boards (IRBs):** Ethics committees that review study protocols to protect the rights and welfare of human subjects.

b. **Data Safety Monitoring Boards (DSMBs)**: Independent groups that monitor patient safety and study integrity during clinical trials.

4. Post-Approval Requirements

a. **Phase IV Trials**: Conduct post-marketing studies to monitor the drug's long-term safety and effectiveness.

b. **Pharmacovigilance**: Continuous monitoring of adverse events and updating the safety profile of the drug.

CLINICAL RESEARCH PROTOCOLS

Clinical research protocols are detailed documents that outline the plan for conducting clinical trials. These protocols are essential for ensuring that studies are scientifically sound, ethically conducted, and comply with regulatory requirements. Here's an in-depth look at the key elements of clinical research protocols and the regulatory requirements involved.

Key Elements of Clinical Research Protocols

1. **Title Page**

    a. **Title of the Study:** A concise description of the study.

    b. **Protocol Number**: A unique identifier for the protocol.

    c. **Study Phase**: Phase I, II, III, or IV.

    d. **Sponsor Information**: Name and contact details of the sponsoring organization.

    e. **Principal Investigator**: Name and contact details of the principal investigator(s).

2. **Table of Contents**

    a. A detailed table of contents to help navigate the protocol document.

3. **Introduction**

    a. **Background Information**: Context and rationale for the study, including relevant preclinical and clinical data.

    b. **Study Rationale**: Justification for conducting the study, highlighting the need and potential benefits.

4. **Objectives and Hypotheses**

a. **Primary Objective**: The main goal of the study, usually related to efficacy or safety.

b. **Secondary Objectives**: Additional goals, such as exploring other effects or collecting more data on safety.

c. **Hypotheses**: Specific hypotheses being tested.

5. **Study Design**

a. **Type of Study**: Description of the study design (e.g., randomized, double-blind, placebo-controlled).

b. **Population**: Criteria for selecting participants (inclusion and exclusion criteria).

c. **Sample Size**: Number of participants required and the rationale for this sample size.

d. **Randomization and Blinding**: Methods for randomization and blinding, if applicable.

6. **Study Population**

a. **Inclusion Criteria**: Specific characteristics required for participants to be eligible.

b. **Exclusion Criteria**: Characteristics that disqualify potential participants.

c. **Recruitment Strategies**: Methods for identifying and recruiting participants.

7. **Interventions**

a. **Study Drug/Intervention**: Detailed description of the investigational product(s) and any comparator(s).

b. **Dosing Regimen**: Dosage, administration route, frequency, and duration of treatment.

c. **Concomitant Medications**: Guidelines on the use of additional medications during the study.

8. **Endpoints**

a. **Primary Endpoints**: Key outcomes that will be measured to determine the effect of the intervention.

b. **Secondary Endpoints**: Additional outcomes that will be measured to provide more information on the intervention's effects.

9. **Assessments and Procedures**

    a. **Schedule of Assessments**: Timeline for conducting assessments and procedures (e.g., blood tests, imaging, questionnaires).

    b. **Methods:** Detailed description of how each assessment and procedure will be performed.

10. **Statistical Considerations**

    a. **Statistical Analysis** Plan: Detailed plan for analyzing the data, including statistical methods and software to be used.

    b. **Interim Analyses**: Plans for any interim analyses and criteria for early termination of the study.

11. **Safety Monitoring**

    a. **Adverse Event Reporting**: Procedures for identifying, recording, and reporting adverse events.

    b. **Safety Assessments**: Regular assessments to monitor participant safety throughout the study.

12. **Data Management**

    a. **Data Collection**: Methods and tools for collecting study data.

    b. **Data Handling and Storage**: Procedures for managing and storing data, ensuring confidentiality and integrity.

13. **Ethical Considerations**

    a. **Informed Consent**: Process for obtaining informed consent from participants.

    b. **Ethics Committee** Approval: Confirmation of approval from relevant ethics committees or institutional review boards (IRBs).

14. **Quality Control and Assurance**

a. **Monitoring Plan**: Strategy for monitoring the study to ensure compliance with the protocol and regulatory requirements.

b. **Audits and Inspections**: Procedures for conducting audits and inspections by regulatory authorities.

15.**Regulatory Compliance**

a. **Compliance with Reg**ulations: Assurance that the study will comply with applicable regulations and guidelines (e.g., GCP, ICH E6).

16.**Study Administration**

a. **Roles and Responsibilities:** Detailed description of the roles and responsibilities of all study personnel.

b. **Study Timeline**: Projected timeline for study initiation, enrollment, completion, and data analysis.

Regulatory Requirements for Clinical Research Protocols

1. Good Clinical Practice (GCP)

a. **ICH E6 (R2) Guidelines**: These international guidelines provide a unified standard for designing, conducting, recording, and reporting clinical trials.

b. **Ethical Principles**: Ensuring the rights, safety, and well-being of trial participants are protected.

2. Regulatory Submissions

a. **Investigational New Drug (IND) Application**: In the United States, an IND must be filed with the FDA before beginning clinical trials. The IND includes the clinical protocol, preclinical data, and manufacturing information.

b. **Clinical Trial Application (CTA):** In the European Union and other regions, a CTA must be submitted to regulatory authorities.

3. Ethics Committee Approval

- ☐ **Institutional Review Boards (IRBs)**: Ethics committees that review and approve clinical trial protocols to ensure they meet ethical standards.
- ☐ **Informed Consent:** Protocols must include a process for obtaining informed consent from all participants.

4. Safety Reporting

- a. **Adverse Event Reporting**: Procedures for timely reporting of adverse events to regulatory authorities and ethics committees.
- b. **Data Safety Monitoring Boards (DSMBs)**: Independent committees that monitor data during the trial to ensure participant safety.

5. Documentation and Record Keeping

- a. **Trial Master File (TMF):** Comprehensive documentation of all trial-related activities to ensure compliance and facilitate audits and inspections.
- b. **Case Report Forms (CRFs)**: Standardized forms for recording study data for each participant.

6. Quality Assurance and Audits

- a. **Monitoring:** Regular monitoring of the trial to ensure compliance with the protocol and regulatory requirements.
- b. **Audits:** Independent reviews of trial processes and data to ensure accuracy and adherence to guidelines.

BIOSTATISTICS IN PHARMACEUTICAL PRODUCT DEVELOPMENT

Biostatistics plays a crucial role in pharmaceutical product development, providing the statistical methods and analyses necessary to design, conduct, and interpret clinical trials and other studies. Regulatory agencies such as the FDA (Food and Drug Administration) and EMA (European Medicines Agency) require robust statistical analyses to ensure the validity and reliability of data submitted for drug approval. Here's a detailed look at the role of biostatistics in pharmaceutical product development and its regulatory requirements:

Key Roles of Biostatistics in Pharmaceutical Product Development

1. **Study Design**: Biostatisticians collaborate with researchers to design clinical trials, ensuring they are appropriately powered, randomized, and controlled to produce valid and interpretable results.

2. **Sample Size Calculation**: Biostatisticians determine the sample size needed for clinical trials to detect clinically significant effects while minimizing the risk of type I and type II errors.

3. **Randomization and Allocation Concealment**: Biostatisticians develop randomization procedures and allocation concealment methods to ensure unbiased treatment assignment in clinical trials.

4. **Statistical Analysis Plan (SAP)**: Biostatisticians create SAPs outlining the statistical methods and analyses that will be used to analyze the data collected in clinical trials, including primary and secondary endpoints.

5. **Interim Analyses**: Biostatisticians conduct interim analyses to monitor the accumulating data for safety and efficacy, often using statistical methods such as group sequential designs or Bayesian approaches.

6. **Data Monitoring and Safety Boards (DSMBs)**: Biostatisticians provide statistical support to DSMBs, which review interim data to make recommendations regarding trial continuation, modification, or termination based on safety or efficacy concerns.

7. **Meta-Analysis**: Biostatisticians perform meta-analyses to synthesize data from multiple studies, providing more robust estimates of treatment effects and enhancing the evidence base for drug efficacy and safety.

8. **Regulatory Submissions**: Biostatisticians prepare statistical sections of regulatory submissions, including Investigational New Drug (IND) applications, New Drug Applications (NDAs), and Marketing Authorization Applications (MAAs), ensuring compliance with regulatory requirements.

Regulatory Requirements for Biostatistics in Drug Approval

1. Good Clinical Practice (GCP)

a. **ICH E6 (R2) Guidelines**: Biostatistical analyses in clinical trials must adhere to the principles outlined in the International Council for Harmonisation of Technical Requirements for Pharmaceuticals for Human Use (ICH) E6 (R2) guideline on Good Clinical Practice.

b. **Data Integrity and Reliability**: Biostatisticians ensure that data collection, management, and analysis processes meet GCP standards to ensure the integrity and reliability of trial results.

2. Regulatory Submissions

a. **Statistical Analysis Plan (SAP)**: Regulatory agencies require a detailed SAP outlining the statistical methods, analysis populations, and handling of missing data for each clinical trial included in regulatory submissions.

b. **Integrated Summary of Efficacy and Safety (ISE/ISS)**: Biostatisticians contribute to the ISE/ISS, which synthesizes data from multiple studies to provide comprehensive evidence of drug efficacy and safety.

3. Sample Size Justification

Power Calculations: Biostatisticians must justify the sample size for clinical trials based on power calculations, ensuring that trials are adequately powered to detect clinically meaningful treatment effects.

4. Randomization and Blinding

a. **Randomization Procedures**: Biostatisticians ensure that randomization procedures are appropriate and adequately implemented to minimize selection bias.

b. **Blinding:** Statistical methods are employed to assess the success of blinding procedures and minimize the risk of bias in treatment assignment and outcome assessment.

5. Interim Analyses and Adaptive Designs

a. **Data Monitoring Committees (DMCs)**: Biostatisticians provide statistical support to DMCs, which review interim data to ensure patient safety and trial integrity.

b. **Adaptive Designs**: Regulatory agencies may accept adaptive trial designs, but they require careful planning and justification, with statistical methods for controlling type I error rates and preserving trial integrity.

6. Meta-Analysis

Meta-Analytic Techniques: Biostatisticians must use appropriate meta-analytic techniques to combine data from multiple studies, accounting for heterogeneity and potential biases to provide reliable estimates of treatment effects.

DATA PRESENTATION FOR FDA SUBMISSIONS

Data presentation for FDA submissions is a critical aspect of regulatory requirements for drug approval. The FDA expects clear and comprehensive presentation of data to support the safety, efficacy, and quality of new drugs. Here's a detailed overview of the key considerations for data presentation in FDA submissions:

1. Common Technical Document (CTD) Format

The FDA requires submissions to follow the Common Technical Document (CTD) format, which provides a standardized structure for organizing and presenting regulatory information. **The CTD is divided into five modules:**

a. **Module** 1: Administrative and prescribing information.

b. **Module 2**: Summaries of the quality, safety, and efficacy information.

c. **Module 3**: Quality information (Chemistry, Manufacturing, and Controls - CMC).

d. **Module 4**: Non-clinical study reports.

e. **Module 5:** Clinical study reports.

2. Quality Information (Module 3)

a. Chemistry, Manufacturing, and Controls (CMC)

a. **Drug Substance:** Detailed information on the chemical composition, manufacturing process, and characterization of the drug substance.

b. **Drug Product**: Description of the drug product formulation, manufacturing process, and controls to ensure quality and consistency.

c. **Stability Studie**s: Data demonstrating the stability of the drug product under various storage conditions.

3. Non-clinical Study Reports (Module 4)

a. Pharmacology and Toxicology

a. **Pharmacodynamic Studies**: Presentation of pharmacological effects and mechanism of action data.

b. **Pharmacokinetic Studies**: Data on drug absorption, distribution, metabolism, and excretion.

c. **Toxicology Studies**: Presentation of results from acute, sub-chronic, chronic toxicity, genotoxicity, reproductive toxicity, and carcinogenicity studies.

4. Clinical Study Reports (Module 5)

a. Efficacy and Safety Data

a. **Study Design**: Description of study design, patient population, and treatment regimen.

b. **Primary and Secondary Endpoints**: Presentation of efficacy endpoints and results, including statistical analyses.

c. **Safety Profile**: Summary of adverse events, laboratory abnormalities, and other safety data collected during the study.

d. **Integrated Summary of Efficacy and Safety (ISE/ISS):** Comprehensive analysis of efficacy and safety data from multiple studies if applicable.

5. Statistical Analysis Plan (SAP)

A detailed Statistical Analysis Plan (SAP) should be included in the submission, outlining the statistical methods and analyses used to analyze the data. The SAP should cover:

a. **Primary and Secondary Analyses**: Description of planned analyses for primary and secondary endpoints.

b. **Handling of Missing Data**: Strategies for handling missing data, including imputation methods if applicable.

c. **Interim Analyses:** Plans for interim analyses and criteria for early termination of the study.

6. Graphs, Tables, and Figures

Graphical representation of data is essential for clarity and interpretation. Graphs, tables, and figures should be appropriately labeled and titled, with clear legends and annotations to aid understanding. Common types of graphs and figures include:

a. **Line Plots**: Showing trends over time or dose.

b. **Bar Charts**: Comparing categorical data.

c. **Kaplan-Meier Curves**: Illustrating time-to-event data.

d. **Forest Plots**: Summarizing results from multiple studies in meta-analyses.

7. Compliance with FDA Guidance Documents

The FDA provides guidance documents that outline specific requirements for data presentation in different types of submissions (e.g., INDs, NDAs, BLAs). It's essential to review and comply with relevant FDA guidance documents to ensure that data presentation meets regulatory expectations.

8. Clarity, Accuracy, and Consistency

Data presentation should be clear, accurate, and consistent throughout the submission. Any discrepancies or inconsistencies should be addressed and explained in the submission.

MANAGEMENT OF CLINICAL STUDIES

Managing clinical studies in accordance with regulatory requirements is crucial for ensuring the integrity, reliability, and ethical conduct of trials in the drug approval process. Here's a detailed overview of the key aspects involved in the management of clinical studies within regulatory requirements:

1. Protocol Development and Review

a. **Protocol Design**: Development of a detailed study protocol outlining the objectives, study design, methodology, endpoints, and statistical analysis plan.

b. **Ethical Considerations**: Ensuring that the protocol adheres to ethical principles and is reviewed and approved by an Institutional Review Board (IRB) or Ethics Committee (EC).

c. **Regulatory Compliance**: Ensuring that the protocol complies with regulatory requirements set forth by agencies such as the FDA or EMA.

2. Investigator Selection and Training

a. **Principal Investigator (PI)**: Selection of qualified investigators with appropriate expertise and experience to conduct the study.

b. **Site Selection:** Identifying investigational sites capable of enrolling and managing study participants effectively.

c. **Training**: Providing training to investigators and site staff on study protocols, Good Clinical Practice (GCP) guidelines, and regulatory requirements.

3. Study Initiation

a. **Regulatory Submissions**: Submitting necessary regulatory documents, such as Investigational New Drug (IND) applications or Clinical Trial Authorizations (CTAs), to obtain approval to initiate the study.

b. **Site Initiation** Visits (SIVs): Conducting SIVs to ensure that investigational sites are adequately prepared to initiate the study, including training of site staff and review of study procedures.

4. Participant Recruitment and Enrollment

a. **Informed Consent**: Obtaining informed consent from study participants in accordance with regulatory and ethical guidelines.

b. **Recruitment Strategies**: Implementing effective strategies to recruit and enroll eligible participants, while ensuring diversity and representation in the study population.

5. Study Conduct and Monitoring

a. **Data Collection and Management**: Implementing procedures for accurate and timely collection, recording, and management of study data.

b. **Quality Control (QC)**: Conducting regular monitoring visits to ensure that study procedures are being followed, data are being collected accurately, and participant safety is being protected.

c. **Adverse Event Reporting**: Implementing procedures for the timely reporting and documentation of adverse events in accordance with regulatory requirements.

6. Safety Monitoring and Reporting

a. **Data Safety Monitoring Board (DSMB)**: Establishing a DSMB to oversee safety data and make recommendations regarding the continuation, modification, or termination of the study based on safety concerns.

b. **Serious Adverse Event (SAE) Reporting**: Ensuring that SAEs are promptly reported to regulatory authorities, IRBs/ECs, and other relevant parties in accordance with regulatory requirements.

7. Protocol Amendments

a. **Protocol Deviations**: Implementing procedures for documenting and reporting protocol deviations or violations.

b. **Protocol Amendments**: Obtaining approval for protocol amendments from regulatory authorities and IRBs/ECs, and ensuring that all study personnel are informed of and trained on the changes.

8. Study Closeout

a. **Study Completion**: Conducting study closeout visits to ensure that all study-related activities are completed, including data collection, participant follow-up, and site closeout procedures.

b. **Data Analysis and Reporting**: Analyzing study data, preparing study reports, and submitting final study reports to regulatory authorities in accordance with regulatory requirements.

9. Regulatory Inspections and Audits

a. **Preparation**: Ensuring that all study documentation is organized, complete, and readily accessible for regulatory inspections or audits.

b. **Compliance:** Addressing any findings or observations identified during inspections or audits and implementing corrective and preventive actions as necessary.

Multiple-Choice Questions (MCQs)

1. What is the primary purpose of the Investigational New Drug (IND) application?

    A) To market a new drug

    B) To request permission to start clinical trials

    C) To provide marketing strategies

    D) To establish manufacturing facilities

2. Which phase in clinical trials mainly assesses the drug's safety and determines a safe dosage range?

    A) Phase I

    B) Phase II

    C) Phase III

    D) Phase IV

3. What is the main focus of Phase III clinical trials?

    A) To confirm drug effectiveness and monitor side effects

    B) To assess safety and tolerability

    C) To evaluate drug metabolism

    D) To investigate long-term effects

4. Which regulatory body is responsible for drug approval in the United States?

    A) FDA

    B) EMA

    C) PMDA

    D) NMPA

5. What does the term "bioequivalence" primarily refer to?

    A) The therapeutic effect of a drug

    B) The rate and extent a drug is absorbed

    C) A drug's side effects

    D) The stability of a drug

6. In the context of clinical trials, what does GCP stand for?

    A) Good Clinical Practice

    B) General Clinical Protocol

    C) Global Clinical Pharmacology

    D) General Compliance Practice

7. What is the main goal of bioequivalence studies?

    A) To compare a generic drug's bioavailability with that of the innovator drug

    B) To determine the clinical efficacy of new drugs

    C) To evaluate the packaging standards of drugs

    D) To assess the global market reach of the drug

8. Which phase in clinical trials is a drug's efficacy and side effects are first tested in patients?

    A) Phase I

B) Phase II

C) Phase III

D) Phase IV

9. What does CMC stand for in regulatory submissions?

A) Clinical Manufacturing Control

B) Chemistry, Manufacturing, and Controls

C) Clinical Management Committee

D) Chemical and Medical Compliance

10. What is the role of the FDA during the NDA review process?

A) To provide funding for drug development

B) To oversee the ethical treatment of clinical trial subjects

C) To evaluate data to determine if the drug's benefits outweigh its risks

D) To develop marketing strategies for new drugs

11. What is the purpose of an Investigator's Brochure (IB)?

A) To advertise new drugs to the public

B) To inform clinical investigators about the investigational product

C) To record the financial details of clinical trials

D) To list the participants of a study

12. What document must be filed to the FDA before initiating Phase I trials in the U.S.?

A) NDA

B) ANDA

C) IND

D) IB

13. Which document is critical for generic drugs to demonstrate bioequivalence?

A) IND

B) NDA

C) ANDA

D) IB

14. Which guidelines must biostatistics adhere to ensure the integrity and reliability of trial results?

A) ICH E6 (R2)

B) GCP

C) Both A and B

D) None of the above

15. Which team is responsible for ensuring that clinical trials adhere to regulatory standards?

A) Legal and Compliance Team

B) Clinical Development Team

C) Quality Assurance Team

D) Marketing and Commercial Team

16. During which phase is the therapeutic index first assessed?

A) Phase I

B) Phase II

C) Phase III

D) Phase IV

17. What is the role of Data Safety Monitoring Boards (DSMBs)?

A) To market pharmaceutical products

B) To oversee safety data and recommend continuation or termination of a study

C) To handle the financial aspects of a clinical trial

D) To recruit participants for clinical studies

18. What is the main objective of Phase IV clinical trials?

A) To perform initial human trials on safety and dosage

B) To test the drug in a small group of patients for efficacy and side effects

C) To confirm efficacy and monitor adverse effects in a large patient group

D) To monitor long-term safety and effectiveness post-approval

19. What does the Common Technical Document (CTD) Module 3 contain?

    A) Quality information

    B) Clinical study reports

    C) Non-clinical study reports

    D) Administrative information

20. Who reviews and approves clinical trial protocols to ensure ethical standards are met?

    A) The FDA

    B) Institutional Review Boards (IRBs)

    C) The principal investigator

    D) The sponsor

Short Answer Type Questions (Subjective)

1. What is the primary purpose of preclinical testing in drug development?

2. Describe the key components of an Investigational New Drug (IND) application.

3. What are the main objectives of Phase I clinical trials?

4. How do regulatory authorities such as the FDA evaluate a New Drug Application (NDA)?

5. Explain the importance of post-marketing surveillance in drug approval.

6. What role does the International Council for Harmonisation (ICH) play in drug approval processes globally?

7. Outline the responsibilities of a Regulatory Affairs Team in drug development.

8. What is the function of Quality Assurance (QA) teams in pharmaceutical development?

9. Describe the typical studies involved in non-clinical drug development.

10. What is the significance of pharmacodynamics studies in assessing a drug's therapeutic potential?

11. How are drug-drug interactions assessed in drug metabolism studies?

12. Explain the purpose of genotoxicity testing in toxicology studies.

13. What are the ethical considerations in clinical research protocols?

14. How does Good Clinical Practice (GCP) influence clinical trials?

15. What are the main considerations for study design in biostatistics within pharmaceutical product development?

16. Discuss the role of data safety monitoring boards in clinical trials.

17. What are the regulatory requirements for a bioequivalence study in generic drug approval?

18. Describe the process and importance of obtaining informed consent in clinical research.

19. What is the role of pharmacokinetics in evaluating a drug's efficacy and safety?

20. How do biostatisticians contribute to the regulatory submission process for new drugs?

Long Answer Type Questions (Subjective)

1. Discuss the various phases of clinical trials and their specific objectives in the context of drug development.

2. Explain the regulatory pathway for a new drug approval including key documentation such as IND and NDA.

3. Describe the role and importance of the Investigator's Brochure (IB) in the context of clinical trials.

4. Elaborate on the challenges and considerations in managing multi-phase clinical studies from initiation to closeout.

5. Discuss the impact of international guidelines, such as those from ICH, on harmonizing drug approval processes across different regulatory bodies.

6. Explain the significance of pharmacokinetics and pharmacodynamics studies in the development and approval of new drugs.

7. Analyze the role of biostatistics in ensuring the validity and reliability of clinical trial results.

8. Detail the process of conducting bioequivalence studies and their importance in the approval of generic drugs.

9. Describe the ethical considerations and regulatory requirements that must be met in conducting human clinical trials.

10. Discuss the role of post-marketing surveillance in maintaining drug safety and efficacy in the general population after approval.

Answer Key

1. (B) To request permission to start clinical trials
2. (A) Phase I
3. (A) To confirm drug effectiveness and monitor side effects
4. (A) FDA
5. (B) The rate and extent a drug is absorbed
6. (A) Good Clinical Practice
7. (A) To compare a generic drug's bioavailability with that of the innovator drug
8. (B) Phase II
9. (B) Chemistry, Manufacturing, and Controls
10. (C) To evaluate data to determine if the drug's benefits outweigh its risks
11. (B) To inform clinical investigators about the investigational product
12. (C) IND
13. (C) ANDA

14.(C) Both A and B

15.(C) Quality Assurance Team

16.(A) Phase I

17.(B) To oversee safety data and recommend continuation or termination of a study

18.(D) To monitor long-term safety and effectiveness post-approval

19.(A) Quality information

20.(B) Institutional Review Boards (IRBs)

CHAPTER - 5

QUALITY MANAGEMENT SYSTEMS

INTRODUCTION:

Quality Management Systems (QMS) are formalized frameworks that document processes, procedures, and responsibilities for achieving quality policies and objectives. They help coordinate and direct an organization's activities to meet customer and regulatory requirements and improve its effectiveness and efficiency on a continuous basis.

Key Concepts of QMS

1. **Quality:** The degree to which a set of inherent characteristics fulfills requirements. It is not limited to products and services but also includes processes, systems, and organizational performance.

2. **Management System**: A set of interrelated or interacting elements of an organization to establish policies and objectives and processes to achieve those objectives. In the context of quality, this includes quality planning, quality control, quality assurance, and quality improvement.

Importance of QMS

1. **Customer Satisfaction**: Ensuring products and services meet customer requirements and expectations.

2. **Compliance**: Meeting regulatory and statutory requirements.

3. **Risk Management**: Identifying and mitigating risks related to quality.

4. **Efficiency**: Streamlining processes to reduce waste and improve efficiency.

5. **Continuous Improvement**: Ongoing efforts to improve products, services, or processes.

Core Elements of a QMS

1. **Quality Policy and Objectives**: A statement of the organization's commitment to quality and its overarching quality goals.

2. **Quality Manual**: A document that outlines the scope of the QMS, including details of the main quality processes and their interactions.

3. **Document Control**: Procedures to control documents and records, ensuring they are accurate and accessible.

4. **Process Control**: Defining and controlling the processes needed for production or service delivery.

5. **Non-Conformance Management**: Identifying, documenting, and managing non-conforming products or processes.

6. **Corrective and Preventive Actions (CAPA):** Steps to address non-conformities and prevent their recurrence.

7. **Internal Audits**: Regular checks to ensure the QMS is implemented effectively and is compliant with the standards.

8. **Training and Competence**: Ensuring employees are adequately trained and competent to perform their roles.

9. **Management Review**: Periodic reviews by top management to ensure the QMS remains suitable, adequate, and effective.

ISO 9001:2015 - The Standard for QMS

ISO 9001:2015 is the most widely recognized QMS standard, providing a set of standardized requirements for a quality management system. The standard is based on several quality management principles, including:

1. **Customer Focus**: Meeting and exceeding customer expectations.

2. **Leadership**: Establishing unity of purpose and direction.

3. **Engagement of People**: Ensuring the involvement of all employees.

4. **Process Approach**: Managing activities as processes.

5. **Improvement**: Continuous improvement of the QMS.

6. **Evidence-based Decision Making**: Basing decisions on the analysis of data.

7. **Relationship Management**: Managing relationships with interested parties.

Implementation of a QMS

Implementing a QMS involves several steps:

1. **Planning**: Define the scope, objectives, and framework for the QMS.

2. **Documentation**: Develop the necessary documents, such as quality manuals, procedures, and records.

3. **Training**: Train employees on QMS principles and their roles within the system.

4. **Implementation**: Roll out the QMS processes across the organization.

5. **Auditing**: Conduct internal audits to ensure compliance and identify areas for improvement.

6. **Review and Improvement**: Use the results of audits and feedback to improve the QMS continually.

Benefits of a QMS

1. **Enhanced Customer Satisfaction**: Consistently meeting customer requirements and improving service.

2. **Increased Efficiency**: Streamlined operations and reduced waste.

3. **Improved Risk Management**: Proactively identifying and mitigating risks.

4. **Better Compliance**: Meeting regulatory requirements.

5. **Continual Improvement**: Ongoing enhancements to processes and products.

A well-implemented QMS fosters a culture of quality, encourages continuous improvement, and ensures that the organization consistently delivers high-quality products and services to its customers.

QUALITY MANAGEMENT & CERTIFICATIONS: CONCEPT OF QUALITY

Quality Management involves the coordinated activities to direct and control an organization with regard to quality. This entails the implementation of a Quality Management System (QMS) to ensure that an organization's products or services are consistent, meet customer requirements, and comply with relevant regulations. The concept of quality in QMS is multifaceted, encompassing several core principles and practices.

Concept of Quality in QMS

1. **Definition of Quality:**
   a. Quality is the degree to which a set of inherent characteristics meets requirements. These requirements are usually defined by the customer, regulatory bodies, or the organization itself.
   b. In the context of a QMS, quality is about fulfilling customer expectations and ensuring satisfaction by delivering products or services that meet specified standards.

2. **Quality Principles:**

3. Quality management principles form the foundation of QMS standards, like ISO 9001. These principles include:
   a. **Customer Focus**: Understanding and meeting the needs of current and future customers.
   b. **Leadership**: Establishing a vision and direction for the organization, creating an environment that encourages quality.
   c. **Engagement of People**: Ensuring that employees are competent, empowered, and engaged in delivering value.
   d. **Process Approach**: Managing activities and related resources as processes to achieve consistent and predictable results.
   e. **Improvement**: Continual improvement should be a permanent objective.

f. **Evidence-Based Decision Making**: Basing decisions on the analysis of data and information.

g. **Relationship Management**: Managing relationships with interested parties (such as suppliers) to optimize performance.

4. **Components of Quality in QMS:**

a. **Quality Planning**: Defining quality objectives and specifying the necessary operational processes and resources to fulfill quality goals.

b. **Quality Assurance (QA):** Ensuring that processes are in place to achieve the quality objectives and prevent defects.

c. **Quality Control (QC):** Monitoring specific results to determine if they comply with relevant quality standards and identifying ways to eliminate causes of unsatisfactory performance.

d. **Quality Improvement**: Continuously improving organizational processes, products, or services to enhance quality.

Certifications in Quality Management

Quality management certifications are credentials that demonstrate an organization's adherence to quality standards and its commitment to continuous improvement. The most prominent certifications include:

1. **ISO 9001:2015:**

a. **ISO 9001**:2015 is the international standard for QMS. It outlines the criteria for a QMS and is based on several quality management principles.

b. **Organizations that implement ISO 9001**:2015 demonstrate their ability to consistently provide products and services that meet customer and regulatory requirements and aim to enhance customer satisfaction through continuous improvement.

c. Certification involves an external audit by a third-party certification body to verify compliance with the standard.

2. **Other ISO Standards:**
   a. **ISO 14001**: Focuses on environmental management systems.
   b. **ISO 45001**: Pertains to occupational health and safety management systems.
   c. **ISO/TS 16949**: Specific to automotive sector QMS.

3. **Sector-Specific Certifications:**
   a. **AS9100:** Aerospace industry.
   b. **ISO 13485**: Medical devices.
   c. **IATF 16949**: Automotive industry.

Steps to Achieve Certification

1. **Gap Analysis**: Assess current processes against the requirements of the chosen standard.

2. **Planning**: Develop a plan to address gaps and align processes with standard requirements.

3. **Implementation**: Execute the plan, ensuring that processes, documentation, and training are in place.

4. **Internal Audit**: Conduct internal audits to verify compliance and effectiveness.

5. **Management Review**: Review the QMS to ensure it meets objectives and identify areas for improvement.

6. **Certification Audit**: An external auditor from a certification body evaluates the QMS for compliance with the standard.

7. **Certification**: If the organization meets the requirements, it receives certification, usually valid for three years with periodic surveillance audits.

Benefits of Quality Management Certifications

1. **Enhanced Credibility and Image**: Certification demonstrates commitment to quality, improving the organization's reputation.

2. **Increased Customer Satisfaction**: Consistently meeting customer expectations leads to higher satisfaction and loyalty.

3. **Access to New Markets**: Certification can be a requirement for doing business in certain markets or with specific customers.

4. **Operational Efficiency**: Streamlined processes and reduced waste lead to cost savings and improved efficiency.

5. **Continuous Improvement**: Certification promotes a culture of ongoing improvement, driving innovation and long-term success.

In summary, quality in QMS is about meeting and exceeding customer expectations through effective management of processes and continuous improvement. Certifications like ISO 9001 provide a structured framework for achieving and demonstrating high-quality standards, offering numerous benefits to organizations in terms of credibility, efficiency, and customer satisfaction.

TOTAL QUALITY MANAGEMENT

Total Quality Management (TQM) is a comprehensive and structured approach to organizational management that seeks to improve the quality of products and services through ongoing refinements in response to continuous feedback. It is an integral part of Quality Management Systems (QMS), emphasizing long-term success through customer satisfaction and benefits to all members of the organization and society.

Core Concepts of Total Quality Management

1. **Customer Focus:**
   a. Understanding and meeting customer needs and expectations is paramount.
   b. Continuous efforts to exceed customer expectations lead to enhanced customer satisfaction and loyalty.

2. **Total Employee Involvement:**
   a. All members of the organization are involved in working towards common goals.

b. Employee empowerment and involvement in decision-making processes enhance ownership and accountability.

3. **Process-Centered Approach:**
   a. A fundamental part of TQM is focusing on process thinking.
   b. Processes are the sequences of activities that take inputs and transform them into outputs, aiming for efficiency and consistency.

4. **Integrated System:**
   a. All functions and processes are interconnected and should work together towards common objectives.
   b. An integrated system aligns organizational processes with quality objectives, creating synergy across departments.

5. **Strategic and Systematic Approach:**
   a. Strategic planning involves setting quality goals and identifying processes that can be improved.
   b. A systematic approach ensures that processes are aligned with the strategic goals of the organization.

6. **Continual Improvement:**
   a. An ongoing effort to improve products, services, or processes.
   b. Continuous improvement involves incremental improvements over time or breakthrough improvements all at once.

7. **Fact-Based Decision Making:**
   a. Decisions are made based on the analysis of data and information.
   b. Fact-based decision making ensures that the actions taken are effective and based on accurate insights.

8. **Communication:**
   a. Effective communication at all levels is essential for TQM.
   b. Clear, open, and frequent communication ensures that everyone understands the goals, processes, and the importance of quality.

Key Principles of TQM

1. **Customer-Centric:**
   a. Ensuring that customer needs and expectations are met or exceeded.
   b. Gathering customer feedback and incorporating it into product and service improvements.

2. **Leadership Commitment:**
   a. Strong leadership to create a vision and direction for quality improvement.
   b. Leaders must be committed to the principles of TQM and inspire the same commitment in employees.

3. **Employee Empowerment:**
   a. Involving employees in decision-making processes and problem-solving.
   b. Providing training and development to enhance skills and knowledge.

4. **Quality Culture:**
   a. Developing a culture where quality is a core value and everyone is committed to achieving high standards.
   b. Recognition and reward systems to promote quality efforts and achievements.

5. **Strategic Planning:**
   a. Establishing a clear mission, vision, and objectives related to quality.
   b. Aligning resources and processes with strategic quality goals.

6. **Systematic Approach:**
   a. Viewing the organization as a collection of interrelated processes.
   b. Managing these processes to optimize performance and achieve quality objectives.

7. **Use of Quality Tools:**

a. Utilizing various quality tools and techniques for problem-solving and continuous improvement.

b. Tools like Pareto charts, fishbone diagrams, control charts, and Six Sigma methodologies.

Implementation of TQM

Implementing TQM requires a structured approach involving several stages:

1. **Preparation:**

   a. Gain commitment from top management.

   b. Establish a quality steering committee and quality councils.

   c. Develop a clear vision and mission statement related to quality.

2. **Planning:**

   a. Conduct a quality assessment to understand current performance.

   b. Develop a strategic plan for TQM implementation.

   c. Set measurable quality objectives and targets.

3. **Training:**

   a. Train employees on TQM principles, tools, and techniques.

   b. Foster a culture of continuous improvement through education and development.

4. **Process Improvement:**

   a. Identify key processes and areas for improvement.

   b. Implement process improvement initiatives using quality tools and techniques.

   c. Monitor and measure performance to ensure improvements are effective.

5. **Implementation:**

   a. Roll out TQM initiatives across the organization.

   b. Communicate the importance of quality and the role of each employee in achieving it.

c. Encourage teamwork and collaboration for problem-solving and innovation.

6. **Evaluation and Feedback:**

   a. Regularly evaluate the effectiveness of TQM initiatives.

   b. Collect feedback from customers, employees, and stakeholders.

   c. Use feedback to refine and improve processes and strategies.

7. **Continuous Improvement:**

   a. Promote a culture of continuous improvement where quality is an ongoing objective.

   b. Encourage innovative ideas and solutions for quality enhancement.

   c. Recognize and reward efforts and achievements in quality improvement.

Benefits of TQM

1. **Enhanced Customer Satisfaction**: Consistently meeting or exceeding customer expectations leads to higher satisfaction and loyalty.

2. **Improved Efficiency**: Streamlined processes reduce waste and inefficiencies, leading to cost savings.

3. **Higher Employee Morale**: Employee involvement and empowerment boost morale and job satisfaction.

4. **Better Decision Making**: Fact-based decision-making leads to more effective and accurate outcomes.

5. **Reduced Costs**: Continuous improvement and defect prevention reduce the costs associated with rework and waste.

6. **Increased Market Share**: High-quality products and services enhance reputation and competitiveness.

7. **Sustainability**: TQM promotes long-term success through a focus on continuous improvement and customer satisfaction.

QUALITY BY DESIGN (QBD)

Quality by Design (QbD) is a proactive approach to ensuring quality in products and processes. Originating from the pharmaceutical industry, QbD involves designing and developing formulations and manufacturing processes to ensure predefined quality criteria are met. It is a systematic approach that incorporates quality into the product development process rather than testing for quality after production.

Core Concepts of Quality by Design (QbD)

1. **Product Understanding:**
   a. Thorough understanding of the product, including its intended use, target specifications, and critical quality attributes (CQAs).
   b. CQAs are the physical, chemical, biological, or microbiological properties that must be controlled to ensure product quality.

2. **Process Understanding:**
   a. In-depth knowledge of the manufacturing process and the identification of critical process parameters (CPPs) that influence CQAs.
   b. CPPs are the variables that need to be controlled to ensure the process produces the desired quality consistently.

3. **Risk Management:**
   a. Systematic identification, assessment, and control of risks related to product and process development.
   b. Use of risk management tools like Failure Mode and Effects Analysis (FMEA) and risk matrices.

4. **Design of Experiments (DoE):**
   a. Structured approach to experimentation that helps understand the relationship between factors affecting a process and the output of that process.
   b. DoE helps in optimizing process parameters to achieve the best possible product quality.

5. **Control Strategy:**
   a. Comprehensive plan that describes how quality will be maintained throughout the product lifecycle.
   b. Includes in-process controls, end-product testing, and monitoring strategies to ensure consistent quality.

6. **Continuous Improvement:**
   a. Ongoing efforts to improve the product and process based on feedback, process data, and advancements in technology.
   b. Emphasis on learning from production data and implementing changes to enhance quality and efficiency.

Implementation of QbD

1. **Define Quality Target Product Profile (QTPP):**
   a. Establish the intended use, dosage form, route of administration, and desired attributes of the product.
   b. QTPP serves as a guide for the development process, ensuring all efforts are aligned with achieving the final product specifications.

2. **Identify Critical Quality Attributes (CQAs):**
   a. Determine the key characteristics that need to be controlled to ensure product quality.
   b. CQAs are derived from the QTPP and include attributes like purity, potency, and stability.

3. **Determine Critical Process Parameters (CPPs):**
   a. Identify the process parameters that have a significant impact on CQAs.
   b. CPPs are the variables that need to be tightly controlled to ensure consistent product quality.

4. **Conduct Risk Assessment:**
   a. Evaluate potential risks to product quality and implement measures to mitigate these risks.

b. Use risk assessment tools to prioritize and manage risks effectively.

5. **Develop and Optimize Formulation and Process:**

   a. Use Design of Experiments (DoE) to explore the effects of different variables on product quality.

   b. Optimize the formulation and manufacturing process to achieve desired quality attributes.

6. **Establish Control Strategy:**

   a. Develop a robust control strategy to maintain quality throughout the manufacturing process.

   b. Implement in-process controls, real-time monitoring, and end-product testing to ensure compliance with quality standards.

7. **Implement Continuous Improvement:**

   a. Use process data and feedback to continuously improve the product and manufacturing process.

   b. Encourage a culture of innovation and quality improvement within the organization.

Benefits of QbD

1. **Enhanced Product Quality:**

   a. By designing quality into the product and process, QbD ensures that the final product consistently meets quality specifications.

2. **Reduced Variability:**

   a. Understanding and controlling critical parameters reduces variability in the manufacturing process, leading to more consistent products.

3. **Improved Efficiency:**

   a. Optimized processes and fewer quality issues lead to increased efficiency and reduced production costs.

4. **Regulatory Compliance:**

a. QbD aligns with regulatory expectations for a systematic and science-based approach to product development.

b. Facilitates smoother regulatory approvals and inspections.

5. Risk Mitigation:

a. Proactive identification and control of risks enhance product safety and reliability.

6. Flexibility and Innovation:

a. QbD encourages continuous learning and improvement, fostering innovation and adaptability in product development.

Application of QbD in Different Industries

While QbD is most commonly associated with the pharmaceutical industry, its principles are applicable across various sectors:

1. Pharmaceuticals:

a. Ensuring the efficacy, safety, and quality of drugs through robust development processes and thorough understanding of formulation and manufacturing.

2. Biotechnology:

a. Applying QbD principles to the development of biopharmaceutical products, ensuring the stability and activity of biologics.

3. Medical Devices:

a. Designing medical devices with a focus on quality attributes and critical parameters to ensure performance and safety.

4. Consumer Goods:

a. Implementing QbD to enhance the quality and consistency of consumer products, such as cosmetics and household items.

5. Automotive:

a. Using QbD to improve the design and manufacturing processes of automotive components, ensuring reliability and safety.

SIX SIGMA CONCEPT, OUT OF SPECIFICATIONS (OOS), CHANGE CONTROL

Six Sigma, Out of Specifications (OOS), and Change Control are integral components of a robust Quality Management System (QMS). Each plays a critical role in ensuring that products meet quality standards and regulatory requirements, contributing to overall operational excellence.

Six Sigma in Quality Management Systems

Six Sigma is a data-driven methodology focused on improving process quality by identifying and removing causes of defects and variability. It uses statistical tools and techniques to achieve near-perfect quality levels, targeting no more than 3.4 defects per million opportunities.

Key Concepts of Six Sigma

1. **DMAIC Methodology:**
   a. **Define**: Identify the problem, project goals, and customer (internal and external) requirements.
   b. **Measure**: Collect data and determine current performance levels.
   c. **Analyze**: Identify root causes of defects and areas for improvement.
   d. **Improve**: Implement solutions to eliminate defects and improve processes.
   e. **Control**: Establish controls to sustain improvements and ensure consistent performance.

2. **Six Sigma Belts:**
   a. **White Belt**: Basic understanding of Six Sigma principles.
   b. **Yellow Belt:** Involvement in project teams and understanding of fundamental concepts.
   c. **Green Belt**: Leads small projects and supports Black Belts.

d. **Black Belt**: Leads complex projects, mentors Green Belts, and applies advanced analysis.

e. **Master Black Belt**: Expert in Six Sigma, responsible for strategy, training, and project oversight.

3. **Critical-to-Quality (CTQ) Characteristics:**

a. Specific attributes of a product or process that have a significant impact on quality and customer satisfaction.

4. **Statistical Tools:**

a. Techniques like Pareto Analysis, Control Charts, Root Cause Analysis, and Hypothesis Testing are used to analyze data and drive improvements.

Benefits of Six Sigma

1. **Improved Quality**: Reduction in defects and variability leads to higher quality products and services.

2. **Cost Savings**: Efficiency improvements and waste reduction result in significant cost savings.

3. **Customer Satisfaction**: Higher quality products increase customer satisfaction and loyalty.

4. **Employee Engagement**: Involving employees in improvement projects fosters a culture of quality and continuous improvement.

Out of Specifications (OOS)

Out of Specifications (OOS) refers to test results that fall outside established acceptance criteria set by regulatory guidelines, specifications, or internal quality standards. OOS results indicate potential issues with the product or process and require thorough investigation.

Managing OOS Results

1. **Immediate Actions:**

a. Quarantine affected products to prevent release.

b. Notify relevant stakeholders and initiate a preliminary investigation.

2. **Investigation Process:**

    a. Phase I Investigation: Initial assessment to determine if there was a laboratory error (e.g., instrument malfunction, analyst error). If a lab error is identified, retesting may be justified.

    b. Phase II Investigation: Comprehensive review involving the production process, raw materials, and environmental conditions if no lab error is found. The goal is to identify potential process-related issues.

3. **Root Cause Analysis:**

    a. Use tools like Fishbone Diagrams, Five Whys, and Failure Mode and Effects Analysis (FMEA) to identify the root cause of the OOS result.

4. **Corrective and Preventive Actions (CAPA):**

    a. Develop and implement CAPAs to address the root cause and prevent recurrence. This may include process adjustments, additional training, or changes in material handling.

5. **Documentation and Reporting:**

    a. Document the investigation, findings, and CAPAs in detail. Report to regulatory authorities if required.

6. **Impact Assessment:**

    a. Evaluate the impact of the OOS result on previously manufactured batches and determine if additional testing or recall is necessary.

Importance of OOS Management

1. Ensures product quality and compliance with regulatory standards.

2. Protects consumer safety and maintains product integrity.

3. Prevents potential recalls, regulatory actions, and reputational damage.

Change Control in Quality Management Systems

Change Control is a systematic approach to managing changes in processes, procedures, equipment, and documents within an organization. It ensures that changes are evaluated, approved, and implemented in a controlled manner to prevent unintended consequences on product quality and compliance.

Change Control Process

1. **Change Proposal:**
   a. Identify the need for change and propose it formally. The proposal should include a detailed description, rationale, and potential impact on product quality.

2. **Impact Assessment:**
   a. Evaluate the potential impact of the proposed change on processes, product quality, regulatory compliance, and other aspects of the QMS.
   b. Conduct risk assessments to identify and mitigate potential risks.

3. **Approval Process:**
   a. Review the change proposal and impact assessment by a cross-functional change control committee or designated authorities.
   b. Approval is based on the assessment of risks and benefits, ensuring all potential impacts are addressed.

4. **Implementation:**
   a. Develop an implementation plan, including timelines, resources, and responsibilities.
   b. Communicate the change to all relevant stakeholders and provide necessary training.

5. **Verification and Validation:**
   a. Verify that the change has been implemented as planned and validate its effectiveness.
   b. Conduct testing and collect data to ensure the change achieves the desired outcomes without negative impacts on product quality.

6. **Documentation:**
   a. Maintain detailed records of the change control process, including the change proposal, impact assessment, approvals, implementation, and validation results.
   b. Update relevant documents (e.g., SOPs, batch records) to reflect the change.

7. **Post-Implementation Review:**
   a. Conduct a review after implementation to assess the long-term impact of the change and ensure ongoing compliance and effectiveness.

Benefits of Change Control

1. **Quality Assurance**: Ensures that all changes are thoroughly evaluated and controlled, maintaining product quality.
2. **Regulatory Compliance**: Demonstrates compliance with regulatory requirements and provides traceability for changes.
3. **Risk Management**: Identifies and mitigates potential risks associated with changes.
4. **Continuous Improvement**: Facilitates ongoing improvements while controlling the impact on product quality.

INTRODUCTION TO ISO 9000 SERIES OF QUALITY SYSTEMS STANDARDS

The ISO 9000 series is a set of international standards for quality management and quality assurance designed to help organizations ensure they meet customer and other stakeholder needs within statutory and regulatory requirements related to a product or service. These standards are developed and published by the International Organization for Standardization (ISO), and they provide a framework for consistent quality management practices across different industries and sectors.

Overview of ISO 9000 Series

The ISO 9000 series consists of several standards, with ISO 9001 being the most notable. Each standard in the series focuses on different aspects of quality management systems.

1. **ISO 9000: Quality Management Systems - Fundamentals and Vocabulary:**
   a. Provides the fundamental concepts, principles, and vocabulary used in the entire ISO 9000 series.
   b. Establishes a common language for quality management to avoid misunderstandings and ensure consistent interpretation.

2. **ISO 9001: Quality Management Systems - Requirements:**
   a. Specifies the criteria for a quality management system.
   b. It is the only standard in the series that organizations can be certified against.
   c. Provides a framework to ensure consistent product or service quality, customer satisfaction, and continuous improvement.

3. **ISO 9004: Quality Management - Quality of an Organization - Guidance to Achieve Sustained Success:**
   a. Offers guidance on extending the benefits of ISO 9001 to all stakeholders, not just customers.
   b. Focuses on long-term performance improvement and provides a broader perspective on quality management.

4. **ISO 19011: Guidelines for Auditing Management Systems:**
   a. Provides guidance on auditing management systems, including the principles of auditing, managing audit programs, and conducting audits.
   b. Applicable to internal and external audits of quality management systems and other types of management systems.

Key Principles of ISO 9001:2015

ISO 9001:2015 is based on seven quality management principles that guide organizations towards improved performance and customer satisfaction:

1. **Customer Focus:**
   a. Understanding and meeting customer needs and expectations.
   b. Striving to exceed customer requirements to enhance satisfaction and loyalty.

2. **Leadership:**
   a. Establishing a clear vision and direction for the organization.
   b. Creating an environment where people are fully involved in achieving the organization's quality objectives.

3. **Engagement of People:**
   a. Ensuring that employees at all levels are competent, empowered, and engaged in delivering value.
   b. Recognizing that motivated and engaged employees contribute to improved performance.

4. **Process Approach:**
   a. Managing activities and resources as interrelated processes that function as a coherent system.
   b. Enhancing efficiency and effectiveness by understanding how results are produced.

5. **Improvement:**
   a. Fostering a culture of continuous improvement.
   b. Using a systematic approach to achieve sustained success.

6. **Evidence-Based Decision Making:**
   a. Making decisions based on the analysis and evaluation of data and information.
   b. Ensuring that decisions are well-informed and lead to desired outcomes.

7. **Relationship Management:**

a. Managing relationships with interested parties (such as suppliers) to enhance performance.

b. Recognizing that a well-managed supply chain can improve the organization's ability to create value.

Structure of ISO 9001:2015

The structure of ISO 9001:2015 follows the High-Level Structure (HLS) adopted by ISO for all its management system standards. This makes it easier to integrate ISO 9001 with other management systems, such as ISO 14001 (Environmental Management) and ISO 45001 (Occupational Health and Safety).

The main sections of ISO 9001:2015 are:

1. **Scope:**

    a. Defines the scope and applicability of the standard.

2. **Normative References:**

    a. Lists the documents that are indispensable for the application of the standard.

3. **Terms and Definitions:**

    a. Provides terms and definitions specific to ISO 9001.

4. **Context of the Organization:**

    a. Understanding the organization and its context.

    b. Understanding the needs and expectations of interested parties.

    c. Determining the scope of the quality management system.

    d. Establishing the quality management system and its processes.

5. **Leadership:**

    a. Leadership and commitment.

    b. Establishing a quality policy.

    c. Organizational roles, responsibilities, and authorities.

6. **Planning:**

    a. Actions to address risks and opportunities.

b. Quality objectives and planning to achieve them.

c. Planning of changes.

7. Support:

a. Resources.

b. Competence.

c. Awareness.

d. Communication.

e. Documented information.

8. Operation:

a. Operational planning and control.

b. Requirements for products and services.

c. Design and development of products and services.

d. Control of externally provided processes, products, and services.

e. Production and service provision.

f. Release of products and services.

g. Control of nonconforming outputs.

9. Performance Evaluation:

a. Monitoring, measurement, analysis, and evaluation.

b. Internal audit.

c. Management review.

10.Improvement:

a. General improvement.

b. Nonconformity and corrective action.

c. Continual improvement.

Certification Process

1. Preparation:

a. Understand the requirements of ISO 9001 and conduct a gap analysis to determine what needs to be done to comply.

2. Documentation:

a. Develop and implement the necessary documentation, including the quality manual, procedures, and records.

3. **Implementation:**

    a. Implement the QMS across the organization, ensuring all employees are trained and understand their roles.

4. **Internal Audit:**

    a. Conduct internal audits to verify that the QMS is effectively implemented and identify any areas for improvement.

5. **Management Review:**

    a. Conduct a management review to ensure the QMS is suitable, adequate, and effective.

6. **Certification Audit:**

    a. Engage a certification body to perform an external audit.

    b. The audit is typically conducted in two stages: Stage 1 (Document Review) and Stage 2 (Implementation Review).

7. **Certification:**

    a. If the organization meets the requirements, the certification body issues an ISO 9001 certificate, usually valid for three years with annual surveillance audits.

Benefits of ISO 9000 Series Certification

1. **Improved Product Quality**: Ensures consistent quality in products and services.

2. **Enhanced Customer Satisfaction**: Meeting customer expectations leads to increased satisfaction and loyalty.

3. **Operational Efficiency**: Streamlined processes reduce waste and increase efficiency.

4. **Regulatory Compliance**: Helps ensure compliance with statutory and regulatory requirements.

5. **Market Competitiveness**: Certification can enhance market access and competitiveness.

6. **Risk Management**: Identifies and mitigates risks related to quality.

7. **Continuous Improvement**: Promotes a culture of continuous improvement within the organization.

ISO 14000

The ISO 14000 series is a family of standards related to environmental management that helps organizations minimize their negative impact on the environment, comply with applicable laws and regulations, and continually improve in these areas. The most prominent standard in this series is ISO 14001, which specifies the requirements for an effective Environmental Management System (EMS).

Overview of ISO 14000 Series

1. **ISO 14001: Environmental Management Systems - Requirements with Guidance for Use:**
   a. The primary standard in the ISO 14000 series, it specifies the requirements for an EMS that an organization can use to enhance its environmental performance.
   b. It provides a framework for organizations to protect the environment, respond to changing environmental conditions, and integrate environmental management into their business processes.

2. **ISO 14004: Environmental Management Systems - General Guidelines on Principles, Systems, and Support Techniques:**
   a. Provides additional guidance on the development, implementation, maintenance, and improvement of an EMS.
   b. Helps organizations interpret the requirements of ISO 14001.

3. **ISO 14006: Environmental Management Systems - Guidelines for Incorporating Ecodesign:**

a. Offers guidelines to assist organizations in integrating ecodesign into their EMS.

b. Focuses on minimizing the environmental impact of products throughout their life cycle.

4. **ISO 14040 Series: Environmental Management - Life Cycle Assessment (LCA):**

    a. Provides principles and framework for conducting Life Cycle Assessment, which evaluates the environmental impacts of products and services from cradle to grave.

5. **ISO 14020 Series: Environmental Labels and Declarations:**

    a. Offers guidance on environmental labeling and declarations, helping organizations communicate the environmental aspects of their products and services effectively.

Key Principles of ISO 14001

ISO 14001:2015 is built on the Plan-Do-Check-Act (PDCA) cycle, which ensures continuous improvement of the environmental management system. Here are the core elements:

1. **Plan:**

    a. Establish environmental objectives and processes necessary to deliver results in accordance with the organization's environmental policy.

    b. Identify and assess environmental aspects and impacts, legal and other requirements, and risks and opportunities.

2. **Do:**

    a. Implement the processes as planned.

    b. Allocate resources, assign roles and responsibilities, and ensure competence and awareness.

3. **Check:**

a. Monitor and measure processes against environmental policy, objectives, legal and other requirements, and report the results.

b. Conduct internal audits and management reviews to assess the EMS's performance.

4. Act:

a. Take actions to continually improve the EMS to achieve intended outcomes.

b. Address non-conformities and implement corrective actions.

Structure of ISO 14001:2015

ISO 14001:2015 adopts the High-Level Structure (HLS) for management system standards, facilitating integration with other management systems, such as ISO 9001. The main sections include:

1. Scope:

a. Defines the scope of the standard and its applicability.

2. Normative References:

a. Lists the documents necessary for the application of the standard.

3. Terms and Definitions:

a. Provides specific terms and definitions used in ISO 14001.

4. Context of the Organization:

a. Understanding the organization and its context.

b. Understanding the needs and expectations of interested parties.

c. Determining the scope of the EMS.

d. Establishing the EMS.

5. Leadership:

a. Leadership and commitment.

b. Environmental policy.

c. Organizational roles, responsibilities, and authorities.

6. Planning:

a. Actions to address risks and opportunities.

b. Environmental objectives and planning to achieve them.

c. Planning of changes.

7. **Support:**

a. Resources.

b. Competence.

c. Awareness.

d. Communication.

e. Documented information.

8. **Operation:**

a. Operational planning and control.

b. Emergency preparedness and response.

9. **Performance Evaluation:**

a. Monitoring, measurement, analysis, and evaluation.

b. Internal audit.

c. Management review.

10. **Improvement:**

a. General improvement.

b. Nonconformity and corrective action.

c. Continual improvement.

Benefits of ISO 14001 Certification

1. **Enhanced Environmental Performance:**

a. Systematic approach to managing environmental responsibilities contributes to sustainable development.

2. **Regulatory Compliance:**

a. Helps ensure compliance with environmental laws and regulations, reducing the risk of legal penalties.

3. **Reduced Environmental Impact:**

a. Identifying and managing environmental aspects and impacts leads to reduced pollution and resource consumption.

4. **Cost Savings:**

   a. Improved efficiency in resource use, waste management, and energy consumption results in cost savings.

5. **Improved Stakeholder Relationships:**

   a. Demonstrating environmental responsibility can enhance relationships with customers, regulators, and the community.

6. **Risk Management:**

   a. Proactive identification and mitigation of environmental risks protect the organization from potential liabilities.

7. **Enhanced Market Opportunities:**

   a. Certification can provide a competitive advantage, opening up new market opportunities and improving brand reputation.

Implementation of ISO 14001

1. **Gap Analysis:**

   a. Conduct a gap analysis to determine the current status of environmental management practices against ISO 14001 requirements.

2. **Planning:**

   a. Develop an implementation plan, including timelines, resources, and responsibilities.

   b. Establish environmental policy and objectives aligned with the organization's context and strategic direction.

3. **Documentation:**

   a. Develop necessary documentation, such as environmental policy, procedures, and records.

   b. Ensure documents are controlled and maintained as per ISO 14001 requirements.

4. **Training and Awareness:**

a. Provide training to employees at all levels to ensure understanding and competence in EMS requirements.

b. Promote awareness of environmental issues and the importance of compliance.

5. **Implementation:**

a. Implement the EMS, including operational controls and monitoring mechanisms.

b. Ensure processes are followed, and environmental objectives are pursued.

6. **Internal Audit:**

a. Conduct internal audits to verify the effectiveness of the EMS and identify areas for improvement.

7. **Management Review:**

a. Top management reviews the EMS to ensure its continuing suitability, adequacy, and effectiveness.

8. **Certification Audit:**

a. Engage an accredited certification body to conduct the certification audit, typically in two stages: Stage 1 (Document Review) and Stage 2 (Implementation Review).

9. **Continuous Improvement:**

a. Maintain and continually improve the EMS through regular reviews, audits, and updates based on performance data and changing circumstances.

NABL

The National Accreditation Board for Testing and Calibration Laboratories (NABL) is an autonomous body under the Quality Council of India (QCI). It provides accreditation to laboratories in India for their competence in performing testing and calibration activities. NABL accreditation ensures that these laboratories meet international standards, enhancing their credibility and acceptance globally.

Overview of NABL

National Accreditation Board for Testing and Calibration Laboratories (NABL) is an autonomous body under the Quality Council of India (QCI). NABL provides accreditation to laboratories in India that perform testing, calibration, and medical services. Accreditation by NABL signifies that the laboratory operates according to international standards and generates reliable and credible data.

Importance of NABL in Quality Management Systems

NABL accreditation ensures that laboratories adhere to high standards of quality and competence. This is crucial for laboratories that aim to be recognized globally and seek to instill confidence in their testing and calibration results among stakeholders.

Key Components and Standards of NABL Accreditation

1. **ISO/IEC 17025:2017 - General Requirements for the Competence of Testing and Calibration Laboratories:**
   a. This standard applies to all types of testing and calibration laboratories.
   b. It includes management and technical requirements that ensure the quality and reliability of laboratory results.

2. **ISO 15189:2012 - Medical Laboratories - Requirements for Quality and Competence:**
   a. Specifically designed for medical laboratories.
   b. Focuses on both quality management system requirements and technical requirements for medical laboratories.

3. **ISO/IEC 17043:2010 - Conformity Assessment - General Requirements for Proficiency Testing:**
   a. Applicable to organizations that provide proficiency testing schemes.
   b. Ensures the proficiency testing provider operates competently and consistently.
4. **ISO 17034:2016 - General Requirements for the Competence of Reference Material Producers:**
   a. Pertains to the production of reference materials used in testing and calibration.

Key Principles of NABL Accreditation

1. **Impartiality and Confidentiality:**
   a. Laboratories must demonstrate impartiality and protect the confidentiality of client information.
2. **Competence:**
   a. Laboratories must have competent personnel, adequate facilities, and proper equipment to perform tests and calibrations.
3. **Management System:**
   a. Laboratories must implement a management system compliant with ISO/IEC 17025, ISO 15189, or relevant standards.
4. **Traceability of Measurements:**
   a. Laboratories must ensure that all measurements are traceable to national or international standards.
5. **Internal Audits and Management Reviews:**
   a. Regular internal audits and management reviews must be conducted to ensure ongoing compliance and continual improvement.

NABL Accreditation Process

1. **Application Submission:**

a. Laboratories apply for accreditation by submitting the required forms and documentation to NABL.

b. The application includes details about the scope of accreditation, facilities, personnel, and management systems.

2. **Pre-Assessment:**

a. An optional pre-assessment can be conducted to identify any major non-conformities and help laboratories prepare for the full assessment.

3. **Document Review:**

a. NABL reviews the laboratory's documentation, including quality manuals, procedures, and records, to ensure compliance with relevant standards.

4. **On-Site Assessment:**

a. A team of NABL assessors visits the laboratory to evaluate its technical competence and management system.

b. The assessment includes an evaluation of testing/calibration methods, personnel competence, equipment, and facilities.

5. **Non-Conformity Resolution:**

a. If any non-conformities are identified during the assessment, the laboratory must address them and provide evidence of corrective actions.

6. **Accreditation Decision:**

a. Based on the assessment report and corrective actions taken, NABL decides whether to grant accreditation.

b. If successful, the laboratory receives an accreditation certificate, usually valid for two years.

7. **Surveillance and Reassessment:**

a. NABL conducts periodic surveillance assessments to ensure continued compliance.

b. Laboratories undergo a full reassessment every two years to renew accreditation.

Benefits of NABL Accreditation

1. **Enhanced Credibility and Market Acceptance:**

   a. Accreditation enhances the credibility of laboratory results and increases acceptance by clients and regulatory bodies.

2. **Regulatory Compliance:**

   a. Accredited laboratories are more likely to comply with national and international regulations, reducing the risk of legal issues.

3. **Improved Quality and Reliability:**

   a. Implementation of robust quality management systems leads to more reliable and consistent results.

4. **Competitive Advantage:**

   a. Accreditation provides a competitive edge in the marketplace, attracting more clients and business opportunities.

5. **Global Recognition:**

   a. NABL accreditation is recognized under mutual recognition agreements (MRAs) with international bodies, facilitating global trade and collaboration.

Integration of NABL Accreditation in Quality Management Systems

1. **Alignment with Existing Standards:**

   a. Laboratories with existing ISO 9001 certification can align their quality management systems with NABL requirements for easier integration.

2. **Comprehensive Documentation:**

   a. Develop detailed documentation that includes quality manuals, SOPs, and records to demonstrate compliance with NABL criteria.

3. **Training and Competence Development:**

a. Conduct regular training programs to ensure personnel are competent and aware of NABL standards and requirements.

4. Internal Audits and Management Reviews:

a. Implement a rigorous internal audit schedule to continuously monitor compliance and identify areas for improvement.

b. Conduct regular management reviews to assess the effectiveness of the quality management system and make necessary adjustments.

5. Customer Feedback and Improvement:

a. Use customer feedback to drive improvements in laboratory processes and enhance service quality.

Key Standards for NABL Accreditation

NABL accreditation is based on internationally recognized standards that ensure the competence and quality of testing and calibration laboratories. The key standards for NABL accreditation include:

1. ISO/IEC 17025:2017 - General Requirements for the Competence of Testing and Calibration Laboratories:

a. This standard specifies the general requirements for the competence, impartiality, and consistent operation of testing and calibration laboratories.

b. It covers both management and technical requirements, including personnel competence, facilities, equipment, measurement traceability, sampling, and handling of test items.

c. ISO/IEC 17025 provides a framework for laboratories to demonstrate their ability to produce reliable and accurate test and calibration results.

2. ISO 15189:2012 - Medical Laboratories - Requirements for Quality and Competence:

a. ISO 15189 is specifically designed for medical laboratories and focuses on both quality management system requirements and technical requirements.

b. It covers areas such as management responsibility, document control, internal audits, corrective actions, proficiency testing, and quality indicators.

c. ISO 15189 ensures that medical laboratories operate efficiently and produce reliable results, contributing to patient safety and healthcare quality.

3. **ISO/IEC 17043:2010 - Conformity Assessment - General Requirements for Proficiency Testing:**

    a. This standard pertains to organizations that provide proficiency testing schemes, which are used to assess the performance of laboratories.

    b. ISO/IEC 17043 specifies general requirements for the design and operation of proficiency testing schemes, including the selection and preparation of test samples, statistical evaluation of results, and reporting of performance scores.

    c. It ensures that proficiency testing providers operate competently and consistently, thereby enhancing the reliability of proficiency testing results.

4. **ISO 17034:2016 - General Requirements for the Competence of Reference Material Producers:**

    a. ISO 17034 applies to organizations that produce reference materials used in testing and calibration activities.

    b. It specifies requirements for the competence of reference material producers, including quality management system requirements, production processes, and characterization of reference materials.

c. ISO 17034 ensures the quality and reliability of reference materials, which are essential for ensuring the accuracy and traceability of measurement results.

These standards provide a comprehensive framework for laboratories to demonstrate their technical competence, adherence to quality management principles, and commitment to continuous improvement. NABL accreditation is based on compliance with these standards, ensuring that accredited laboratories meet internationally accepted criteria for quality and competence.

Key Requirements for NABL Accreditation

NABL accreditation is granted to testing, calibration, and medical laboratories that meet specific requirements set forth by the National Accreditation Board for Testing and Calibration Laboratories (NABL). These requirements ensure that accredited laboratories operate with competence, impartiality, and consistency, producing reliable and accurate results. Below are the key requirements for NABL accreditation:

1. **ISO/IEC 17025 or ISO 15189 Compliance:**
   a. Laboratories seeking NABL accreditation must comply with ISO/IEC 17025 for testing and calibration laboratories or ISO 15189 for medical laboratories.
   b. These standards specify general requirements for the competence of laboratories and cover areas such as management system requirements, personnel competence, facilities and equipment, measurement traceability, and testing/calibration procedures.

2. **Impartiality and Confidentiality:**
   a. Laboratories must demonstrate impartiality and independence in their operations, ensuring that testing, calibration, and medical services are conducted objectively and free from bias.

b. Confidentiality of client information and test results must be maintained at all times to protect proprietary information and comply with applicable privacy laws and regulations.

3. Management System Documentation:

a. Laboratories must establish and maintain a documented quality management system (QMS) that includes policies, procedures, and records necessary for effective operation.

b. The QMS documentation should cover all aspects of laboratory activities, including quality objectives, organizational structure, roles and responsibilities, document control, and record keeping.

4. Personnel Competence and Training:

a. Laboratories must ensure that personnel are competent and adequately trained to perform their assigned tasks.

b. Competence requirements should be defined for each job function, and personnel must receive appropriate training, education, and experience to meet these requirements.

c. Records of personnel qualifications, training, and competency assessments must be maintained and periodically reviewed.

5. Facilities and Equipment:

a. Laboratories must have appropriate facilities, equipment, and infrastructure to support their testing, calibration, or medical activities.

b. Facilities should be designed, maintained, and equipped to ensure the integrity of samples, minimize contamination, and provide a suitable environment for conducting tests or calibrations.

c. Equipment must be properly calibrated, maintained, and validated to ensure accurate and reliable measurement results.

6. Measurement Traceability:

a. Laboratories must establish and maintain traceability of measurement results to national or international standards.

b. Calibration and measurement standards used in testing, calibration, or medical activities must be traceable to recognized standards, ensuring the accuracy and reliability of measurement results.

7. **Testing/Calibration Procedures and Methods:**

a. Laboratories must use validated testing, calibration, or medical procedures and methods that are appropriate for the intended purpose and scope of their activities.

b. Procedures should be documented, controlled, and followed consistently to ensure repeatability and reproducibility of results.

c. Any deviations from established procedures must be documented and justified.

8. **Quality Assurance and Control:**

a. Laboratories must implement a comprehensive quality assurance and quality control program to monitor and verify the validity and reliability of test, calibration, or medical results.

b. Quality assurance activities may include internal audits, proficiency testing, inter-laboratory comparisons, instrument checks, and data review procedures.

c. Non-conformities and corrective actions must be promptly addressed to prevent recurrence and ensure continuous improvement.

9. **Reporting of Results:**

a. Laboratories must generate accurate, reliable, and clear test, calibration, or medical reports that are understandable to the intended users.

b. Reports should include all relevant information, such as sample identification, test methods used, measurement results, uncertainty estimates, and any applicable reference standards or regulations.

10. Compliance with Legal and Regulatory Requirements:

a. Laboratories must comply with all applicable legal and regulatory requirements related to their testing, calibration, or medical activities.

b. This may include adherence to specific industry standards, health and safety regulations, environmental regulations, and data protection laws.

11. Continuous Improvement:

a. Laboratories must demonstrate a commitment to continuous improvement by regularly reviewing their processes, procedures, and performance against established objectives and benchmarks.

b. Opportunities for improvement should be identified, documented, and addressed through corrective and preventive actions.

Meeting these key requirements ensures that laboratories seeking NABL accreditation operate with integrity, competence, and reliability, thereby instilling confidence in their testing, calibration, or medical services among clients, stakeholders, and regulatory authorities.

Benefits of NABL Accreditation

NABL accreditation offers numerous benefits to laboratories, organizations, and stakeholders involved in testing, calibration, and medical services. These benefits encompass improved quality, reliability, credibility, market acceptance, and regulatory compliance. Here are the **key benefits of NABL accreditation:**

1. **Enhanced Credibility and Trust**: NABL accreditation signifies that a laboratory operates according to internationally recognized standards and meets stringent quality and competence requirements. This enhances the

credibility and trustworthiness of the laboratory's testing, calibration, or medical services among clients, regulators, and stakeholders.

2. **Compliance with International Standards**: Accredited laboratories adhere to ISO/IEC 17025 or ISO 15189 standards, ensuring that their management systems, technical procedures, personnel competence, and measurement traceability meet global best practices. Compliance with these standards facilitates acceptance of test results and data exchange across borders.

3. **Improved Quality and Reliability**: NABL accreditation promotes a culture of quality, continual improvement, and excellence within accredited laboratories. It encourages the implementation of robust quality management systems, standardized procedures, and quality assurance measures, leading to improved accuracy, reliability, and repeatability of test, calibration, and medical results.

4. **Regulatory Compliance**: Accreditation by NABL demonstrates that a laboratory complies with relevant national and international regulations, standards, and guidelines governing testing, calibration, and medical activities. This helps laboratories meet regulatory requirements, minimize legal risks, and avoid potential penalties or sanctions.

5. **Access to Markets and Opportunities**: NABL accreditation enhances a laboratory's market acceptance and competitiveness, opening up opportunities for business growth, collaboration, and partnerships. Accredited laboratories are preferred by clients, industry stakeholders, and government agencies seeking reliable and competent testing, calibration, or medical services.

6. **Recognition and Acceptance**: NABL accreditation is widely recognized and accepted by industry, government, and regulatory bodies in India and internationally. Accredited laboratories are listed on NABL's directory of

accredited laboratories, providing visibility and recognition within the industry and facilitating access to new markets and clients.

7. **Enhanced Customer Confidence**: Clients and stakeholders have greater confidence in the quality, accuracy, and reliability of test, calibration, and medical results produced by NABL-accredited laboratories. This confidence stems from the rigorous assessment, monitoring, and surveillance conducted by NABL to ensure compliance with accreditation requirements.

8. **Continuous Improvement**: NABL accreditation encourages laboratories to continuously monitor, evaluate, and improve their processes, procedures, and performance. Through internal audits, corrective actions, and management reviews, accredited laboratories identify areas for improvement and implement measures to enhance efficiency, effectiveness, and customer satisfaction.

9. **Mutual Recognition and Global Acceptance**: NABL has signed mutual recognition arrangements (MRAs) with international accreditation bodies, facilitating the acceptance of NABL-accredited test, calibration, and medical results in other countries. This promotes global trade, harmonization of standards, and mutual recognition of laboratory competence and capabilities.

10. **Risk Management and Quality Assurance**: Accredited laboratories implement robust quality assurance and quality control measures to mitigate risks, prevent errors, and ensure the integrity of test, calibration, and medical results. This enhances client confidence, reduces the likelihood of disputes or disputes, and protects the reputation and integrity of the laboratory.

Integration of NABL Accreditation into Quality Management Systems

Integrating NABL accreditation requirements into a laboratory's quality management system (QMS) is essential for ensuring compliance with international standards, continuous improvement, and the delivery of high-quality testing, calibration, or medical services. Here's how NABL accreditation can be integrated into quality management systems:

1. **Alignment with ISO Standards:**
   a. NABL accreditation requirements are aligned with ISO/IEC 17025 for testing and calibration laboratories or ISO 15189 for medical laboratories.
   b. Laboratories should align their existing QMS with the requirements of these standards to ensure comprehensive coverage of accreditation criteria.

2. **Documentation and Record Keeping:**
   a. Develop and maintain detailed documentation that encompasses both NABL accreditation requirements and ISO standard requirements.
   b. Document control procedures should ensure that all documents, including policies, procedures, manuals, and records, are up-to-date, accessible, and controlled.

3. **Training and Competence Development:**
   a. Implement a training program that covers both ISO requirements and NABL accreditation criteria.
   b. Ensure that personnel are trained on relevant procedures, techniques, equipment operation, quality control measures, and safety protocols.

4. **Internal Audits and Management Reviews:**
   a. Conduct regular internal audits to assess compliance with ISO and NABL requirements.
   b. Management reviews should include a comprehensive assessment of the QMS, including performance metrics, customer feedback, corrective actions, and opportunities for improvement.

5. **Facilities and Equipment Management:**

   a. Ensure that laboratory facilities and equipment meet the requirements of both ISO standards and NABL accreditation criteria.

   b. Implement procedures for equipment calibration, maintenance, and validation, as per NABL guidelines and ISO requirements.

6. **Testing/Calibration Procedures and Methods:**

   a. Develop and validate testing, calibration, or medical procedures that comply with ISO and NABL requirements.

   b. Ensure that procedures are documented, controlled, and followed consistently to achieve reliable and repeatable results.

7. **Quality Assurance and Control:**

   a. Implement a comprehensive quality assurance program that encompasses both ISO and NABL requirements.

   b. Include measures such as proficiency testing, inter-laboratory comparisons, instrument checks, data review, and corrective actions to ensure the validity and reliability of test results.

8. **Customer Feedback and Improvement:**

   a. Solicit feedback from customers regarding the quality, timeliness, and effectiveness of laboratory services.

   b. Use customer feedback to identify areas for improvement and implement corrective and preventive actions to address any issues or concerns.

9. **Compliance with Legal and Regulatory Requirements:**

   a. Ensure that the QMS addresses all relevant legal and regulatory requirements related to testing, calibration, or medical services.

   b. Stay informed about changes in regulations and standards and update the QMS accordingly to maintain compliance.

10. **Continuous Improvement Culture:**

a. Foster a culture of continuous improvement within the laboratory by encouraging employees to identify opportunities for enhancement and innovation.

b. Implement mechanisms for capturing and implementing improvement ideas, such as suggestion boxes, improvement projects, and process optimization initiatives.

11.Integration of NABL Accreditation Criteria:

a. Integrate specific NABL accreditation criteria into existing QMS procedures, manuals, and processes.

b. Ensure that all requirements related to impartiality, competence, facilities, equipment, measurement traceability, and reporting are addressed and implemented effectively.

By integrating NABL accreditation requirements into the laboratory's quality management system, laboratories can ensure compliance with international standards, enhance the quality and reliability of their services, and demonstrate their commitment to excellence and continuous improvement. This integration fosters a culture of quality, transparency, and accountability, leading to increased customer satisfaction, market acceptance, and regulatory compliance.

GLP

Good Laboratory Practice (GLP) is a quality system concerned with the organizational process and the conditions under which non-clinical health and environmental safety studies are planned, performed, monitored, recorded, archived, and reported. GLP principles ensure the generation of high-quality and reliable test data.

Overview of GLP

GLP principles were first established by the Organisation for Economic Co-operation and Development (OECD) in the 1970s to promote the quality and validity of test data used for determining the safety of chemicals and other products. These principles are now adopted internationally.

Key Principles of GLP

1. **Organization and Personnel:**
   a. **Responsibilities**: Clearly defined roles and responsibilities for all personnel involved in the study.
   b. **Training:** Personnel should be adequately trained and qualified for their tasks.
   c. **Management:** A study director is responsible for the overall conduct of the study, and a quality assurance unit monitors compliance with GLP.

2. **Facilities:**
   a. **Test Facility Organization**: Facilities should be appropriately designed and equipped to conduct the study.
   b. **Environmental Conditions**: Control of environmental conditions (e.g., temperature, humidity) to ensure the integrity of the study.

3. **Equipment and Materials:**
   a. **Maintenance and Calibration**: Regular maintenance and calibration of equipment to ensure accuracy and reliability.
   b. **Materials**: Use of certified and properly labeled materials and reagents.

4. **Standard Operating Procedures (SOPs):**
   a. **Documentation**: Detailed SOPs for all aspects of the study to ensure consistency and repeatability.
   b. **Approval and Review**: SOPs should be regularly reviewed and approved by authorized personnel.

5. **Test Systems:**
   a. **Selection and Handling**: Proper selection, handling, and care of test systems (e.g., animals, plants, microorganisms).

b. **Monitoring**: Regular monitoring of test systems to ensure their health and stability.

6. **Test and Reference Items:**
   a. **Characterization:** Thorough characterization of test and reference items, including purity, stability, and storage conditions.
   b. **Handling:** Proper handling, storage, and documentation of test and reference items.

7. **Study Plan:**
   a. **Content:** A detailed study plan should outline objectives, methodology, data collection, and analysis procedures.
   b. **Approval:** The study plan must be approved by the study director before the study begins.

8. **Conduct of Study:**
   a. **Execution**: Studies should be conducted according to the approved plan and SOPs.
   b. **Data Collection**: Accurate and timely recording of all data generated during the study.

9. **Reporting of Results:**
   a. **Final Report**: A comprehensive final report should document all aspects of the study, including methodology, results, discussion, and conclusions.
   b. **Archiving**: Retention of all records and materials related to the study in an organized and secure manner.

10. **Quality Assurance:**
    a. **Audits:** Regular audits by the quality assurance unit to ensure compliance with GLP.
    b. **Inspections**: Facility and process inspections to identify and correct non-compliance issues.

Implementation of GLP in Quality Management Systems

1. **Establishing a GLP Framework:**
   a. Develop a GLP framework tailored to the organization's needs, based on OECD principles or other relevant guidelines.
   b. Define the scope, objectives, and responsibilities for implementing GLP within the organization.

2. **Developing SOPs:**
   a. Create detailed SOPs covering all laboratory activities, from sample handling to data reporting.
   b. Ensure SOPs are accessible to all relevant personnel and regularly updated.

3. **Training and Competence:**
   a. Implement a training program to ensure all staff understand GLP principles and their specific roles.
   b. Maintain records of training and competence assessments.

4. **Facility and Equipment Management:**
   a. Ensure laboratory facilities and equipment meet GLP requirements, including regular maintenance and calibration.
   b. Document all maintenance and calibration activities.

5. **Study Planning and Conduct:**
   a. Develop comprehensive study plans for each study, outlining objectives, methods, and quality assurance measures.
   b. Conduct studies in strict accordance with the approved plans and SOPs.

6. **Data Management:**
   a. Implement robust data management practices to ensure the integrity, accuracy, and traceability of all study data.
   b. Use secure and validated systems for data recording, storage, and retrieval.

7. **Quality Assurance and Auditing:**

a. Establish a quality assurance unit responsible for auditing studies, facilities, and processes.

b. Conduct regular internal audits and inspections to verify compliance with GLP.

8. **Continuous Improvement:**

a. Use audit findings, non-conformance reports, and other feedback to identify areas for improvement.

b. Implement corrective and preventive actions to address issues and enhance GLP compliance.

Benefits of Implementing GLP

1. **Improved Data Quality and Reliability:**

a. Ensures that data generated are accurate, reliable, and reproducible.

2. **Regulatory Compliance:**

a. Facilitates compliance with national and international regulatory requirements.

3. **Enhanced Credibility and Reputation:**

a. Demonstrates commitment to high-quality research and data integrity, enhancing the laboratory's reputation.

4. **Efficient Risk Management:**

a. Identifies and mitigates risks related to laboratory activities, ensuring the safety and validity of studies.

5. **Streamlined Processes:**

a. Standardized procedures lead to more efficient and consistent operations.

6. **Global Acceptance of Data:**

a. GLP compliance is recognized internationally, increasing the acceptance of data by regulatory bodies worldwide.

Multiple Choice Questions (MCQs)

1. What is the primary purpose of a Quality Management System (QMS)?

    a) To document organizational hierarchy

    b) To improve marketing strategies

    c) To coordinate and direct activities to meet customer and regulatory requirements

    d) To manage financial operations

2. Which of the following is a key principle of ISO 9001:2015?

    a) Profit Maximization

    b) Leadership

    c) Environmental Conservation

    d) Market Expansion

3. What does "Customer Focus" in ISO 9001:2015 emphasize?

    a) Reducing costs

    b) Increasing market share

    c) Meeting and exceeding customer expectations

    d) Expanding product lines

4. What is the purpose of a Quality Manual in a QMS?

    a) To outline the company's financial plans

    b) To detail marketing strategies

    c) To outline the scope of the QMS and its processes

    d) To document employee salaries

5. What is the first step in implementing a QMS?

    a) Conducting internal audits

    b) Planning the scope and objectives

    c) Training employees

    d) Developing a quality manual

6. What does "Process Control" involve in a QMS?

    a) Managing financial transactions

    b) Defining and controlling production or service delivery processes

c) Hiring new employees

d) Conducting market research

7. What is a core benefit of implementing a QMS?

a) Increased customer satisfaction

b) Higher marketing costs

c) Reduced compliance

d) Lower product quality

8. Which standard is the most widely recognized for Quality Management Systems?

a) ISO 14001

b) ISO 45001

c) ISO 9001:2015

d) ISO 17025

9. What does the acronym "CAPA" stand for in a QMS context?

a) Customer and Product Analysis

b) Corrective and Preventive Actions

c) Cost and Price Analysis

d) Certification and Policy Assessment

10. What is the focus of Total Quality Management (TQM)?

a) Short-term profits

b) Customer satisfaction and continuous improvement

c) Marketing expansion

d) Reducing employee training

11. In the context of GLP, what is the role of a study director?

a) To handle financial audits

b) To manage marketing strategies

c) To oversee the conduct of the study

d) To conduct employee performance reviews

12. What is a key benefit of NABL accreditation?

a) Improved financial performance

b) Enhanced credibility and market acceptance

c) Increased employee turnover

d) Decreased regulatory compliance

13. What does ISO 14001:2015 focus on?

a) Quality Management

b) Environmental Management

c) Financial Management

d) Marketing Management

14. What is the purpose of ISO 9004?

a) To provide guidelines for sustained success

b) To establish financial controls

c) To define environmental policies

d) To manage employee benefits

15. What is a major component of Quality by Design (QbD)?

a) Reducing marketing costs

b) Designing and developing processes to ensure quality

c) Managing financial investments

d) Expanding product lines

16. What does "Non-Conformance Management" involve in a QMS?

a) Tracking employee attendance

b) Identifying and managing non-conforming products or processes

c) Conducting market research

d) Developing new product lines

17. What is the goal of continuous improvement in a QMS?

a) Increasing costs

b) Expanding market share

c) Enhancing products, services, or processes continuously

d) Reducing employee training

18. What standard is specific to the automotive sector QMS?

   a) ISO 9001

   b) ISO 14001

   c) IATF 16949

   d) ISO 45001

19. What does "Document Control" ensure in a QMS?

   a) Documents are accessible and accurate

   b) Financial records are audited

   c) Marketing plans are implemented

   d) Employee attendance is tracked

20. What is the purpose of conducting internal audits in a QMS?

   a) To review marketing strategies

   b) To ensure the QMS is effectively implemented and compliant

   c) To manage financial investments

   d) To hire new employees

Short Answer Type Questions (Subjective)

1. Define a Quality Management System (QMS) and its primary purpose.

2. What are the core elements of a QMS?

3. Explain the importance of customer satisfaction in a QMS.

4. What is the role of a Quality Manual in a QMS?

5. Describe the concept of continuous improvement in a QMS.

6. What is the significance of document control in a QMS?

7. Explain the process of conducting internal audits in a QMS.

8. What are the key principles of ISO 9001:2015?

9. Define the term "Quality Policy" in the context of a QMS.

10. How does ISO 9001:2015 ensure evidence-based decision-making?

11. What is Total Quality Management (TQM)?

12. Describe the concept of "Customer Focus" in TQM.

13. Explain the role of employee involvement in TQM.

14. What is Quality by Design (QbD)?

15. How does QbD differ from traditional quality assurance methods?

16. What is the purpose of the DMAIC methodology in Six Sigma?

17. Explain the significance of managing Out of Specifications (OOS) results.

18. What is Change Control in the context of a QMS?

19. How does ISO 14001:2015 contribute to environmental management?

20. What is the primary objective of Good Laboratory Practice (GLP)?

Long Answer Type Questions (Subjective)

1. Discuss the key concepts and importance of a Quality Management System (QMS) in organizational effectiveness.

2. Explain the steps involved in implementing a QMS and the challenges organizations might face during implementation.

3. Analyze the benefits of obtaining ISO 9001:2015 certification for an organization.

4. Discuss the principles of Total Quality Management (TQM) and how they contribute to organizational success.

5. Explain the process of Quality by Design (QbD) and its application in the pharmaceutical industry.

6. Describe the DMAIC methodology in Six Sigma and its role in improving process quality.

7. Discuss the process and importance of managing Out of Specifications (OOS) results in a QMS.

8. Explain the Change Control process in a QMS and its significance in maintaining product quality and compliance.

9. Discuss the structure and key principles of ISO 14001:2015 and its role in environmental management.

10. Explain the principles of Good Laboratory Practice (GLP) and how they ensure the reliability and integrity of non-clinical study data.

Answer Key

1. c) To coordinate and direct activities to meet customer and regulatory requirements
2. b) Leadership
3. c) Meeting and exceeding customer expectations
4. c) To outline the scope of the QMS and its processes
5. b) Planning the scope and objectives
6. b) Defining and controlling production or service delivery processes
7. a) Increased customer satisfaction
8. c) ISO 9001:2015
9. b) Corrective and Preventive Actions
10. b) Customer satisfaction and continuous improvement
11. c) To oversee the conduct of the study
12. b) Enhanced credibility and market acceptance
13. b) Environmental Management
14. a) To provide guidelines for sustained success
15. b) Designing and developing processes to ensure quality
16. b) Identifying and managing non-conforming products or processes
17. c) Enhancing products, services, or processes continuously
18. c) IATF 16949
19. a) Documents are accessible and accurate
20. b) To ensure the QMS is effectively implemented and compliant

CHAPTER - 6

INDIAN REGULATORY REQUIREMENTS

INTRODUCTION:

Indian regulatory requirements encompass a broad spectrum of laws, regulations, and standards that govern various sectors and industries within the country. Here's an introduction to some of the key areas:

Pharmaceuticals and Healthcare:

Regulatory requirements in India for pharmaceuticals and healthcare are comprehensive and stringent, overseen primarily by the Central Drugs Standard Control Organization (CDSCO) and various State Licensing Authorities (SLAs). These regulations cover a wide range of aspects related to the development, manufacturing, distribution, and marketing of pharmaceuticals, medical devices, biological products, and cosmetics. Here's a detailed overview of the regulatory requirements for pharmaceuticals and healthcare in India:

1. **Drug Approval Process:**
   a. The approval process for pharmaceuticals involves rigorous evaluation by CDSCO. It includes preclinical studies, clinical trials, and submission of a New Drug Application (NDA) for marketing authorization.
   b. CDSCO assesses the safety, efficacy, and quality of drugs before granting marketing approval. Post-approval, it continues monitoring through pharmacovigilance activities.

2. **Clinical Trials Oversight:**
   a. CDSCO regulates and monitors clinical trials conducted in India to ensure participant safety and ethical conduct. It reviews trial protocols, monitors trial progress, and evaluates data to assess safety and efficacy.

3. **Manufacturing Standards:**

   a. Compliance with Good Manufacturing Practices (GMP) is mandatory for pharmaceutical manufacturing facilities. CDSCO conducts inspections to ensure adherence to quality standards.

4. **Quality Control:**

   a. CDSCO establishes and enforces quality standards for pharmaceuticals. It conducts testing and analysis to ensure compliance with pharmacopoeial standards.

5. **Import and Export Regulations:**

   a. CDSCO regulates the import and export of pharmaceuticals, ensuring compliance with regulatory requirements and standards.

6. **Medical Devices Regulation:**

   a. The regulation of medical devices involves registration, licensing, and adherence to quality standards set by CDSCO. Import and manufacturing of medical devices are subject to regulatory approval.

7. **Biological Products:**

   a. Biological products, including vaccines, blood products, and recombinant products, are subject to stringent regulatory oversight by CDSCO to ensure safety and efficacy.

8. **Cosmetics Regulation:**

   a. CDSCO regulates cosmetics, including their import, manufacture, distribution, and sale. Compliance with quality standards and labeling requirements is mandatory.

9. **Advertising and Promotion:**

   a. Advertising and promotion of pharmaceuticals and healthcare products are regulated to ensure accuracy, fairness, and compliance with regulatory requirements.

10. **Post-Marketing Surveillance:**

a. CDSCO conducts post-marketing surveillance to monitor the safety and efficacy of pharmaceuticals and healthcare products in the market. It collects and analyzes reports of adverse events and takes regulatory action as necessary.

11. Pharmacy Practice:

a. Regulations govern the practice of pharmacy, including licensing of pharmacists and premises, prescription requirements, and dispensing practices.

12. Telemedicine and Digital Health:

a. With the growth of telemedicine and digital health platforms, regulatory frameworks are evolving to address issues such as patient privacy, data security, and quality of care.

13. Public Health Initiatives:

a. Regulatory authorities collaborate with healthcare stakeholders to implement public health initiatives, such as immunization programs, disease surveillance, and drug pricing policies.

Food Safety:

Food safety regulations in India are governed by the Food Safety and Standards Authority of India (FSSAI), which was established under the Food Safety and Standards Act, 2006. FSSAI is responsible for ensuring food safety, hygiene, and quality throughout the food supply chain. Here's a detailed overview of food safety in Indian regulatory requirements:

1. Food Safety Standards:

a. FSSAI establishes and enforces food safety standards to ensure the safety and quality of food products available in the market.

b. These standards cover various aspects such as permissible limits for contaminants, residues, additives, and labeling requirements.

2. Licensing and Registration:

a. Food businesses are required to obtain licenses or register with FSSAI, depending on the scale and nature of their operations.

b. Licensing and registration ensure that food businesses comply with food safety standards and maintain hygiene and sanitation practices.

3. Food Safety Management Systems:

a. FSSAI promotes the adoption of food safety management systems, such as Hazard Analysis and Critical Control Points (HACCP) and Good Manufacturing Practices (GMP), by food businesses.

b. These systems help prevent, eliminate, or reduce food safety hazards throughout the food production process.

4. Food Testing and Analysis:

a. FSSAI operates a network of food testing laboratories to analyze food samples for compliance with safety and quality standards.

b. These laboratories conduct tests for microbiological, chemical, and physical parameters to ensure food safety.

5. Food Additives and Contaminants:

a. FSSAI regulates the use of food additives and contaminants to ensure that they do not exceed permissible limits and do not pose risks to consumer health.

b. It establishes standards for the use of food additives and monitors compliance through testing and inspection.

6. Labeling and Packaging:

a. FSSAI mandates labeling requirements for packaged food products to provide consumers with accurate and relevant information.

b. Labels must include details such as ingredients, nutritional information, allergen information, and FSSAI license or registration number.

7. Import and Export Regulations:

a. FSSAI regulates the import and export of food products to ensure compliance with food safety standards.

b. Imported food products must meet Indian standards and undergo inspection and testing before clearance.

8. **Food Safety Training and Awareness:**

a. FSSAI conducts food safety training programs and awareness campaigns to educate food businesses, consumers, and food handlers about safe food practices.

b. Training programs cover topics such as personal hygiene, food handling, sanitation, and food safety management.

9. **Enforcement and Compliance:**

a. FSSAI conducts inspections, audits, and surveillance activities to enforce food safety regulations and ensure compliance by food businesses.

b. Non-compliance may result in penalties, license suspension or cancellation, and prosecution under the Food Safety and Standards Act.

10. **Surveillance and Monitoring:**

a. FSSAI conducts surveillance and monitoring activities to assess the safety and quality of food products available in the market.

b. It collects data on foodborne illnesses, outbreaks, and food safety incidents to identify emerging risks and take preventive measures.

Banking and Finance:

Banking and finance in India are regulated by various authorities to ensure stability, integrity, and transparency within the financial system. Here's a detailed overview of regulatory requirements in Indian banking and finance:

1. **Reserve Bank of India (RBI):**

a. The Reserve Bank of India is the central bank of the country and the primary regulatory authority for banking and financial institutions.

b. RBI formulates and implements monetary policy to maintain price stability and promote economic growth.

c. It regulates and supervises banks, non-banking financial companies (NBFCs), payment systems, and foreign exchange transactions.

d. RBI issues licenses, sets prudential norms, and conducts inspections to ensure the soundness and stability of the banking system.

2. Banking Regulation:

a. RBI regulates banks operating in India, including public sector banks, private sector banks, foreign banks, cooperative banks, and regional rural banks.

b. It sets capital adequacy requirements, liquidity norms, and asset classification and provisioning norms to ensure the financial health of banks.

c. RBI also regulates mergers, acquisitions, and restructuring of banks to maintain a competitive and resilient banking sector.

3. Non-Banking Financial Companies (NBFCs):

a. RBI regulates NBFCs, which provide banking and financial services but do not hold a banking license.

b. It sets prudential norms, capital adequacy requirements, and governance standards for NBFCs to mitigate risks and protect investors.

4. Securities and Exchange Board of India (SEBI):

a. SEBI is the regulatory authority for the securities market in India, overseeing stock exchanges, brokers, mutual funds, and other market intermediaries.

b. It regulates securities offerings, insider trading, market manipulation, and corporate governance to ensure investor protection and market integrity.

c. SEBI also promotes the development and regulation of the capital markets by introducing reforms and enhancing transparency and disclosure standards.

5. **Insurance Regulatory and Development Authority of India (IRDAI):**

    a. IRDAI regulates and supervises the insurance industry in India, including life insurance, general insurance, and reinsurance companies.

    b. It sets solvency and capital adequacy requirements, product guidelines, and distribution norms to safeguard policyholders' interests and ensure the stability of the insurance sector.

6. **Financial Stability and Development Council (FSDC):**

    a. FSDC is an apex body chaired by the Finance Minister of India, comprising regulators, policymakers, and government officials.

    b. It coordinates financial sector reforms, monitors systemic risks, and promotes financial stability, development, and inclusion in the economy.

7. **Anti-Money Laundering (AML) and Combating the Financing of Terrorism (CFT):**

    a. Indian regulatory authorities, including RBI, SEBI, and IRDAI, implement AML/CFT measures to prevent money laundering and terrorist financing.

    b. They require banks, financial institutions, and intermediaries to conduct customer due diligence, monitor transactions, and report suspicious activities to the Financial Intelligence Unit-India (FIU-IND).

8. **Consumer Protection:**

a. Regulatory authorities enforce consumer protection measures to safeguard the interests of banking and financial services consumers.

b. They regulate fair practices, transparency, grievance redressal mechanisms, and disclosure requirements to ensure consumer rights are protected.

Securities and Exchange:

Regulatory requirements for securities and exchanges in India are overseen by the Securities and Exchange Board of India (SEBI). SEBI is the regulatory authority responsible for regulating the securities market, protecting investors, and promoting fair and transparent practices within the market. Here's a detailed overview of regulatory requirements for securities and exchanges in India:

1. **Regulation of Securities Market:**

   a. SEBI regulates various segments of the securities market, including equity, debt, derivatives, commodities, and mutual funds.

   b. It formulates regulations, guidelines, and frameworks for securities offerings, trading, and market operations to ensure investor protection and market integrity.

2. **Issuance and Listing of Securities:**

   a. SEBI regulates the issuance, listing, and trading of securities such as stocks, bonds, debentures, and derivatives.

   b. It reviews and approves prospectuses and offer documents for securities offerings to ensure disclosure of material information and compliance with regulatory requirements.

   c. SEBI oversees the listing process and monitors listed companies' compliance with listing requirements, corporate governance norms, and disclosure obligations.

3. **Market Intermediaries Regulation:**

a. SEBI regulates market intermediaries such as stock exchanges, brokers, depositories, clearing corporations, and registrars to ensure their compliance with regulatory standards.

b. It sets eligibility criteria, registration requirements, and conduct norms for market intermediaries to maintain market integrity and protect investor interests.

4. **Investor Protection:**

a. SEBI implements investor protection measures to safeguard investors' interests and rights in the securities market.

b. It regulates fair practices, transparency, disclosure requirements, and grievance redressal mechanisms to enhance investor confidence and trust.

5. **Market Surveillance and Enforcement:**

a. SEBI conducts surveillance and enforcement activities to monitor market activities, detect market manipulation, insider trading, and other malpractices.

b. It investigates violations of securities laws and takes disciplinary action against entities found to be non-compliant with regulatory requirements.

6. **Regulation of Market Infrastructure:**

a. SEBI regulates market infrastructure institutions such as stock exchanges, clearing corporations, and depositories to ensure their efficiency, safety, and reliability.

b. It sets operational and technological standards, risk management frameworks, and governance norms for market infrastructure institutions.

7. **Corporate Governance:**

a. SEBI promotes corporate governance practices among listed companies to enhance transparency, accountability, and shareholder value.

b. It issues corporate governance guidelines and mandates disclosure of corporate governance practices in annual reports and other filings.

8. Mutual Funds Regulation:

a. SEBI regulates mutual funds and asset management companies to protect the interests of unit holders and ensure the integrity of mutual fund operations.

b. It sets investment norms, disclosure requirements, and fund management standards to promote investor confidence and trust in mutual funds.

9. Derivatives Regulation:

a. SEBI regulates the derivatives market to ensure the integrity and stability of derivative transactions.

b. It sets eligibility criteria, position limits, margin requirements, and risk management norms for derivative trading to mitigate risks and protect market participants.

Telecommunications:

In India, telecommunications are regulated by the Department of Telecommunications (DoT) and the Telecom Regulatory Authority of India (TRAI). These regulatory bodies oversee the telecommunications sector to ensure fair competition, consumer protection, and the growth of the industry. Here's a detailed overview of the regulatory requirements for telecommunications in India:

1. Licensing and Spectrum Management:

a. DoT is responsible for issuing licenses and managing the allocation of spectrum for telecommunications services.

b. It grants licenses to telecom operators for providing various services such as voice, data, and value-added services.

c. DoT allocates spectrum through auctions and administers spectrum usage charges to ensure efficient utilization of radio frequencies.

2. **Regulation of Telecommunications Services:**

   a. TRAI is the statutory regulatory authority for telecommunications services in India.

   b. TRAI formulates regulations, guidelines, and recommendations for telecom services to promote competition, consumer interests, and the orderly growth of the sector.

   c. It sets tariff regulations, quality of service norms, interconnection regulations, and licensing guidelines for telecom operators.

3. **Interconnection and Interoperability:**

   a. TRAI regulates interconnection arrangements between telecom operators to ensure seamless connectivity and interoperability of networks.

   b. It mandates fair and non-discriminatory interconnection agreements to facilitate competition and consumer choice.

4. **Spectrum Auctions and Management:**

   a. DoT conducts spectrum auctions to allocate radio frequencies to telecom operators for providing wireless services.

   b. It formulates spectrum management policies, pricing norms, and auction rules to ensure transparency, efficiency, and equitable access to spectrum.

5. **Quality of Service (QoS) Regulations:**

   a. TRAI mandates quality of service standards for telecom operators to ensure the delivery of reliable and high-quality services to consumers.

b. It sets benchmarks for parameters such as call drop rates, network availability, and data speed to measure and monitor service quality.

6. Consumer Protection:

a. TRAI implements consumer protection measures to safeguard the interests and rights of telecom consumers.

b. It regulates billing practices, dispute resolution mechanisms, and grievance redressal procedures to address consumer complaints and grievances.

7. Network Security and Data Privacy:

a. DoT and TRAI collaborate with other government agencies to address network security concerns and protect telecom infrastructure from cyber threats.

b. They formulate regulations and guidelines to ensure compliance with data privacy and security standards, including the storage and transmission of sensitive information.

8. Promotion of Broadband and Digital Connectivity:

a. DoT and TRAI promote the expansion of broadband and digital connectivity to bridge the digital divide and enhance access to telecom services.

b. They formulate policies, incentives, and initiatives to promote the deployment of broadband infrastructure, including fiber optic networks and wireless broadband technologies.

9. Competition Policy and Market Regulation:

a. TRAI monitors market dynamics and enforces competition policies to prevent anti-competitive practices and promote a level playing field in the telecom sector.

b. It conducts market assessments, market studies, and market analysis to identify competition issues and take corrective measures as necessary.

Environmental Regulations:

Environmental regulations in India are governed by various laws, policies, and regulatory bodies at the central and state levels. These regulations aim to protect the environment, prevent pollution, conserve natural resources, and promote sustainable development. Here's a detailed overview of environmental regulations in Indian regulatory requirements:

1. **The Environment (Protection) Act, 1986:**
   a. The Environment (Protection) Act is the principal legislation for environmental protection in India.
   b. It empowers the central government to take measures to protect and improve the quality of the environment and to prevent and control pollution.

2. **The Air (Prevention and Control of Pollution) Act, 1981:**
   a. The Air Act aims to prevent and control air pollution by regulating emissions from industries, vehicles, and other sources.
   b. It empowers state pollution control boards to enforce emission standards, conduct air quality monitoring, and take measures to mitigate air pollution.

3. **The Water (Prevention and Control of Pollution) Act, 1974:**
   a. The Water Act aims to prevent and control water pollution by regulating the discharge of pollutants into water bodies.
   b. It mandates the establishment of state pollution control boards to enforce water quality standards, regulate industrial effluents, and promote wastewater treatment.

4. **The Environment Impact Assessment (EIA) Notification, 2006:**
   a. The EIA Notification mandates environmental clearance for projects that may have significant environmental impacts.
   b. It requires project proponents to assess the environmental impacts of their projects, consult stakeholders, and obtain clearance from

the Ministry of Environment, Forest and Climate Change (MoEFCC) or State Environment Impact Assessment Authorities (SEIAAs).

5. **The Hazardous and Other Wastes (Management and Transboundary Movement) Rules, 2016:**

   a. These rules regulate the generation, storage, treatment, and disposal of hazardous wastes in India.

   b. They require hazardous waste generators to obtain authorization, follow waste management practices, and comply with disposal requirements.

6. **The Forest (Conservation) Act, 1980:**

   a. The Forest Act regulates the diversion of forest land for non-forest purposes such as mining, infrastructure projects, and industrial activities.

   b. It mandates prior approval from the MoEFCC or state forest departments for any diversion of forest land.

7. **The Wildlife Protection Act, 1972:**

   a. The Wildlife Act aims to protect and conserve wildlife and their habitats in India.

   b. It prohibits hunting, poaching, and trade in endangered species and regulates activities in wildlife sanctuaries and national parks.

8. **The Coastal Regulation Zone (CRZ) Notification, 2019:**

   a. The CRZ Notification regulates development activities along the coastal areas to protect coastal ecosystems and livelihoods.

   b. It restricts certain activities within coastal zones and mandates prior clearance for development projects in CRZ areas.

9. **The National Green Tribunal (NGT):**

   a. The NGT is a specialized environmental court established to adjudicate environmental disputes and enforce environmental laws.

b. It has the authority to hear cases related to environmental violations, pollution incidents, and non-compliance with environmental regulations.

10. State Pollution Control Boards (SPCBs):

a. SPCBs are responsible for implementing environmental laws and regulations at the state level.

b. They issue permits, conduct inspections, monitor pollution levels, and take enforcement actions against violators of environmental regulations.

Intellectual Property Rights (IPR):

Intellectual Property Rights (IPR) in India are governed by various laws and regulations to protect creations of the intellect, such as inventions, literary and artistic works, trademarks, designs, and trade secrets. Here's a detailed overview of IPR in Indian regulatory requirements:

1. The Patents Act, 1970:

a. The Patents Act provides for the grant and protection of patents in India.

b. It defines the criteria for patentability, including novelty, inventive step, and industrial applicability.

c. The Act establishes the process for filing patent applications, examination, grant, and enforcement of patents.

d. It also outlines the rights and obligations of patent holders, including the exclusive right to make, use, sell, or import the patented invention.

2. The Copyright Act, 1957:

a. The Copyright Act protects literary, artistic, musical, and dramatic works, as well as cinematographic films and sound recordings.

b. It grants creators exclusive rights to reproduce, distribute, perform, and adapt their works.

c. The Act outlines the duration of copyright protection, rights of copyright owners, and exceptions to copyright infringement.

d. It also establishes copyright registration procedures and enforcement mechanisms.

3. The Trade Marks Act, 1999:

a. The Trade Marks Act provides for the registration and protection of trademarks in India.

b. It defines trademarks as distinctive signs used to identify goods or services of a particular source.

c. The Act outlines the process for trademark registration, including examination, publication, and opposition proceedings.

d. It also prohibits the unauthorized use of registered trademarks and provides remedies for trademark infringement.

4. The Designs Act, 2000:

a. The Designs Act governs the registration and protection of industrial designs in India.

b. It defines industrial designs as the visual appearance of products, including shape, configuration, pattern, or ornamentation.

c. The Act establishes the process for design registration, examination, and enforcement of design rights.

d. It grants design owners exclusive rights to use and license their designs for a specified period.

5. The Geographical Indications of Goods (Registration and Protection) Act, 1999:

a. The Geographical Indications Act provides for the registration and protection of geographical indications (GIs) in India.

b. It defines GIs as indications that identify goods as originating from a specific geographical location, which possess qualities, reputation, or characteristics attributable to that location.

c. The Act outlines the procedure for GI registration, protection of GI rights, and enforcement against unauthorized use of GIs.

6. **The Protection of Plant Varieties and Farmers' Rights Act, 2001 (PPVFR Act):**

   a. The PPVFR Act provides for the protection of plant varieties and the rights of farmers in India.

   b. It establishes a national registry for the registration of plant varieties and grants breeders exclusive rights over registered varieties.

   c. The Act also recognizes the rights of farmers to save, use, exchange, and sell farm-saved seeds of registered varieties.

7. **Enforcement and Protection:**

   a. Various enforcement mechanisms, including civil and criminal remedies, injunctions, and damages, are available to protect IPR in India.

   b. Specialized intellectual property offices, such as the Patent Office, Copyright Office, and Trademark Registry, handle registration and enforcement of IPR.

   c. The judiciary adjudicates disputes related to IPR infringement and violation of intellectual property rights.

Labour Laws:

Labour laws in India are designed to regulate employment relationships, protect the rights of workers, and promote social justice and welfare. These laws cover a wide range of aspects related to employment, including wages, working conditions, social security, industrial relations, and occupational health and safety. Here's a detailed overview of labour laws in Indian regulatory requirements:

1. **The Factories Act, 1948:**

a. The Factories Act regulates the working conditions in factories, ensuring the safety, health, and welfare of workers.

b. It prescribes standards for workplace amenities, such as ventilation, lighting, sanitation, and safety measures.

c. The Act also addresses issues such as working hours, overtime, holidays, and employment of women and young persons.

2. The Minimum Wages Act, 1948:

a. The Minimum Wages Act sets minimum wage rates for different categories of workers to ensure fair remuneration and prevent exploitation.

b. It mandates payment of wages not less than the prescribed minimum wage rates and regulates wage payment intervals and deductions.

3. The Payment of Wages Act, 1936:

a. The Payment of Wages Act regulates the payment of wages to workers employed in any industry.

b. It mandates timely payment of wages, prohibition of unauthorized deductions, and maintenance of wage records by employers.

4. The Employees' Provident Funds and Miscellaneous Provisions Act, 1952 (EPF Act):

a. The EPF Act provides for the establishment of provident fund schemes for employees in certain industries.

b. It mandates contributions to provident funds by both employers and employees and governs the administration of provident fund schemes.

5. The Employees' State Insurance Act, 1948 (ESI Act):

a. The ESI Act provides for social security benefits, including medical, sickness, maternity, disablement, and dependent benefits, to employees in certain industries.

b. It mandates contributions to the Employees' State Insurance (ESI) scheme by employers and employees and governs the administration of ESI benefits.

6. The Industrial Disputes Act, 1947:

a. The Industrial Disputes Act regulates industrial relations and provides mechanisms for the resolution of disputes between employers and workers.

b. It covers issues such as strikes, lockouts, layoffs, retrenchment, and unfair labour practices.

7. The Trade Unions Act, 1926:

a. The Trade Unions Act provides for the registration and regulation of trade unions in India.

b. It grants legal recognition to trade unions and confers certain rights and privileges, such as collective bargaining and representation of workers.

8. The Contract Labour (Regulation and Abolition) Act, 1970:

a. The Contract Labour Act regulates the employment of contract labour in certain industries and establishments.

b. It mandates registration of establishments engaging contract labour, regulation of working conditions, and welfare measures for contract workers.

9. The Maternity Benefit Act, 1961:

a. The Maternity Benefit Act provides for maternity leave and benefits to women employees.

b. It mandates paid maternity leave, medical benefits, and nursing breaks for women employees during pregnancy and childbirth.

10. The Sexual Harassment of Women at Workplace (Prevention, Prohibition and Redressal) Act, 2013:

a. The Sexual Harassment Act provides for the prevention and redressal of sexual harassment of women at the workplace.

b. It mandates the establishment of internal complaints committees and provides for the investigation and resolution of complaints of sexual harassment.

CENTRAL DRUG STANDARD CONTROL ORGANIZATION (CDSCO) AND STATE LICENSING AUTHORITY

The Central Drugs Standard Control Organization (CDSCO) is India's primary regulatory body for pharmaceuticals and medical devices. It operates under the Ministry of Health and Family Welfare. CDSCO's main responsibilities include:

Central Drugs Standard Control Organization (CDSCO):

The Central Drugs Standard Control Organization (CDSCO) is India's primary regulatory body for pharmaceuticals, medical devices, and cosmetics. Established under the Drugs and Cosmetics Act, 1940, and the Drugs and Cosmetics Rules, 1945, CDSCO operates under the Ministry of Health and Family Welfare. Its primary objective is to ensure the quality, safety, and efficacy of drugs and healthcare products in the country. Here's a detailed overview of CDSCO's roles, functions, and organizational structure:

1. **Regulatory Functions:**

a. **Regulatory Approvals**: CDSCO is responsible for granting regulatory approvals for the import, manufacture, distribution, and sale of drugs, medical devices, and cosmetics in India. This includes the review and evaluation of applications for marketing authorization, clinical trials, import licenses, and manufacturing licenses.

b. **Quality Control**: CDSCO establishes and enforces quality standards for pharmaceuticals, medical devices, and cosmetics. It ensures compliance with Good Manufacturing Practices (GMP), Good Laboratory Practices

(GLP), and other quality requirements through inspections, audits, and testing.

c. **Clinical Trials Oversight**: CDSCO regulates and monitors clinical trials conducted in India to ensure participant safety and ethical conduct. It reviews and approves trial protocols, monitors trial progress, and evaluates trial data to assess the safety and efficacy of investigational products.

d. **Pharmacovigilance**: CDSCO conducts post-marketing surveillance to monitor the safety of drugs and medical devices in the market. It collects and analyzes reports of adverse drug reactions (ADRs) and takes regulatory action, such as product recalls or labeling changes, to protect public health.

e. **Registration of Medical Devices**: CDSCO oversees the registration process for medical devices in India, ensuring compliance with applicable regulatory requirements for safety, performance, and quality.

2.   Organizational Structure:

CDSCO is structured into various divisions, offices, and laboratories, each with specific responsibilities related to regulatory oversight, approval processes, and enforcement. Some key components of CDSCO's organizational structure include:

a. **Office of the Drugs Controller General of India (DCGI):** The DCGI is the head of CDSCO and is responsible for overall coordination and supervision of regulatory activities related to drugs, medical devices, and cosmetics in India.

b. **Drug Regulatory Affairs Division**: This division is responsible for regulatory approvals, including the review and evaluation of applications for new drugs, clinical trials, import and export licenses, and manufacturing licenses.

c. **Medical Device Division**: This division focuses on regulatory oversight of medical devices, including classification, registration, and quality control.

d. **Biological Division**: This division deals with regulatory aspects related to biological products, including vaccines, blood products, and biotechnology-derived products.

e. **Quality Control Laboratories**: CDSCO operates a network of Central Drugs Testing Laboratories (CDTLs) and Regional Drugs Testing Laboratories (RDTLs) across India. These laboratories are responsible for testing and analyzing drug samples to ensure compliance with quality standards.

3.   International Collaboration:

CDSCO collaborates with international regulatory agencies and organizations to harmonize regulatory standards, exchange information, and facilitate the import and export of pharmaceuticals and medical devices. This includes participation in forums such as the International Council for Harmonisation of Technical Requirements for Pharmaceuticals for Human Use (ICH) and the World Health Organization (WHO).

In summary, the Central Drugs Standard Control Organization (CDSCO) plays a crucial role in regulating pharmaceuticals, medical devices, and cosmetics in India. Its functions encompass regulatory approvals, quality control, clinical trials oversight, pharmacovigilance, and registration of medical devices. Through its organizational structure and international collaborations, CDSCO works to ensure the safety, quality, and efficacy of healthcare products available in the Indian market.

State Licensing Authority:

In addition to CDSCO, each Indian state has its own State Licensing Authority (SLA) responsible for regulating pharmaceuticals and medical devices within its jurisdiction. The SLA typically operates under the State Drugs Control

Department or similar authority. The roles and responsibilities of the SLA include:

State Licensing Authorities (SLAs) play a significant role in the regulatory framework for pharmaceuticals, medical devices, and cosmetics in India. These authorities operate at the state level and are responsible for enforcing regulatory requirements within their respective states. Here's a detailed overview of SLAs' roles, functions, and organizational structure:

1. **Regulatory Functions:**

a. **Licensing and Registration**: SLAs issue licenses and registrations to manufacturers, wholesalers, distributors, and retailers of drugs, medical devices, and cosmetics operating within their respective states. They ensure compliance with regulatory requirements and standards.

b. **Inspections and Enforcement**: SLAs conduct inspections of manufacturing facilities, storage facilities, and retail outlets to verify compliance with regulatory standards. They take enforcement actions against violators, such as issuing warnings, suspending licenses, or initiating legal proceedings.

c. **Monitoring and Surveillance**: SLAs monitor the market within their states to detect and address violations of regulatory requirements. They investigate complaints, conduct product sampling and testing, and take corrective actions to protect public health and safety.

d. **Training and Capacity Building**: SLAs provide training programs and educational initiatives to stakeholders involved in the pharmaceutical and healthcare sectors within their states. This helps enhance awareness of regulatory requirements and promotes compliance with standards.

e. **Public Awareness and Education**: SLAs engage in public awareness campaigns and educational initiatives to inform consumers and healthcare professionals about the safe and rational use of pharmaceuticals, medical devices, and cosmetics.

2.   **Organizational Structure:**

The organizational structure of SLAs may vary from state to state, but typically includes the following components:

a. **Office of the Drugs Controller**: The Drugs Controller at the state level is responsible for overseeing regulatory activities within the state, including licensing, inspections, and enforcement.

b. **Licensing Section**: This section handles the issuance of licenses and registrations to pharmaceutical manufacturers, wholesalers, distributors, and retailers operating within the state.

c. **Inspection and Enforcement Division**: This division conducts inspections of manufacturing facilities, storage facilities, and retail outlets to ensure compliance with regulatory standards. It takes enforcement actions against violators and investigates complaints related to drug safety and quality.

d. **Testing Laboratories**: Some states may have their own state-level testing laboratories for analyzing drug samples and conducting quality control tests. These laboratories support the regulatory functions of the SLA by ensuring the quality and safety of pharmaceutical products.

3.   **Coordination with Central Authorities:**

SLAs coordinate with central regulatory authorities such as the Central Drugs Standard Control Organization (CDSCO) to ensure consistency and uniformity in the implementation and enforcement of regulatory requirements. They may seek guidance from CDSCO on interpretation of regulations and facilitate communication between manufacturers and CDSCO as needed.

ORGANIZATION

CDSCO is structured into various divisions and offices, each with specific responsibilities related to regulatory oversight, approval processes, and enforcement. Here are some key components of CDSCO's organizational structure:

Central Drugs Standard Control Organization (CDSCO):

The Central Drugs Standard Control Organization (CDSCO) is India's primary regulatory body for pharmaceuticals, medical devices, biological products, and cosmetics. It operates under the regulatory framework provided by the Drugs and Cosmetics Act, 1940, and the Drugs and Cosmetics Rules, 1945. CDSCO is responsible for ensuring the safety, efficacy, and quality of healthcare products in India. Here's a detailed overview of CDSCO's organization within the Indian regulatory framework:

1. **Office of the Drugs Controller General of India (DCGI):**

   a. **Role**: The Drugs Controller General of India (DCGI) is the head of CDSCO and is responsible for overall coordination, supervision, and direction of regulatory activities related to drugs, medical devices, biological products, and cosmetics in India.

   b. **Functions:**

      o Oversees and directs the activities of various divisions and offices within CDSCO.

      o Provides guidance and interpretation of regulations to ensure uniform implementation and enforcement across India.

      o Represents CDSCO in national and international forums related to regulatory affairs.

      o Acts as the final authority for decisions on regulatory approvals and enforcement actions.

2. **Divisions and Offices:**

CDSCO is organized into several divisions and offices, each with specific responsibilities related to regulatory oversight, approval processes, and enforcement. Some key divisions and offices include:

a. **Drug Regulatory Affairs Division**: Responsible for regulatory approvals, including the review and evaluation of applications for new drugs, clinical trials, import and export licenses, and manufacturing licenses.

b. **Medical Device Division**: Regulates medical devices, including classification, registration, and quality control.

c. **Biological Division**: Deals with regulatory aspects related to biological products, including vaccines, blood products, and biotechnology-derived products.

d. **Quality Control Laboratories**: Operates a network of Central Drugs Testing Laboratories (CDTLs) and Regional Drugs Testing Laboratories (RDTLs) across India. These laboratories test and analyze drug samples to ensure compliance with quality standards.

3. **Functions and Responsibilities:**

a. **Regulatory Approvals**: CDSCO grants regulatory approvals for the import, manufacture, distribution, and sale of drugs, medical devices, biological products, and cosmetics in India. This includes evaluating applications for marketing authorization, clinical trials, import licenses, and manufacturing licenses.

b. **Quality Control**: CDSCO establishes and enforces quality standards for healthcare products. It ensures compliance with Good Manufacturing Practices (GMP), Good Laboratory Practices (GLP), and other quality requirements through inspections, audits, and testing.

c. **Clinical Trials Oversight**: Regulates and monitors clinical trials conducted in India to ensure participant safety and ethical conduct. Reviews and approves trial protocols, monitors trial progress, and evaluates trial data.

d. **Pharmacovigilance:** Conducts post-marketing surveillance to monitor the safety of drugs and medical devices in the market. Collects and analyzes reports of adverse drug reactions (ADRs) and takes regulatory action to protect public health.

e. **Registration and Licensing**: Oversees the registration and licensing of pharmaceutical manufacturers, wholesalers, distributors, and retailers operating in India.

4.   International Collaboration:

CDSCO collaborates with international regulatory agencies and organizations to harmonize regulatory standards, exchange information, and facilitate the import and export of pharmaceuticals and medical devices. This includes participation in forums such as the International Council for Harmonisation of Technical Requirements for Pharmaceuticals for Human Use (ICH) and the World Health Organization (WHO).

In summary, the Central Drugs Standard Control Organization (CDSCO) plays a crucial role in regulating pharmaceuticals, medical devices, biological products, and cosmetics in India. Its organizational structure, functions, and responsibilities are designed to ensure the safety, efficacy, and quality of healthcare products available in the Indian market.

State Licensing Authority (SLA):

State Licensing Authorities operate at the state level and are responsible for regulating pharmaceuticals, medical devices, and cosmetics within their respective states. While the specific organizational structure may vary from state to state, here are the typical components of an SLA:

State Licensing Authorities (SLAs) are pivotal in the regulatory framework for pharmaceuticals, medical devices, and cosmetics within India. Operating at the state level, SLAs are entrusted with enforcing regulatory requirements and standards within their respective states. Here's a detailed breakdown of the organization of SLAs within the Indian regulatory landscape:

1. **Office of the Drugs Controller (ODC):**

a. **Role**: The Drugs Controller heads the SLA and oversees all regulatory activities concerning pharmaceuticals, medical devices, and cosmetics within the state.

b. **Functions:**

  i. Supervision and management of all regulatory operations within the state, including licensing, inspections, and enforcement.

  ii. Interpretation and implementation of relevant laws and regulations governing healthcare products.

  iii. Coordination with other regulatory bodies, such as the Central Drugs Standard Control Organization (CDSCO), for consistency in regulatory practices.

2. **Divisions and Sections:**

SLAs are typically organized into various divisions and sections, each with distinct responsibilities related to regulatory oversight and enforcement. Some common divisions and sections include:

a. **Licensing Section**: Handles the issuance of licenses and registrations to manufacturers, wholesalers, distributors, and retailers of healthcare products operating within the state.

b. **Inspection and Enforcement Division**: Conducts regular inspections of manufacturing facilities, storage units, and retail outlets to ensure compliance with regulatory standards. Takes appropriate enforcement actions against violators of regulations.

c. **Drug Testing Laboratory**: Some SLAs may have their own drug testing laboratories responsible for analyzing samples to verify compliance with quality standards. These laboratories play a crucial role in ensuring the safety and efficacy of healthcare products available within the state.

3. **Functions and Responsibilities:**

a. **Licensing and Registration**: SLAs issue licenses and registrations to healthcare product establishments operating within the state. This includes manufacturers, wholesalers, distributors, and retailers.

b. **Inspections and Enforcement**: Regularly inspect facilities to ensure compliance with regulatory standards regarding manufacturing practices, storage conditions, and distribution processes. Take enforcement actions against violators, including issuing warnings, suspending licenses, or initiating legal proceedings.

c. **Monitoring and Surveillance**: Conduct ongoing monitoring and surveillance activities to detect and address violations of regulatory requirements. Investigate complaints, conduct product sampling and testing, and take corrective actions to protect public health and safety.

d. **Training and Capacity Building**: Organize training programs and educational initiatives for stakeholders within the state to enhance awareness of regulatory requirements and promote compliance with standards.

e. **Public Awareness and Education**: Engage in public awareness campaigns and educational initiatives to inform consumers and healthcare professionals about the safe and rational use of healthcare products.

4.   Coordination with Central Authorities:

SLAs coordinate closely with central regulatory authorities such as CDSCO to ensure consistency and uniformity in the implementation and enforcement of regulatory requirements across the country. Seek guidance and support from central authorities as needed for interpretation of regulations and resolution of complex regulatory issues.

In summary, State Licensing Authorities (SLAs) play a critical role in enforcing regulatory requirements and ensuring the safety, efficacy, and quality of healthcare products within their respective states. Through their organizational structure, functions, and responsibilities, SLAs contribute significantly to the overall regulatory framework for healthcare products in India.

RESPONSIBILITIES

Central Drug Standard Control Organization (CDSCO):

The Central Drugs Standard Control Organization (CDSCO) in India holds significant responsibilities within the regulatory landscape, ensuring the safety, efficacy, and quality of pharmaceuticals, medical devices, biological products, and cosmetics. Below is a detailed breakdown of CDSCO's responsibilities within the Indian regulatory requirements:

1. **Regulatory Approvals:**
    a. CDSCO is responsible for evaluating and granting regulatory approvals for the import, manufacture, distribution, and sale of drugs, medical devices, biological products, and cosmetics in India.
    b. This includes reviewing and assessing applications for marketing authorization, clinical trials, import licenses, and manufacturing licenses.

2. **Quality Control:**
    a. CDSCO establishes and enforces quality standards for pharmaceuticals, medical devices, and cosmetics.
    b. It ensures compliance with Good Manufacturing Practices (GMP), Good Laboratory Practices (GLP), and other quality requirements through inspections, audits, and testing.

3. **Clinical Trials Oversight:**
    a. CDSCO regulates and monitors clinical trials conducted in India to ensure participant safety and ethical conduct.
    b. It reviews and approves trial protocols, monitors trial progress, and evaluates trial data to assess the safety and efficacy of investigational products.

4. **Pharmacovigilance:**

   a. CDSCO conducts post-marketing surveillance to monitor the safety of drugs, medical devices, biological products, and cosmetics in the market.

   b. It collects and analyzes reports of adverse drug reactions (ADRs) and takes regulatory action, such as product recalls or labeling changes, to protect public health.

5. **Registration and Licensing:**

   a. CDSCO oversees the registration process for medical devices, biological products, and cosmetics in India, ensuring compliance with applicable regulatory requirements for safety, performance, and quality.

   b. It also manages the licensing of pharmaceutical manufacturers, wholesalers, distributors, and retailers operating in India.

6. **International Collaboration:**

   a. CDSCO collaborates with international regulatory agencies and organizations to harmonize regulatory standards, exchange information, and facilitate the import and export of pharmaceuticals and medical devices.

   b. This includes participation in forums such as the International Council for Harmonisation of Technical Requirements for Pharmaceuticals for Human Use (ICH) and the World Health Organization (WHO).

7. **Research and Development:**

   a. CDSCO may engage in research and development activities related to regulatory science, including the development of new testing methodologies, standards, and guidelines.

   b. It may also conduct studies and evaluations to assess the safety and efficacy of new technologies and products entering the market.

Responsibilities of State Licensing Authorities (SLAs):

State Licensing Authorities (SLAs) in India are crucial components of the regulatory framework for pharmaceuticals, medical devices, biological products, and cosmetics within their respective states. Their responsibilities encompass various aspects of regulatory oversight and enforcement. Below is a detailed breakdown of the responsibilities of State Licensing Authorities (SLAs) within the Indian regulatory requirements:

1. **Licensing and Registration:**
   a. SLAs issue licenses and registrations to manufacturers, wholesalers, distributors, and retailers of pharmaceuticals, medical devices, biological products, and cosmetics operating within their respective states.
   b. They ensure compliance with regulatory requirements and standards before granting licenses or registrations.

2. **Inspections and Audits:**
   a. SLAs conduct regular inspections and audits of manufacturing facilities, storage facilities, and retail outlets to verify compliance with regulatory standards.
   b. They assess adherence to Good Manufacturing Practices (GMP), Good Distribution Practices (GDP), and other relevant quality standards.

3. **Enforcement Actions:**
   a. SLAs take enforcement actions against violators of regulatory requirements within their jurisdiction.
   b. This may include issuing warnings, suspending or revoking licenses or registrations, imposing fines, or initiating legal proceedings.

4. **Monitoring and Surveillance:**

a. SLAs monitor the market within their states to detect and address violations of regulatory requirements.

b. They investigate complaints, conduct product sampling and testing, and take corrective actions to protect public health and safety.

5. **Training and Capacity Building:**

a. SLAs organize training programs and educational initiatives for stakeholders within their states.

b. These programs aim to enhance awareness of regulatory requirements, promote compliance with standards, and build capacity.among regulatory personnel and industry stakeholders.

6. **Public Awareness and Education:**

a. SLAs engage in public awareness campaigns and educational initiatives to inform consumers and healthcare professionals about the safe and rational use of pharmaceuticals, medical devices, biological products, and cosmetics.

b. They disseminate information on regulatory requirements, product safety, and reporting mechanisms for adverse events.

7. **Coordination with Central Authorities:**

a. SLAs coordinate with central regulatory authorities, such as the Central Drugs Standard Control Organization (CDSCO), to ensure consistency and uniformity in the implementation and enforcement of regulatory requirements.

b. They seek guidance from central authorities on interpretation of regulations and facilitate communication between manufacturers and central regulatory bodies as needed.

Effective coordination and collaboration between CDSCO and State Licensing Authorities are essential for ensuring the safety, quality, and efficacy of pharmaceuticals and medical devices throughout India. Compliance with regulatory requirements at both the national and state levels is crucial for companies operating in the healthcare and pharmaceutical sectors.

CERTIFICATE OF PHARMACEUTICAL PRODUCT (COPP)

The Certificate of Pharmaceutical Product (COPP) is an essential document in the regulatory framework of pharmaceuticals in India. Both the Central Drugs Standard Control Organization (CDSCO) and State Licensing Authorities (SLAs) play a role in its issuance and regulation:

Central Drugs Standard Control Organization (CDSCO):

The Certificate of Pharmaceutical Product (COPP) is a crucial document in the Indian regulatory framework overseen by the Central Drugs Standard Control Organization (CDSCO). Below is a detailed overview of the COPP in the context of Indian regulatory requirements and CDSCO's role:

1. **Definition of COPP:**
   a. The Certificate of Pharmaceutical Product (COPP) is a certificate issued by the regulatory authority of a country to confirm that a pharmaceutical product is approved for sale in that country and meets the necessary regulatory requirements.

2. **Role of CDSCO:**
   a. CDSCO is responsible for issuing the COPP to pharmaceutical manufacturers in India for products intended for export.
   b. The issuance of COPP signifies that the pharmaceutical product meets the standards and requirements of the importing country or countries.

3. **Application Process:**
   a. Pharmaceutical manufacturers seeking COPP for their products must submit an application to CDSCO.
   b. The application typically includes detailed information about the manufacturing process, quality control measures, product

specifications, and evidence of compliance with regulatory standards.

4. Documentation and Review:

   a. CDSCO reviews the application and supporting documentation to ensure compliance with regulatory requirements.

   b. This involves verifying that the manufacturing process adheres to Good Manufacturing Practices (GMP) and that the product meets quality standards.

5. Inspections and Audits:

   a. CDSCO may conduct inspections and audits of manufacturing facilities to verify compliance with GMP and other quality standards.

   b. The findings of these inspections are taken into consideration during the review process for COPP issuance.

6. Validity and Renewal:

   a. Once issued, the COPP is typically valid for a certain period, after which it may need to be renewed.

   b. CDSCO may require manufacturers to submit updated information or undergo re-inspection before renewing the COPP.

7. International Collaboration:

   a. CDSCO collaborates with regulatory authorities in other countries to facilitate the acceptance of COPP for pharmaceutical exports.

   b. This includes harmonizing documentation requirements and exchanging information to streamline the regulatory process.

8. Role in Export:

   a. The COPP serves as a key document for pharmaceutical exports from India, providing assurance to importing countries that the products meet regulatory standards.

b. It facilitates smooth clearance of pharmaceutical shipments at customs checkpoints in importing countries.

State Licensing Authorities (SLAs):

State Licensing Authorities (SLAs) in India are primarily responsible for regulating pharmaceutical manufacturing and distribution within their respective states. However, the issuance of the Certificate of Pharmaceutical Product (COPP) is typically handled by the Central Drugs Standard Control Organization (CDSCO), which operates at the national level. Below is an overview of how SLAs may be involved in the COPP process within the Indian regulatory framework:

1. **Compliance Verification:**
   a. SLAs may play a role in verifying compliance with regulatory requirements at the state level before a pharmaceutical manufacturer applies for COPP.
   b. This may involve ensuring that manufacturing facilities within the state adhere to Good Manufacturing Practices (GMP) and other quality standards.

2. **Documentation Support:**
   a. SLAs may assist pharmaceutical manufacturers in preparing and submitting documentation required for COPP application to CDSCO.
   b. This may include providing guidance on the information and supporting documents needed for the application.

3. **Inspections and Audits:**
   a. SLAs may conduct inspections and audits of manufacturing facilities within their states to verify compliance with regulatory standards.
   b. The findings of these inspections may be considered by CDSCO during the review process for COPP issuance.

4. **Coordination with CDSCO:**
   a. SLAs coordinate with CDSCO, the national regulatory authority responsible for issuing COPP, to ensure smooth processing of applications.
   b. They may facilitate communication between pharmaceutical manufacturers and CDSCO and provide any necessary assistance during the application process.

5. **Monitoring Compliance:**
   a. SLAs monitor compliance with regulatory requirements among pharmaceutical manufacturers within their states on an ongoing basis.
   b. They may require manufacturers to maintain compliance with regulatory standards as a condition for holding a state-level manufacturing license.

6. **Public Health Oversight:**
   a. SLAs oversee pharmaceutical manufacturing and distribution within their states to safeguard public health and safety.
   b. They ensure that only products meeting regulatory standards are manufactured and distributed within their jurisdiction.

While SLAs do not typically issue the COPP themselves, they play a supporting role in ensuring that pharmaceutical manufacturers comply with regulatory requirements at the state level. Compliance with state-level regulations is essential for manufacturers to obtain and maintain the necessary approvals from CDSCO, including the COPP, for exporting pharmaceutical products from India.

Overall, the Certificate of Pharmaceutical Product (COPP) plays a crucial role in facilitating the export of pharmaceutical products from India by certifying compliance with regulatory standards of importing countries. CDSCO and State

Licensing Authorities collaborate to ensure the proper issuance, verification, and enforcement of COPP requirements to maintain the integrity and quality of pharmaceutical products exported from India.

REGULATORY REQUIREMENTS

Central Drug Standard Control Organization (CDSCO):

The Central Drugs Standard Control Organization (CDSCO) is the primary regulatory body responsible for ensuring the safety, efficacy, and quality of pharmaceuticals, medical devices, biological products, and cosmetics in India. Its regulatory requirements encompass a wide range of aspects to oversee the entire lifecycle of healthcare products, from preclinical development to post-marketing surveillance. Here's a detailed breakdown of CDSCO's regulatory requirements within the Indian regulatory framework:

1. **Preclinical Development:**
   a. Before a pharmaceutical product can progress to clinical trials, CDSCO requires comprehensive preclinical data demonstrating the safety and efficacy of the product in animal studies.
   b. This includes data on pharmacology, toxicology, and pharmacokinetics to assess the potential risks and benefits of the product.

2. **Clinical Trials Oversight:**
   a. CDSCO regulates and monitors clinical trials conducted in India to ensure participant safety and ethical conduct.
   b. It reviews and approves trial protocols, monitors trial progress, and evaluates trial data to assess the safety and efficacy of investigational products.

3. **Marketing Authorization:**

a. CDSCO evaluates applications for marketing authorization, which are submitted by pharmaceutical manufacturers seeking approval to market and sell their products in India.

b. The evaluation includes comprehensive data on the quality, safety, and efficacy of the product obtained from preclinical and clinical studies.

4. **Good Manufacturing Practices (GMP):**

a. CDSCO mandates compliance with GMP regulations for pharmaceutical manufacturing facilities to ensure that products are consistently produced and controlled to meet quality standards.

b. GMP inspections are conducted by CDSCO to verify compliance with regulatory requirements and to assess the quality management systems of manufacturing facilities.

5. **Quality Control:**

a. CDSCO establishes and enforces quality standards for pharmaceuticals, medical devices, biological products, and cosmetics.

b. It conducts testing and analysis of drug samples to ensure compliance with quality standards, including pharmacopoeial standards.

6. **Post-Marketing Surveillance:**

a. CDSCO conducts post-marketing surveillance to monitor the safety and efficacy of healthcare products in the market.

b. It collects and analyzes reports of adverse drug reactions (ADRs) and takes regulatory action, such as product recalls or labeling changes, to protect public health.

7. **Import and Export Regulations:**

a. CDSCO regulates the import and export of pharmaceuticals, medical devices, biological products, and cosmetics to ensure compliance with regulatory requirements.

b. It issues import and export licenses and evaluates applications for import and export of healthcare products.

8. Pharmacovigilance:

a. CDSCO oversees pharmacovigilance activities to monitor the safety of drugs and medical devices in the market.

b. It collects, analyzes, and evaluates data on adverse drug reactions (ADRs) and takes regulatory action to mitigate risks to public health.

9. Licensing and Registration:

a. CDSCO issues licenses and registrations to pharmaceutical manufacturers, wholesalers, distributors, and retailers operating in India.

b. It ensures compliance with regulatory requirements for licensing and registration of healthcare products.

State Licensing Authorities (SLAs):

State Licensing Authorities (SLAs) in India play a critical role in enforcing regulatory requirements for pharmaceuticals, medical devices, biological products, and cosmetics at the state level. Their responsibilities are outlined within the broader Indian regulatory framework and involve various aspects of oversight and enforcement. Here's a detailed breakdown of SLAs' regulatory requirements within the Indian regulatory landscape:

1. Licensing and Registration:

a. SLAs are responsible for issuing licenses and registrations to manufacturers, wholesalers, distributors, and retailers of healthcare products operating within their respective states.

b. They ensure compliance with regulatory requirements and standards before granting licenses or registrations.

2. **Quality Control:**

   a. SLAs oversee compliance with Good Manufacturing Practices (GMP), Good Distribution Practices (GDP), and other quality standards among pharmaceutical manufacturers and distributors within their states.

   b. They conduct inspections and audits of manufacturing facilities, storage units, and distribution centers to verify compliance.

3. **Inspections and Audits:**

   a. SLAs conduct regular inspections and audits of healthcare product establishments within their states to ensure adherence to regulatory standards.

   b. These inspections assess various aspects such as manufacturing practices, storage conditions, record-keeping, and personnel training.

4. **Enforcement Actions:**

   a. SLAs take enforcement actions against violators of regulatory requirements within their jurisdiction.

   b. This may include issuing warnings, suspending or revoking licenses or registrations, imposing fines, or initiating legal proceedings.

5. **Monitoring and Surveillance:**

   a. SLAs monitor the market within their states to detect and address violations of regulatory requirements.

   b. They investigate complaints, conduct product sampling and testing, and take corrective actions to protect public health and safety.

6. **Training and Capacity Building:**

a. SLAs organize training programs and educational initiatives for stakeholders within their states.

b. These programs aim to enhance awareness of regulatory requirements, promote compliance with standards, and build capacity among regulatory personnel and industry stakeholders.

7. Public Awareness and Education:

a. SLAs engage in public awareness campaigns and educational initiatives to inform consumers and healthcare professionals about the safe and rational use of healthcare products.

b. They disseminate information on regulatory requirements, product safety, and reporting mechanisms for adverse events.

8. Coordination with Central Authorities:

a. SLAs coordinate closely with central regulatory authorities, such as the Central Drugs Standard Control Organization (CDSCO), to ensure consistency and uniformity in the implementation and enforcement of regulatory requirements.

b. They seek guidance from central authorities on interpretation of regulations and facilitate communication between manufacturers and central regulatory bodies as needed.

These regulatory requirements enforced by CDSCO and State Licensing Authorities are essential for ensuring the safety, quality, and efficacy of pharmaceuticals, medical devices, and cosmetics in India. Compliance with these requirements is crucial for companies operating in the healthcare and pharmaceutical sectors to protect public health and safety.

APPROVAL PROCEDURES FOR NEW DRUGS

The approval procedures for new drugs in India involve both the Central Drugs Standard Control Organization (CDSCO) at the national level and State Licensing Authorities (SLAs) at the state level. Here's a detailed overview of the process:

Central Drugs Standard Control Organization (CDSCO):

The Central Drugs Standard Control Organization (CDSCO) in India regulates the approval procedures for new drugs, ensuring their safety, efficacy, and quality before they are introduced into the market. Here's a detailed overview of the approval procedures for new drugs within the Indian regulatory requirements overseen by CDSCO:

1. **Investigational New Drug (IND) Application:**
   a. Before conducting clinical trials in India, pharmaceutical companies must obtain approval from CDSCO by submitting an Investigational New Drug (IND) application.
   b. The IND application includes preclinical data demonstrating the safety and efficacy of the investigational drug obtained from laboratory studies.
   c. CDSCO reviews the IND application to ensure that the proposed clinical trial meets ethical and regulatory standards.

2. **Clinical Trial Application (CTA):**
   a. Once the IND application is approved, pharmaceutical companies can proceed with submitting a Clinical Trial Application (CTA) to CDSCO.
   b. The CTA includes comprehensive details of the proposed clinical trial, including the study protocol, informed consent documents, investigator brochure, and other relevant information.
   c. CDSCO reviews the CTA to assess the safety and efficacy of the investigational drug in human subjects and evaluates the trial protocol to ensure participant safety and ethical conduct.

3. **Clinical Trials Conduct:**
   a. Upon approval of the CTA, pharmaceutical companies can initiate clinical trials in India under the supervision of CDSCO.

b. CDSCO monitors the progress of clinical trials to ensure compliance with regulatory requirements and ethical standards.

c. It may conduct inspections of trial sites and review trial data to verify adherence to Good Clinical Practices (GCP) and to assess the safety and efficacy of the investigational drug.

4. New Drug Application (NDA):

a. After completion of clinical trials, pharmaceutical companies submit a New Drug Application (NDA) to CDSCO for marketing authorization.

b. The NDA includes comprehensive data on the safety, efficacy, and quality of the new drug obtained from preclinical and clinical studies.

c. CDSCO conducts a thorough review of the NDA to evaluate the risk-benefit profile of the new drug and to assess its suitability for marketing approval.

5. Drug Approval Process:

a. CDSCO evaluates the NDA based on scientific evidence, including preclinical and clinical data, to determine whether the new drug meets regulatory standards.

b. If the new drug is found to be safe, effective, and of acceptable quality, CDSCO grants marketing authorization, allowing the pharmaceutical company to market and sell the drug in India.

c. The approval may be subject to specific conditions or restrictions to ensure safe use of the drug, such as post-marketing surveillance requirements or risk mitigation measures.

6. Post-Marketing Surveillance:

a. After approval, CDSCO continues to monitor the safety of the new drug through post-marketing surveillance.

b. It collects and analyzes reports of adverse drug reactions (ADRs) and takes regulatory action, such as product recalls or labeling changes, to protect public health.

State Licensing Authorities (SLAs):

State Licensing Authorities (SLAs) in India primarily focus on licensing and regulatory oversight at the state level, while the approval procedures for new drugs are predominantly managed by the Central Drugs Standard Control Organization (CDSCO) at the national level. However, SLAs may play a role in certain aspects of the approval process for new drugs within their respective states. Here's an overview of how SLAs may be involved in the approval procedures for new drugs in the Indian regulatory framework:

1. **Preclinical and Clinical Trial Oversight:**
   a. While CDSCO oversees the approval of new drugs through preclinical and clinical trial stages, SLAs may participate in monitoring and oversight activities at the state level.
   b. SLAs may conduct inspections of clinical trial sites within their states to ensure compliance with regulatory standards and ethical guidelines.

2. **Manufacturing and Distribution Licensing:**
   a. SLAs issue licenses to pharmaceutical manufacturers, wholesalers, distributors, and retailers operating within their states.
   b. As part of the approval process for new drugs, SLAs may verify that manufacturing facilities comply with Good Manufacturing Practices (GMP) and other quality standards before granting manufacturing licenses.

3. **Post-Marketing Surveillance:**
   a. After a new drug receives marketing authorization from CDSCO, SLAs play a role in post-marketing surveillance at the state level.

b. They monitor the safety of the new drug within their states by collecting and analyzing reports of adverse drug reactions (ADRs) and taking regulatory action as necessary to protect public health.

4. Enforcement Actions:

a. SLAs may take enforcement actions against violators of regulatory requirements related to the approval, manufacturing, distribution, and sale of new drugs within their states.

b. This may include issuing warnings, suspending or revoking licenses, or imposing fines on entities found to be non-compliant with regulatory standards.

5. Public Awareness and Education:

a. SLAs may engage in public awareness campaigns and educational initiatives within their states to inform healthcare professionals and the public about the approval process for new drugs and the importance of regulatory compliance.

b. They may disseminate information on the safe and rational use of new drugs and the reporting of adverse events.

While SLAs do not typically play a direct role in the approval procedures for new drugs conducted by CDSCO, they contribute to the regulatory framework by ensuring compliance with licensing requirements, conducting post-marketing surveillance, and enforcing regulatory standards at the state level. Collaboration between SLAs and CDSCO helps to maintain consistency and effectiveness in the regulation of new drugs across India.

Multiple Choice Questions (MCQs)

1. What is the primary regulatory body for pharmaceuticals and medical devices in India?

    a) Ministry of Health and Family Welfare

    b) Indian Medical Association

c) Central Drugs Standard Control Organization (CDSCO)

d) State Licensing Authority (SLA)

2. Which organization is responsible for regulating food safety in India?

a) Food Safety and Standards Authority of India (FSSAI)

b) Ministry of Agriculture

c) Indian Council of Medical Research (ICMR)

d) Central Drugs Standard Control Organization (CDSCO)

3. What does CDSCO stand for?

a) Central Drug Supply and Control Organization

b) Central Drugs Standard Control Organization

c) Central Drugs and Safety Control Organization

d) Central Drug Safety and Compliance Organization

4. What is the role of the State Licensing Authority (SLA) in the regulatory framework?

a) Issuing national licenses

b) Conducting clinical trials

c) Enforcing regulatory requirements within their respective states

d) Exporting pharmaceuticals

5. Which document certifies that a pharmaceutical product is approved for sale and meets regulatory requirements?

a) Certificate of Quality

b) Certificate of Pharmaceutical Product (COPP)

c) Good Manufacturing Practice Certificate

d) Import License

6. Who is responsible for issuing the Certificate of Pharmaceutical Product (COPP) in India?

a) Ministry of Health and Family Welfare

b) Central Drugs Standard Control Organization (CDSCO)

c) Food Safety and Standards Authority of India (FSSAI)

d) Indian Medical Association (IMA)

7. Which authority conducts post-marketing surveillance to monitor the safety of drugs in the market?

   a) Ministry of Health and Family Welfare

   b) Indian Council of Medical Research (ICMR)

   c) Central Drugs Standard Control Organization (CDSCO)

   d) State Licensing Authority (SLA)

8. What is the primary focus of the Food Safety and Standards Authority of India (FSSAI)?

   a) Regulating pharmaceuticals

   b) Ensuring food safety and quality

   c) Overseeing clinical trials

   d) Licensing medical devices

9. What does the Environment (Protection) Act, 1986, empower the central government to do?

   a) Conduct clinical trials

   b) Establish quality standards for pharmaceuticals

   c) Take measures to protect and improve the quality of the environment

   d) Issue patents

10. What is the purpose of the Industrial Disputes Act, 1947?

   a) Regulating pharmaceuticals

   b) Protecting intellectual property rights

   c) Regulating industrial relations and resolving disputes between employers and workers

   d) Overseeing clinical trials

11. What is the primary function of the Reserve Bank of India (RBI)?

   a) Regulating food safety

   b) Issuing patents

   c) Formulating and implementing monetary policy

d) Conducting clinical trials

12. What does the term "Good Manufacturing Practices (GMP)" refer to in the context of CDSCO?

   a) Guidelines for food safety

   b) Standards for clinical trials

   c) Regulations ensuring that products are consistently produced and controlled to meet quality standards

   d) Licensing requirements for medical devices

13. Which act regulates the registration and protection of geographical indications (GIs) in India?

   a) The Trade Marks Act, 1999

   b) The Copyright Act, 1957

   c) The Geographical Indications of Goods (Registration and Protection) Act, 1999

   d) The Patents Act, 1970

14. What is the role of the Drug Regulatory Affairs Division within CDSCO?

   a) Conducting food safety inspections

   b) Managing the quality control laboratories

   c) Overseeing regulatory approvals for new drugs, clinical trials, and import/export licenses

   d) Monitoring post-marketing surveillance

15. What does the acronym "TRAI" stand for in the context of telecommunications regulation in India?

   a) Telecommunications Regulatory Authority of India

   b) Telecom Regulation and Administration of India

   c) Telecom Regulatory Authority of India

   d) Telecommunication and Radio Authority of India

16. Which body is responsible for the protection of plant varieties and farmers' rights in India?

a) Food Safety and Standards Authority of India (FSSAI)

b) Indian Council of Medical Research (ICMR)

c) Central Drugs Standard Control Organization (CDSCO)

d) The Protection of Plant Varieties and Farmers' Rights Authority

17. What is the purpose of the COPP in the pharmaceutical industry?

a) To certify that a pharmaceutical product meets quality standards for export

b) To regulate food safety

c) To issue licenses for manufacturing

d) To oversee clinical trials

18. What does the Central Drugs Testing Laboratory (CDTL) do under CDSCO?

a) Issuing patents

b) Conducting post-marketing surveillance

c) Testing and analyzing drug samples to ensure compliance with quality standards

d) Regulating food safety

19. Who regulates the issuance and licensing of medical devices in India?

a) Ministry of Health and Family Welfare

b) Indian Medical Association (IMA)

c) Central Drugs Standard Control Organization (CDSCO)

d) State Licensing Authority (SLA)

20. What does the Patents Act, 1970, in India cover?

a) Protection of geographical indications

b) Licensing of medical devices

c) Grant and protection of patents

d) Regulating food safety

Short Answer Type Questions (Subjective)

1. What is the role of the Central Drugs Standard Control Organization (CDSCO) in India?

2. Explain the significance of Good Manufacturing Practices (GMP) in pharmaceutical manufacturing.

3. How does the CDSCO ensure the safety and efficacy of new drugs before they are approved for marketing?

4. What is the Certificate of Pharmaceutical Product (COPP) and why is it important?

5. Describe the responsibilities of the State Licensing Authorities (SLAs) in the regulation of pharmaceuticals.

6. What are the primary functions of the Food Safety and Standards Authority of India (FSSAI)?

7. How does the Reserve Bank of India (RBI) contribute to the stability of the banking system?

8. What regulatory measures does SEBI implement to protect investors in the securities market?

9. Explain the role of the Telecom Regulatory Authority of India (TRAI) in regulating telecommunications services.

10. What is the Environment Impact Assessment (EIA) Notification, and why is it important?

11. How do intellectual property rights (IPR) laws in India protect the creations of the intellect?

12. What are the main provisions of the Minimum Wages Act, 1948?

13. How does the Maternity Benefit Act, 1961, support women employees?

14. Describe the organizational structure of the CDSCO.

15. What steps are involved in the drug approval process by the CDSCO?

16. How do State Licensing Authorities (SLAs) monitor compliance with regulatory standards?

17.Explain the importance of post-marketing surveillance conducted by the CDSCO.

18.How does FSSAI ensure the safety and quality of imported food products?

19.What role does the National Green Tribunal (NGT) play in environmental regulation in India?

20.How does the Patents Act, 1970, facilitate innovation and protect inventions in India?

Long Answer Type Questions (Subjective)

1. Discuss in detail the regulatory framework for pharmaceuticals and healthcare in India, focusing on the roles of CDSCO and State Licensing Authorities.

2. Explain the approval procedures for new drugs in India, highlighting the different stages involved from preclinical development to post-marketing surveillance.

3. Describe the functions and responsibilities of the Food Safety and Standards Authority of India (FSSAI) and how it ensures food safety and quality throughout the food supply chain.

4. Analyze the regulatory requirements and challenges in the banking and finance sector in India, with a focus on the roles of RBI, SEBI, and IRDAI.

5. Discuss the regulatory framework for securities and exchanges in India, detailing the role of SEBI in ensuring market integrity and investor protection.

6. Explain the regulatory requirements for telecommunications in India, including the roles of the Department of Telecommunications (DoT) and the Telecom Regulatory Authority of India (TRAI).

7. Describe the various environmental regulations in India and their significance in protecting the environment and promoting sustainable development.

8. Explain the importance of intellectual property rights (IPR) in India, focusing on the key laws and regulations that protect patents, trademarks, copyrights, and designs.

9. Discuss the significance of labour laws in India, including key legislations like the Factories Act, Minimum Wages Act, and the Sexual Harassment of Women at Workplace Act.

10. Analyze the role of international collaboration in the functioning of the CDSCO, including how it harmonizes regulatory standards and facilitates the import and export of pharmaceuticals.

Answer Key

1. c) Central Drugs Standard Control Organization (CDSCO)
2. a) Food Safety and Standards Authority of India (FSSAI)
3. b) Central Drugs Standard Control Organization
4. c) Enforcing regulatory requirements within their respective states
5. b) Certificate of Pharmaceutical Product (COPP)
6. b) Central Drugs Standard Control Organization (CDSCO)
7. c) Central Drugs Standard Control Organization (CDSCO)
8. b) Ensuring food safety and quality
9. c) Take measures to protect and improve the quality of the environment
10. c) Regulating industrial relations and resolving disputes between employers and workers
11. c) Formulating and implementing monetary policy
12. c) Regulations ensuring that products are consistently produced and controlled to meet quality standards

13.c) The Geographical Indications of Goods (Registration and Protection) Act, 1999

14.c) Overseeing regulatory approvals for new drugs, clinical trials, and import/export licenses

15.c) Telecom Regulatory Authority of India

16.d) The Protection of Plant Varieties and Farmers' Rights Authority

17.a) To certify that a pharmaceutical product meets quality standards for export

18.c) Testing and analyzing drug samples to ensure compliance with quality standards

19.c) Central Drugs Standard Control Organization (CDSCO)

20.c) Grant and protection of patents